SOCIAL CONFLICT
Escalation, Stalemate, and Settlement

Part of the Topics in
Social Psychology Series

Social Conflict

Escalation, Stalemate, and Settlement

Dean G. Pruitt
State University of New York at Buffalo

Jeffrey Z. Rubin
Tufts University

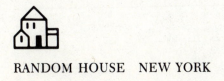

RANDOM HOUSE   NEW YORK

To André, Paul and Charles, David, Sally and Noah.

Permission is acknowledged to reprint the following material:

Page 47: From E. E. Jones and C. Wortman, *Ingratiation: An Attributional Approach* (General Learning Press, 1973). Reprinted by permission of Silver Burdett Company.

Page 129: From R. F. Kennedy, *Thirteen Days: A Memoir of the Cuban Missile Crisis* (New York: Norton, 1969). Reprinted by permission.

Page 150: From *Getting to Yes* by Roger Fisher and William Ury. Copyright © 1981 by Roger Fisher and William Ury. Reprinted by permission of Houghton Mifflin Company.

Certain materials in Chapter 3 appeared in a different form in D. G. Pruitt, Strategic Choice in Negotiation, *American Behavioral Scientist*, 1983, vol. 27, pp. 167–194. Copyright 1983 by Sage Publications, Inc. Reprinted by permission of Sage Publications, Inc. Certain materials in Chapter 9 appeared in a different form in D. G. Pruitt, "Achieving Integrative Agreements," in M. H. Bazerman and R. Lewicki, eds., *Negotiating in Organizations* (Beverly Hills, Calif.: Sage, 1983), pp. 35–50. Copyright 1983 by Sage Publications, Inc. Reprinted by permission of Sage Publications, Inc.

First Edition
987654321
Copyright ©1986 by Newbery Award Records, Inc.

Library of Congress Cataloging in Publication Data
Pruitt, Dean G.
   Social conflict.
   Bibliography: p.
   Includes index.
   1. Social conflict. 2. Social conflict—Psychological aspects. 3. Interpersonal conflict. 4. Problem solving. I. Rubin, Jeffrey Z. II. Title.
HM291.P725   1985   303.6   85-10842
ISBN 0-394-35245-9

Manufactured in the United States of America

PREFACE

This book has been an unhurried product. Its origins date back to a brief encounter about eight years ago when we decided to "think about" doing a book on social conflict. For a long time we specialized in thinking. Our problem was that we could not agree on how to define our basic concept. One of us saw conflict as incompatible activity, the other as divergence of interest. In the face of such a fundamental difference, it seemed hopeless to proceed. Finally, in the summer of 1980, we had a "showdown" meeting—a little conflict (by the former definition) of our own—which unlocked the logjam. We concluded that both concepts were plausible but that there would be greater theoretical flexibility in defining conflict as *perceived* divergence of interest. Four years and five drafts later, the present written product is the result of our efforts.

One reason why it took so long to write this book is that we had no model to lean on. The book fills what we believe to be an important gap in the literature. There are few books on the psychology of social conflict—and still fewer that draw heavily, as we do, on the sophisticated theories about social conflict to be found in other fields of social science, such as sociology, economics, management, industrial relations, and international relations. Adding to this our determination to write a book that is accessible to students at all levels of higher education and to the educated public, we believe that our product, though slow in coming, is unique.

Defining conflict in terms of perception rather than behavior has allowed us to develop a *strategic choice model,* which specifies five basic kinds of behavior that are available when people get into conflict. This model is used for theoretical analysis throughout the book. The title of the book and the sequence of its chapters reflect another model that provides a "dramaturgical" account of the three acts or stages through which many conflicts go. In the first stage, efforts to influence the other party by means of contentious tactics lead to conflict *escalation*, as each party ups the tactical ante in an effort to outdo the other. If neither party is victorious, *stalemate* is likely to ensue. This leads eventually to the final stage of *settlement*, which is characterized by problem solving, often aided by third-party intervention.

Although the basic organizing principles are mainly our own, the ideas presented in this book are solidly based in research evidence and widely accepted theory. We have also tried to illustrate as many concepts as possible, drawing our examples from a wide spectrum of conflict settings, ranging from minor disputes between children to profound events such as the outbreak of the First World War.

A number of people made important contributions to this project. We are particularly grateful to three scholars who read an intermediate draft of the book and gave us copious useful comments: Max H. Bazerman, George Levinger, and William P. Smith. Others who provided helpful critiques include Orly Ben-Yoav, David Lax, Neil McGillicuddy, Jim Sebenius, Helena Syna, Carol Tavris, Michael Van Slyck, and the late Clara Mayo. Our activities would have been completely in vain had it not been for the marathon typing efforts of Jean Intoppa.

CONTENTS

CHAPTER 1

Overview

- It is not easy to become an air traffic controller; one doesn't simply walk into an airport control tower, look down at the field, and begin ordering aircraft to take off and land. The job requires extensive training and experience, and most of the nation's controllers belong—or used to belong—to a single union, Patco. Therefore, when Patco demanded a handsome package of wage and fringe benefit increases during the summer of 1981, its members had every reason to believe that they would get what they wanted. When they didn't, a strike was called, and Patco seemed to have the feds over a barrel. To the union members' great surprise and consternation, President Reagan responded to the Patco demands not by agreeing to them but by firing every one of the striking union members (on the basis that the strike was illegal). Simultaneously the President declared that the amount of air traffic in the country would be reduced immediately and that air traffic controllers would be brought over from the military to keep the planes flying in and out of the nation's busy airports.
- Sales and Production are in the throes of an intense exchange regarding the delivery date for their company's new product. Sales argues that, unless a delivery date can be scheduled no more than *three* months from now, potential new customers will be lost to the competition, visiting a minor disaster upon Sales and the company as a whole. Production argues in return that it has a carefully organized and sequenced production schedule that must be maintained. To break out of that schedule, by making the new product available for distribution earlier than Production intends, would be to incur costs in time and money that would be detrimental to Production and its parent company. No, insists Production, the new product is scheduled for appearance *nine* months hence, and that's when it will appear! After days of acrimony, an agreement is reached in which each department settles for less than it originally wanted: a production schedule of *six* months.
- When Egypt and Israel sat down to negotiate at Camp David in October 1978, it appeared that they had before them an intractable conflict. Egypt demanded the immediate return of the entire Sinai Peninsula; Israel, which had occupied the Sinai since the 1967 Middle East war, refused to return an inch of this land. Efforts to reach agreement, including the proposal of a compromise in which each nation would retain half of the Sinai, proved completely unacceptable to both sides. As the Camp David negotiations proceeded, however, it emerged that the seemingly irreconcilable positions of Israel and Egypt reflected underlying interests that were not at all incompatible. Israel's underlying interest was security; the Israelis wanted to be certain that their borders were safe against Egyptian land or air attack. For its part, Egypt was primarily interested in sovereignty—regaining rule over a piece of land that had been part of Egypt as far back as biblical times. After many days of hard work by the parties and the American mediators, an agreement was eventually

1

reached that satisfied both of these underlying interests. Israel agreed to return the Sinai in exchange for assurances of a demilitarized zone and new Israeli air bases. This agreement was put into effect in April of 1982.
- Two small children are arguing over the use of a bright red tricycle. Each wants the trike, and each wants it first. Unable or unwilling to work out some sort of rule for turn taking, they stand on either side of the little vehicle, grab it in their hands, and yank it back and forth in an effort to seize control. Eventually the smaller child begins to cry and walks away from this torrid scene, leaving the tricycle in the sole possession of the other.

TOWARD A THEORY OF CONFLICT

Though strikingly different in scale and significance, the four incidents just cited have a great deal in common. They all describe a conflict between two sides, a situation in which each party aspires to an outcome that the other is apparently unwilling to provide. The outcome may involve money, time, ease of scheduling, land, security, an item of personal property—or any of a myriad other possibilities. Note, moreover, that each example of conflict involves a distinctive set of moves, or ways of pursuing the conflict in an effort to settle it. Are these moves similar? Not superficially. But they can be sorted into five main classes or strategies that reveal some continuity from case to case. Indeed, one of the major objectives of this book is to describe in detail the different sorts of strategies used by parties experiencing conflict and to examine the causes and consequences of the use of these strategies.

One basic strategy is *contending*—trying to impose one's preferred solution on the other party. President Reagan employed contentious behavior when he unilaterally fired the striking union members. Similarly, both Sales and Production tried at first to argue the other into submission, as did Israel and Egypt in the early stages of the Camp David negotiations. In the dispute between the children, contending took a physical form: wrestling for the tricycle.

A second strategy is *yielding*—lowering one's own aspirations and settling for less than one would have liked. This is the way Sales and Production resolved their dispute over timing. Each side settled for less than it aspired to, and in so doing, they managed to carve out a compromise agreement. Is the agreement a good one? That is, is it likely to be mutually satisfactory? We cannot be sure, but there is reason to wonder whether a "worst of both worlds" solution may not have evolved. A delay of three months may have been sufficient to erode the profits that Sales hoped for, and moving up the production schedule by three months may have seriously disrupted the efficiency of Production's plan. Yielding created a solution, to be sure, but not necessarily a solution of high quality.

A third fundamental strategy is *problem solving*—pursuing an alternative that satisfies the aspirations on both sides. With the assistance of President Carter and his aides, Egypt and Israel engaged in just such a process when they moved toward an agreement to disengage in the Sinai Peninsula.

A fourth strategy for addressing conflict involves *withdrawing*—choosing to leave the scene of the conflict, either physically or psychologically. The retreat of the smaller child, which ended the great trike squabble, exemplifies a very different approach to conflict from problem solving, yielding, and contending. Withdrawing involves abandonment of the controversy, whereas the other three strategies entail different sorts of efforts to cope.

A fifth strategy involves *inaction*—doing nothing. Though the Camp David negotiations ended in a blaze of problem solving, inaction dominated much of the proceedings. This was not because the principals were slow-witted, fumbling decision makers, but by design. Each party waited endlessly for the other's next move. Indeed, in an effort to resolve the deadlock produced by this mutual inaction, President Carter finally imposed a deadline beyond which he indicated he would withdraw from the negotiations. This galvanized the parties into action.

Although it is conceptually useful to distinguish among these five fundamental strategies for addressing conflict, we hasten to add several explanatory and cautionary notes. First, most conflict situations—be they armed exchanges, labor strikes, international negotiations, or the tacit exchanges that occur when two cars jockey for position at an unmarked intersection—call forth a *combination* of the preceding strategies. Rarely is one strategy used to the utter exclusion of the others.

Second, as will be evident in subsequent chapters of this book, each of the five strategies—particularly contending and problem solving—may be implemented through a wide variety of tactics. The terms "strategy" and "tactics" differ in scope. A strategy constitutes a set of (macroscopic) objectives or ends, and tactics are the (relatively microscopic) means to these ends. As will be apparent in our discussion of contending (Chapter 4) and in our analysis of problem solving (Chapter 9), achieving a strategic objective requires individual tactical maneuvers. In this book we will look primarily at strategic considerations, but we will keep a careful eye on the tactics that help transform strategic objectives into reality.

Third, contending, yielding, and problem solving can be thought of as *coping* strategies in the sense that each involves some relatively consistent, coherent effort to settle conflict. By contrast, withdrawing and inaction are strategies not of coping but of pause or abandonment.

Fourth, the meaning of withdrawing and inaction (unlike that of the three other strategies) depends heavily on the context in which they occur. Thus, whereas contending almost invariably reflects a competitive motivation, yielding a wish to surrender, and problem solving a wish to collaborate, the meaning of withdrawing and inaction is less obvious. Withdrawing may denote surrender, as in the strike example. But in the context of President Reagan's decision to stop negotiating with Patco, withdrawing had a far more contentious connotation. Similarly, inaction in the early stages of the Camp David negotiations implied stubborn unwillingness to budge from an extreme opening posture. Later in these discussions, when tentative agreement had almost been reached, inaction denoted an unwillingness to rock the boat and disturb the status quo.

Finally, note that yielding, like withdrawing and inaction, is fundamentally a unilateral strategy. Your consent is not required for me to withdraw or deliberately pursue a strategy of inaction. Similarly, my decision to yield to you is a unilateral one; you may not want or accept what I am prepared to yield, but I can do so anyway. By contrast, contending and problem solving work as intended only when they are accompanied by effective social influence. As we will see in Chapter 4, one person can prevail in a contentious exchange only if the other allows it. Similarly, the successful problem-solving pursuit of a satisfactory solution requires joint effort and the acceptance of social influence that this implies. In short, because they are strategies that can be effected only through social influence, problem solving and contending are far more interesting than the other three. They will therefore receive the preponderance of our attention throughout this book.

As the four opening illustrations were designed to make clear, conflicts differ in their complexity and importance, in the strategies to which they give rise, and in the solutions to which they lead. Despite these differences, we believe that—regardless of the level at which they occur—conflicts have much in common. Conflicts at the interpersonal, intergroup, community, and international level are clearly not one and the same. Nevertheless, we believe it is possible to develop generalizations that cut across, and shed light on, most or all conflicts. Our aim in this book is to organize and report existing contributions to an emerging theory of social conflict and to add a few new ideas of our own. Although we wish to improve the practice of dispute settlement, and therefore will occasionally introduce prescriptive advice for doing so (see Chapter 9), our aim is primarily *descriptive*: to account, as best we can, for the many interesting ways in which people go about addressing social conflict.

WHAT IS CONFLICT?

According to Webster (1966), the term "conflict" originally meant a "fight, battle, or struggle"—that is, a physical confrontation between parties. But its meaning has grown to include a "sharp disagreement or opposition, as of interests, ideas, etc." In other words, the term now embraces the psychological under-pinnings of physical confrontation as well as physical confrontation itself. In short, the term "conflict" has come to be so broadly applied that it is in danger of losing its status as a singular concept.

Our solution to this problem has been to adopt a restrictive meaning that builds on Webster's second definition. For us *conflict* means *perceived divergence of interest*, or *a belief that the parties' current aspirations cannot be achieved simultaneously*. We have chosen this meaning because it seems to be the best place to begin building theory. We find that we are able to construct a simple yet powerful theory (presented in Chapters 2 and 3) by trying to explain the origins of perceived divergence of interest and the impact of this perception on strategic choice and outcome. Undoubtedly our decision in this matter was influenced by the fact that we are both social psychologists and hence are accustomed to thinking in terms of the impact of mental states on social behavior. Nevertheless, we believe that this approach will be of value to scholars and practitioners from many other disciplines.

Note that implicit in our definition of conflict is the deliberate exclusion of certain topics from further analysis. We will have little to say about differences of opinion concerning facts, arguments of interpretation over objective reality, blame for prior failure, or grudges provoked by some earlier betrayal. Nor, for that matter, will we have much to say about overt conflict in the form of physical violence, armed insurrection, or war.

Clearly, each of the foregoing topics is important and worthy of attention in its own right, but we cannot cover everything. Instead we wish to examine closely the psychological realm of perceived divergence of interest and to emphasize conflict as it occurs in the present—with its attendant implications for the future. What will be the disposition of the Sinai? How long will Production take to fill the order? Who will end up with the tricycle, and why? Without ignoring the past altogether (past frustrations can make people concerned about precedents for the future and breed hostility that encourages the future use of heavy contentious tactics), these are the sorts of questions we wish to address.

Furthermore, though our analysis of conflict has been informed, whenever possible, by our awareness that conflict is waged in diverse settings and at multiple levels of complexity, we have deliberately focused primarily on conflicts between two parties. This is not because we feel that multiple-party conflicts are unimportant but because we find ourselves best able to construct plausible theory about the dyad. One has to begin theory construction somewhere, and as social psychologists we are most comfortable doing so in the realm that we know best: the interface between two individuals, two groups, or two organizations. Moreover, although we have tried to make use of the limited field research available on social conflict, most of the relevant conflict research has in fact been conducted in laboratory settings, and it has typically involved the dyad. These are the primary reasons for the book's largely dyadic focus.

Sometimes our analysis will consider the dyad as a social system, waging or addressing conflict as a dynamic duo. On other occasions, we will find it useful or necessary to present our conflict analysis from the vantage point of one person (referred to as Party) doing things to or with a second person (referred to as Other).

SOME GOOD NEWS AND SOME BAD NEWS ABOUT CONFLICT

Although people have been interested in the study of conflict at least since biblical times, the nineteenth century provided the dramatic, energetic thrust whose impact is still felt today. Charles Darwin was interested in the struggle within species for "survival of the fittest." Sigmund Freud studied the internal combat of various psychodynamic forces for control over the ego. And Karl

Marx, reflecting the dialectical philosophy that preceded him, developed a political and economic analysis based on the assumption that conflict is an inevitable part of society.

To conclude, on the basis of the work of these three profound nineteenth-century thinkers, that conflict is necessarily destructive is to miss the point of their work. For Darwin, the productive outcome of the struggle for survival was the emergence of a mutant/misfit who happens to have a genetic anomaly that fosters survival; hence the species as a whole is more likely to survive through the genetic adjustments that the struggle to survive occasions. Freud similarly envisioned individual growth and insight as a result of the struggle to understand and address the conflicts within. And Marx, in his dialectical materialism, also grasped the fact that conflict promotes further conflict; that change is inevitable; and that, at least in his judgment, this change is inexorably moving in the direction of an improved human condition. All three of these men were keenly aware of the virtues and necessity of conflict, and they all saw both the costly and the beneficial consequences that conflict can engender.

The Good News

Although conflict is found in almost every realm of human interaction—as Darwin, Freud, and Marx made abundantly clear—and although episodes of conflict are among the most significant and newsworthy events of human life, it would surely be a mistake to assume that interaction necessarily involves conflict. People manage to get along remarkably well with other individuals, groups, and organizations; they do so with consideration, helpfulness, and skill, and with little evidence of conflict along the way. When conflict *does* arise, more often than not it is settled, even resolved, with little acrimony and to the mutual satisfaction of the parties involved. Although it is tempting to detail only the negative consequences that are associated with conflict and conflict management, let us not lose sight of conflict's several positive functions—in addition to those already suggested by Darwin, Freud, and Marx.

First, conflict is the seedbed that nourishes social change. People who regard their situation as unjust or see the foolishness of current policies must usually do battle with the old order before they can be successful. Almost every new piece of legislation in the Congress of the United States is enacted after a period of debate and cross-pressures from opposing interest groups. Where would we be if, in the interest of avoiding conflict, reformers were routinely stifled, or if they stifled themselves?

A second positive function of social conflict is that it facilitates the reconciliation of people's legitimate interests. Most conflicts do not end with one party winning and the other losing. Rather, some synthesis of the two parties' positions—some integrative agreement—often emerges that fosters the parties' mutual benefit and the benefit of larger collectives of which they are members. If union and management, Egypt and Israel, Sales and Production, or two children fighting over a tricycle can manage to reconcile their interests, they will contribute to their own individual outcomes and, indirectly, to the well being of the larger organization, world community, or neighborhood of which they are members. If, in an effort to avoid conflict, they are not allowed to make claims against one another, such deep-seated reconciliation will seldom be possible. In this sense, conflict can be considered a creative force.

Third, by virtue of the first two functions, conflict fosters group unity. Without the capacity for social change or the reconciliation of individual interests, group solidarity is likely to decline—and with it group effectiveness and enjoyment of the group experience (Coser, 1956). The eventual result is often group disintegration. Without conflict, groups are like the married couple in Ingmar Bergman's film *Couples*, who fail to recognize and confront the issues in their marriage and eventually split up because neither is getting anything out of their relationship.

And Some Less Wonderful News

We have seen that much social exchange does not give rise to conflict. Moreover, when conflict does arise, it is often settled without pain and rancor, while serving a number of positive functions. When all is said and done, however, the fact remains that conflict is fully capable of wreaking havoc on society. Marriages succumb to conflict at an alarming rate. Our daily newspapers are replete with accounts of controversies that—if not especially common— are certainly compelling in their terrible intensity and consequences. And with the Damoclean sword of nuclear annihilation looming over our collective heads, it would be hard to deny that conflict is the major problem of our times.

Although it may seem paradoxical that conflict can have both harmful and beneficial consequences, this paradox is more apparent than real. What often happens is that the positive functions of conflict are swamped by the harmful consequences that derive from the use of heavy contentious tactics. In the throes of insult, threat, and even physical assault, it is difficult to savor the positive functions of conflict.

When people deal with conflict by contending, each trying to do well at the other's expense, a set of moves and countermoves tends to result that drives conflict to increase in intensity. We refer to this increase in intensity as *escalation*. The escalation of conflict is accompanied by a number of transformations, each of which is difficult—though not impossible—to reverse. First, relatively light, friendly, and inoffensive contentious tactics tend to give way to heavier moves; in the Patco case, President Reagan's early promises were later replaced by threats and finally by the unilateral imposition of costs. Second, the number of issues in conflict tends to increase; Patco wage demands were just the tip of the iceberg. Third, a focus on specifics gives way to more global, all-encompassing concerns; first it's only possession of the trike that's called into question but then it's the viability of the two children's entire relationship. Fourth, motivation in escalating conflict shifts from an initial interest in doing well for oneself to beating the other side and (eventually) to making sure that the other is hurt more than oneself. Finally, the number of parties to the conflict tends to increase; first it's just you and me, then our families, and sooner or later the entire clan. Once conflict begins to escalate, the preceding transformations make it increasingly difficult for de-escalation to occur.

In summary, although conflict need not be destructive in its consequences, when it is bad, it may well be horrid. And because destructive conflict—although far less prevalent than its more constructive cousin—is capable of doing so much damage to the people who are caught in its machinery, we want to take a particularly close and careful look in this book at the circumstances that lead conflict along a destructive, escalatory pathway.

PLAN OF THE BOOK

Not surprisingly, the book's organization reflects the set of guiding assumptions and interests that have characterized our introductory remarks. Chapter 2 elaborates on our definition of conflict, introduces simple graphic analysis to clarify the definition, and summarizes the causes of conflict as well as the conditions that make conflict less likely to erupt.

Chapter 3 deals with the topic of strategic choice. We describe in more detail the five strategic approaches to conflict introduced in this chapter. Then we turn to the set of considerations that lead people to choose one strategy over another. This chapter is the theoretical heart of the book, inasmuch as it presents concepts that are used in most of the later chapters.

The next four chapters focus, in one way or another, on the important topic of escalation. Chapter 4 explores the set of contentious tactics that people typically use in an effort to prevail at someone else's expense. Conflict escalation is most likely to occur when such contentious tactics are used. Chapter 5 details the transformations that occur during escalation. It also examines the set of stabilizing constraints that ordinarily prevent conflict from escalating. It is when these constraints are relatively weak, and/or the forces toward conflict intensification are particularly acute, that escalation occurs. Chapter 6 probes the psychological and collective (group and organizational) processes that are responsible for, and that accompany, conflict escalation. Chapter 7 presents the several reasons why conflicts tend to escalate and why such escalation tends to persist. Here we explore the dynamics that help explain why it is easier for conflict to escalate than to de-escalate.

The focus of Chapter 8 is stalemate, the point at which the parties to an escalating conflict are either no longer capable or no longer willing to continue expending the effort necessary to sustain a contentious exchange. Stalemate represents the point of transition in a conflict-intensified exchange between the trajectory of escalation and the pathway of de-escalation and eventual problem solving.

Chapter 9 addresses the extremely important, constructive, and often creative strategy of problem solving. Problem solving, a pervasive and often highly effective solution to conflict, need not occur only in the wake of conflict escalation and stalemate. This chapter describes the several methods of moving toward an integrative solution that satisfies the aspirations of all concerned.

Third-party intervention in conflict (by mediators, arbitrators, or fact-finders) is the subject of Chapter 10. Although third parties can involve themselves in disputes at any point along the way, we are particularly interested here in exploring the several things that third parties can do to ease disputants away from contentious behavior and in the direction of problem solving.

Chapter 11 briefly summarizes the major implications of the preceding analysis for the theory and practice of dispute settlement. In that final chapter, we leave you with a few reminders of the book's most important themes and emphases and indicate the direction that further productive work in this field may take.

CHAPTER 2

Sources of Conflict

Before examining the antecedents of conflict, we must define the concept of conflict more precisely. According to our definition, conflict is perceived divergence of interest. But what is meant by *interest*?

We use the term "interests" where others use "values" or "needs." Interests are people's feelings about what is basically desirable. They tend to be central to people's thinking and action, forming the core of many of their attitudes, goals, and intentions (Raven & Rubin, 1983).

There are several dimensions that can be used to describe interests. Some interests are virtually universal (such as the needs for security, identity, social approval, happiness, clarity about the nature of one's world and some level of physical well-being). Other interests are specific to certain actors (such as the Palestinian desire for a homeland). Some interests are more important (higher in priority) than others, and such priorities differ from person to person. Some interests underlie other interests; for example, America's interest in security underlies its interest in maintaining a strong Western alliance.

Before Party's interests can clash with those of Other, they must be translated into *aspirations,* by which we mean *goals* and *standards.* A *goal* is a more or less precise end toward which one is striving, such as the goal of achieving a $2,000 raise or attaining a moderate level of respect in one's profession. A *standard* is a minimal level of achievement below which one views one's outcomes as inadequate; examples include a "rock bottom" salary requirement of $32,000 or 98% certainty of being able to repel an enemy attack. These aspirations must then be seen as incompatible with Other's aspirations. That is, Party must perceive that satisfaction of his or her own aspirations precludes satisfaction of Other's aspirations, and vice versa. The larger this apparent incompatibility, the greater the perceived divergence of interest.

There are three ways in which this perceived incompatibility can develop—Party's aspirations are high, Other is perceived to have high aspirations, and/or mutually beneficial alternatives do not seem to be available. For example, a union negotiator may perceive a conflict of interest with management because he or she aspires to a 25 percent improvement in the employee hospitalization plan, believes management intends to invest no more money than is presently being invested in this plan, and sees no way of achieving a 25 percent improvement at the current level of investment.

A few graphs may help to clarify what is meant by perceived incompatibility of aspirations. Figure 2.1 represents Party's conception of the joint outcome space for himself or herself and Other.[1] The horizontal axis represents some dimension or combination of dimensions of value to Party, and the vertical axis represents a similar value dimension for Other. The dashed lines represent perceived aspirations. That marked P is Party's own aspiration; that marked O is Party's view of Other's aspiration. The points in the space represent various known alternatives. These alternatives can be a matter of Party's behavior, Other's behavior, or joint action by Party and Other. A and B can be thought of as partisan alternatives, providing value to only one party; C is moderately favorable to both parties, a form of compromise; and D is highly favorable to both, an integrative agreement.

Figure 2.2 shows four possible patterns of perceived alternatives and aspirations. In Figure 2.2a, there is no perceived conflict of interest because a known alternative satisfies both parties' aspirations. (It is represented by the point that lies above and to the right of the intersections of the two dashed lines.) The other three figures (each of which can be contrasted with Figure 2.2a) depict various ways in which perceived conflict of interest can develop. In Figure 2.2b, Party's own aspirations have risen to a level where there is no viable alternative. In Figure 2.2c, Other's aspirations are perceived to have risen to such a level. In Figure 2.2d, the mutually acceptable (integrative) alternative that appeared in Figure 2.2a is no longer available, and the re-

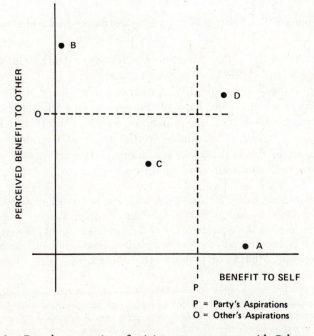

Figure 2.1.   Party's conception of a joint outcome space with Other.

[1]This and subsequent diagrams have elements in common with those used by Thomas (1976).

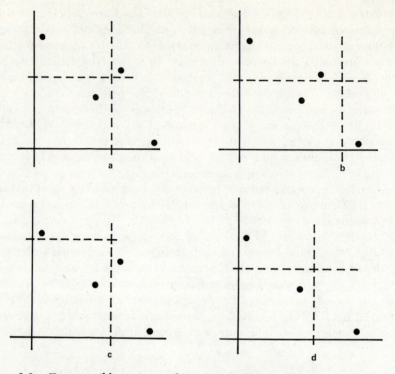

Figure 2.2. **Four possible patterns of perceived alternatives and aspirations.**

maining alternatives have the character of a zero-sum game, wherein each party's advantage implies the other's disadvantage.[2]

In addition to the level (or identity) of own and other's aspirations, participants also judge conflict on the basis of the apparent *rigidity* of these aspirations. When aspirations seem incompatible, conflict is judged to be more profound the more rigid and immutable are the apparent aspirations on both sides. The reason for this is that rigid aspirations make conflict difficult to resolve. There are two main sources of rigidity in aspirations:

1. Very important values underlie these aspirations. Examples include security, identity, and recognition for most people and probably for all nations.
2. The values underlying the aspirations are of the either–or variety; one either achieves them or one does not. Such values produce rigid aspirations, because making any concession requires giving up the value altogether.

[2]Though they do provide an intuitive understanding of our ideas about conflict, graphs of the kind shown in Figures 2.1 and 2.2 have serious limitations in that they treat utility (an individual's level of benefit) as a single dimension. In reality, human needs in most situations are multidimensional. For example, people need both food and adequate housing, and they cannot readily trade more of one for less of the other, as implied by a simple utility concept. Rather than having a single level of aspiration, as implied by Figures 2.1 and 2.2, people are likely to have multiple aspirations, one for each realm of need involved in the controversy. A more sophisticated analysis would employ multidimensional graphs.

In summary, conflict, defined as perceived divergence of interest, occurs when there seems to be no available alternative that will satisfy both parties' aspirations. This can occur because one or both parties have high aspirations or because integrative alternatives seem to be in short supply. When such conflict exists, it will seem especially severe to the extent that own and other's perceived aspirations are rigid and immutable.

By defining conflict as *perceived* rather than *true* divergence of interest, we depart from custom in the social sciences. But we feel that this departure has merit, because perceived divergence of interest is more useful in predicting what people actually will do. This is because perceptions ordinarily have an immediate impact on behavior (that is, in the case of conflict, on the choice among strategies), whereas reality works more slowly and with less certainty. We acknowledge that defining conflict in perceptual terms leaves open the possibility that one party will believe that there is a conflict of interest while the other does not. In such a case, one party must clearly be wrong. Yet that party will probably act on its perceptions anyway.

We turn now to the determinants of the three elements that can produce conflict: Party's level of aspiration, Party's perceptions of Other's level of aspiration, and the apparent lack of integrative alternatives. Finally, we shall turn the question of sources of conflict on its head and examine the antecedents of stability—that is, the conditions under which conflict is especially *unlikely* to occur.

DETERMINANTS OF LEVEL OF ASPIRATION

It is fortunate that people aspire to only a tiny fraction of the objects that might have value for them. Otherwise almost everybody would be in profound conflict with almost everybody else. I would want your house, you my car, etc.

Aspirations rise and produce conflict for one of two reasons. Either parties have reason to believe that they are able to achieve an object of value to themselves, or they come to believe that they are entitled to such an object. The former is a *realistic* consideration, the latter an *idealistic* consideration. These considerations work themselves out in a number of ways.

Past Achievement

An important realistic consideration is what has been achieved in the past; aspirations rise as achievement rises and fall as achievement declines. This is because people become more hopeful as things get better and less hopeful as they worsen. This does not create problems so long as aspirations remain in the vicinity of achievement. But sometimes a discrepancy—a "revolutionary gap"—develops. Aspirations have risen so rapidly that there are no apparent alternatives for satisfying them, and conflict results. Such runaway aspirations are particularly likely to be found in periods of rapidly expanding achievement.

A case in point is the period of intense black agitation during the 1960s. Enforcement of civil rights had improved markedly in the prior decade, especially with the landmark Supreme Court decision outlawing school segregation; and the pace of this advance was accelerated in the 1960s, which saw the passage of much new legislation and widespread changes in the attitudes of whites. Yet, somewhat paradoxically, this period also saw more discontent and agitation among blacks than any other time before or after. What may well have happened is that the progress made in civil rights encouraged expectations of rapid further change, producing unrealistic aspirations. We do not contend that these aspirations were illegitimate, only that they were inconsistent with the aspirations of others and hence produced conflict.

Several authors (such as Davies, 1962, and Gurr, 1970) have amassed evidence that revolutions are especially likely after periods of expanding economic and social development. They argue that aspirations rise rapidly during such periods, often forging well ahead of attainment. When attainment levels off or begins to decline, the gap between aspiration and achievement becomes so large that violence is inevitable. Though we agree with these authors on the importance of rising aspirations, we differ with them on the mechanism that relates rising aspirations to conflict. Rather than stressing the gap between aspirations and attainment, we argue that, as aspirations rise, they seem increasingly at odds with other people's aspirations, setting the scene for conflict.

Periods of unchanging or slowly changing resources tend to be the most free of conflict, even when people are severely deprived. This is because aspirations tend to adjust to attainment. Thus the present period (the 1980s) is notable neither for advances in civil rights nor for conflict about this issue.

Perceived Power

Aspirations also tend to rise—for realistic reasons—when people encounter a person or group whose resources are valued and who seems weaker than themselves. If the other party's aspirations do not decline concomitantly, exploitative conflict becomes quite likely. Rationalizations for this exploitation are commonly devised in order to assuage guilt. Witness the British concept of "white man's burden" or the Nazi notion of *Ubermensch*.

These points suggest that conflict is especially likely when ambiguity exists about the nature of power such that *each* party can conclude—through a process of wishful thinking—that it is stronger than the other. The Vietnam War offers a good example. Because of differing military technologies, both the United States and North Vietnam inferred that they were the probable victor. Many years of war were required to demonstrate which of these parties had drawn the right conclusions (it was, of course, North Vietnam).

Rules and Norms

Societies and the groups within them are constantly developing rules to govern the behavior of their members. Broader and longer-lasting rules are called *norms*. A major function of such rules is to dovetail the aspirations of potential opponents and hence reduce the likelihood of conflict (Thibaut & Kelley, 1959). An example is the norm against stealing. If this norm did not exist, conflict would be so pervasive and severe that society would be virtually unworkable. A less earthshaking example is the minimum wage law. By specifying a single wage level for routine jobs, it limits the aspirations of both workers and employers and thus reduces the likelihood of conflict between them. A similar function is played by the rule, subscribed to in many families, that one spouse cooks and the other does the dishes.

Norms are relevant to conflict because they specify the outcomes to which one is entitled and hence the aspirations to which one has a right. (These are idealistic considerations.) When rightful aspirations seem incompatible with another party's apparent goals, the result is often quite explosive.

The points just made imply that conflict is particularly common at times when social norms are weak and changing. In such periods, people are especially likely to develop idiosyncratic views of their rights, views that do not dovetail with those developed by others. The present troubled period in relations between husbands and wives is a case in point.

Comparison with Others

Gurr (1970) asserts that a "demonstration effect" often underlies political violence. People tend to identify with members of other groups who are close at hand or similar in some way. If such a group is ahead of oneself in attainment or begins to advance in some way, this stimulates a rise in one's aspirations that can lead to conflict. For example, it can be argued that the American Civil War occurred partly because "many Southerners were fundamentally dissatisfied with the relative economic stagnation of the South vis-à-vis the industrialized North" (Gurr, 1970, p. 109).

Similar points can be made about individuals. The importance of a comparison figure for the development of conflict is illustrated by the events in Ibsen's classic play *A Doll's House*. The heroine, Nora, is a traditional housewife who is very much dominated by her husband. She becomes acquainted with Christine, a more liberated woman, and the contrast between their two conditions causes her to aspire to greater freedom and privilege. This brings her into conflict with her husband, whom she eventually leaves.

Such a phenomenon is commonly called *invidious comparison*. It stimulates a rise in aspirations for both realistic reasons (because it seems reasonable that one can do as well as people with whom one compares oneself) and idealistic reasons (because people think that their outcomes should be as good as those of others with whom they compare themselves).

Equity theorists (Adams, 1965; Walster, Walster & Berscheid, 1978) argue that invidious comparisons are especially likely to be made when people whose outcomes are better than our own seem similar to us in basic merit (the technical term for merit is "contributions") or when people whose outcomes are equal to our own appear to have lower merit than we do.

The Formation of Struggle Groups

When several people with similar latent (unrecognized) interests begin to talk with one another, their interests often rise into consciousness. Gaining the courage of their convictions, they may begin to develop and pursue new aspirations, which can lead to conflict with others whose interests are opposed to these aspirations. Such a result is particularly likely if they begin to identify themselves as a group apart from other groups. The common aspirations then become group norms, and the pursuit of these aspirations becomes a manifestation of group loyalty. The result can be called a *struggle group*. One example is the sequence of steps during the 1960s by which individual student distress about the Vietnam War was transformed into a massive student movement that came into conflict with various adult institutions, including many university administrations. A case study of one campus crisis that grew out of this movement is presented in Chapter 5.

Dahrendorf (1959) has specified three conditions that foster development of a struggle group and hence often encourage conflict: (1) continuous communication among the people in question; (2) availability of leadership to help articulate an ideology, organize a group, and formulate a program for group action; and (3) group legitimacy in the eyes of the broader community—or at least the absence of effective community suppression of the group. The role of these conditions and others that contribute to group development is considered in greater detail in Chapter 6, which focuses on the elements of conflict escalation.

DETERMINANTS OF PERCEPTIONS OF OTHER'S ASPIRATIONS

Simply having high aspirations is not enough to get one into conflict. Party must further believe that Other also has high aspirations in a realm where it is not possible for both parties to achieve their aspirations. If Other's aspirations are low or flexible, they do not pose a threat to Party's aspirations, so there is no conflict. Under what circumstances will Party conclude that Other's objectives are too high to be compatible with his or her own?

Hard experience with frustration at the hands of Other is one source of such conclusions. Other occupies land that Party wants, fails to give Party the expected raise, or fights with Party's friend and makes it clear that he or she feels free to do so again. Such experiences dramatize the divergence of interest and also often generate aggressive impulses, making Party especially likely to take action in his or her own behalf. Hence such experiences tend to be important antecedents of conflict behavior. However, we do not believe with Kriesberg (1982) that hard, dissatisfying experiences are always necessary for the development of conflict. Conflict can arise when one is wholly satisfied with one's position and yet perceives that another party threatens this position, as when a small grocer believes that a chain store is about to steal his or her customers. Conflict can also arise when a decision must be made about the future and Party and Other take differing positions about how this decision should go, as when a salesperson and a buyer negotiate about the price of a new line of ceiling tiles.

In the absence of hard experience, it is possible to draw conclusions about Other's objectives on the basis of knowledge of Other's circumstances. All of the points made earlier about the determinants of Party's aspirations can be used by Party in estimating the extent of Other's ambitions. For example, Party can expect Other to have higher aspirations to the extent that Other has had favorable past experience in the area under consideration, has a vaunted view of his or her inputs, or is associated with a group in which people have similar values.

Estimates of another party's objectives are also influenced by trust and distrust. The term "trust" has many meanings, but in this context it implies a belief that Other is positively concerned about our interests. The concern need not necessarily be genuine in the sense of being based on positive feelings toward us. It is quite possible to trust a person because we believe that he or she is dependent on us and for this reason unlikely to risk our anger. Distrust is the opposite of trust. It is a belief that Other is hostile or indifferent to our interests.

Distrust tends to encourage a perception that Other's aspirations are incompatible with our own. If we, the United States, seek closer relations with Saudi Arabia, we are likely to assume that our distrusted adversary, the Soviet Union, opposes the establishment of such relations, simply because we view Russian leaders as generally opposed to our interests. Hence distrust profoundly encourages conflict. Trust, on the other hand, discourages conflict by fostering the belief that Other will try to accommodate our interests in areas of special importance to ourselves.

THE ABSENCE OF MUTUALLY ACCEPTABLE ALTERNATIVES

Having high aspirations and believing that Others do too are necessary for the perception of a conflict of interest, but they are not sufficient. Party must also perceive that the two sets of aspirations are incompatible. This is a matter of perceived alternatives—of plausible states of the world. At times there appear to be no alternatives that allow both parties to succeed. The available pie looks strictly limited: for example, both parties want all the available money. Or each party's efforts to achieve its goals look as though they will impose costs on the other party; for example, one wants to play music and the other wants to study quietly. In these cases there will be conflict. At other times, mutually acceptable alternatives seem to be available, making it appear that both parties can achieve their aims. In these cases, conflict will be absent.

Alternatives that satisfy both parties' aspirations can be called *integrative solutions* because they reconcile—that is, integrate—the two parties' interests. Anything that provides a glimmer of hope of finding an integrative alternative diminishes perceived conflict. For example, when Sadat made his famous trip to Jerusalem in 1977, it began to seem possible that a solution could be found to the major differences between Egypt and Israel. As a result, the tension between Egypt and Israel diminished in the eyes of most people on both sides. The apparent availability of integrative alternatives is called *perceived integrative potential* (PIP).

The perception of an absence of good alternatives is sometimes realistic; for example, critical resources desired by both parties may actually be in short supply. But at other times, PIP is low because of an erroneous perception of shortage. This is often due to zero-sum thinking, the belief that my gain is your loss and vice versa. Zero-sum thinking can result from a negative attitude toward the other party, which makes one unwilling to contribute to the other's welfare, or from a personality disposition akin to authoritarianism, which leads to a view of the world as a jungle in which everybody is in inevitable competition with everybody else (Kelley & Stahelski, 1970).

STABILITY AS THE DISCOURAGEMENT OF CONFLICT

The theory presented so far in this chapter identifies a number of conditions that encourage the development of conflict. When such conditions are not present or the opposite conditions prevail, conflict is unlikely to develop. Such a situation is said to be *stable* in one sense of this term. For reasons that will be presented at the end of this section, stability of this kind is often not desirable; but it is nevertheless important as an object of study.

There is no such thing as a totally stable, conflict-free system, but some systems come closer than others. Compare, for example, the bedroom community of Bethesda, Maryland, whose residents largely treat it as a post office address, with the poor sections of most big American cities or with countries that host guerrilla movements, such as Vietnam during the war and El Salvador today. In Bethesda, people's aspirations are largely compatible. In the latter two kinds of communities, they are not.

We can identify several stability-inducing conditions: Material resources are stable and ample so that people's aspirations do not outstrip what they can provide one another. Neither party sees itself as stronger than the other. There is consensus about a set of norms that produce a dovetailing of aspirations among the different segments of the community. Invidious comparisons are seldom made. The formation of struggle groups is inhibited. Potential adversaries trust each other. And integrative alternatives seem readily available. We will now examine three of the most important of these conditions in greater detail.

Normative Consensus

In low-conflict communities, one typically finds a broad normative consensus involving wide acceptance of certain goals, rules of conduct, role definitions, procedures for decision making, and authority and status systems. In a smoothly functioning automobile assembly plant, for example, established authority relations and work rules ensure the compatibility of most people's aspirations. And in a small New England town in the nineteenth century, the common cultural heritage and the Protestant church served as social cement. By contrast, many conflicts are often found in communities whose norms are breaking down, becase some community members begin to aspire to outcomes that others are not willing to let them have. An example can be seen in the "community" of two people known as a marriage. Many of the difficulties that arise in marriages today can be traced to current uncertainties in our society about what spouses can reasonably expect from one another.

When a set of norms has broad support among the more powerful segments of a community, minorities even if they are sizable are relatively unlikely to develop aspirations that threaten these norms. Most people learn to fit in and make the most of what may be a constricted set of options. Their aspirations fit social reality.

This does not mean that everybody is happy in a community with a broad normative consensus. The least advantaged—be they blacks, women, students, or slaves—may be quite unhappy. But most of them are sufficiently discouraged (by the fact that everyone else seems to support the norms) or frightened (by the techniques used to enforce the norms) to aspire to no better than they have. Of course, there are always some people in such settings who are restless about their rights and benefits. Community stability, in the sense of an absence of conflict, is enhanced if these people can readily escape, as many did by moving to the Western frontier from nineteenth-century New England. Stated more abstractly, the point is that withdrawing may substitute for more active forms of conflict behavior.

In stable communities, there are particularly clear norms governing those interpersonal relationships that are most prone to conflict, such as authority and status relationships. For example, there are plenty of opportunities for conflict to develop between employers and workers, because their activities and wishes are so intimately linked. But most people go into the job situation with a fairly clear idea of their appropriate roles. Workers expect to do more or less as they are told and to try to make a good impression; employers expect to provide clear direction and both positive and negative reinforcement. Considering the potential for controversy, things work amazingly well.

Absence of Invidious Comparisons

Social comparisons become invidious when, in the language of equity theory (see Walster, Walster & Berscheid, 1978), we find that people with whom we compare ourselves have a more favorable ratio of rewards to contributions than we do. For example, imagine that we discover that a fellow worker who seems to be working as hard as, or less hard than, ourselves is paid more than we are. Invidious comparisons lead to increased aspirations and hence, often, to social conflict. It follows that systems that discourage invidious comparisons are likely to be more stable than those that do not.

Invidious comparisons are particularly likely when there is status inconsistency (Kriesberg, 1982). Status inconsistency exists when there are multiple criteria for assessing people's contributions, and some people are higher on one criterion and lower on another criterion than others. In our society, for example, both experience and education are sources of on-the-job status. People with experience tend to feel that experience makes the most relevant contribution, whereas people with education tend to feel the opposite. When these two kinds of people have to work together, each is likely to feel more deserving of rewards than the other, and conflict is especially likely to develop. This is a hard nut for management to crack.

One method some organizations use to avoid invidious comparisons on the job is to conceal information about employee rewards. Salary information is particularly easy to conceal, and many organizations do so in an (often fruitless) effort to avert conflict. Another approach is to develop a firm set of norms that link rewards to a single, easily measured criterion, such as seniority or educational attainment. This is the method used to minimize invidious comparisons in the United States civil service system.

Certain myths about the relative contributions of various community members also foster this form of stability. In his ideal state, the "Republic," Plato recommended the establishment of such a myth. The rulers should be viewed as containing gold in their makeup, the auxiliaries as containing silver, and the farmers and other workers as containing iron and bronze. Myths about racial and sexual inferiority serve a similar purpose. In our society, blacks and women have traditionally been viewed as intellectually and emotionally deficient and hence less deserving of reward. Quite often they have subscribed to these myths themselves. Such myths encourage the belief that the more advantaged segments of a community are more deserving. Hence they promote social stability (though often at the expense of social justice).

Another stabilizing myth in our society is that of social mobility (Apfelbaum, 1979), which holds that anyone with ability can advance. This myth implies that, if some people's outcomes are lower than those of others, it is because of their inferior ability. Accordingly, they have no legitimate claim to greater rewards and no legitimate basis for making invidious comparisons. Because there is some truth to the myth of mobility in America—almost everybody knows someone who has risen from disadvantaged beginnings—it is a particularly important source of stability in our society.

Segregation of people with different levels of reward probably also contributes to stability. Two forms of segregation can be distinguished: psychological segregation, in which social groups do not identify with one another, and physical segregation, in which they do not come in informal contact with one another. Psychological segregation is self-imposed, whereas physical segregation can be either self-imposed or imposed by the community. An example of psychological segregation is the tendency of men to compare themselves with other men, and women with other women, in deciding how much money to ask from an employer (Major & Forcey, 1985). This tendency may well contribute to the perpetuation of lower pay for women. An example of self-imposed physical segregation is the tendency of blacks and whites to sort themselves out according to race in dining halls (Schelling, 1978). Psychological and physical segregation tend to diminish invidious comparisons between social groups, making conflict less likely to occur.

Failure of Struggle Group Formation

As indicated in Chapter 1, disadvantaged members of society are much more likely to develop aspirations for improving their status if they find common cause with one another and develop political struggle groups. It follows that conditions that prevent these developments encourage stability.

Psychological and physical separation of potential dissidents makes it difficult for them to join together. In the psychological realm, if they do not trust, respect, or identify with one another, they are unlikely to find common cause. For example, low-status people often do not respect one another because of the myth of their own inferiority. Hence they have difficulty working together on common problems. Likewise, rulers sometimes follow a policy of divide and rule, contriving controversies between potential opponents who might otherwise unite against them.

Keeping people apart physically can have a similar impact. Separating prison chums is a time-honored method for averting prison revolts. The rules against forming organizations without the approval of the Communist party, which are found in all communist countries, have similar objectives. So do rules that deny legitimacy to collective dissent. A dramatic example of the impact of giving legitimacy to a group of dissenters can be seen in an incident that occurred in the academic department of one of the authors. Associate professors who were unhappy with the organization of the department were allowed to form a committee to recommend changes. With their common interests legitimized in this way, they felt free to push for a sweeping reform of the structure of the department, which reduced the power of the chairman who had allowed them to organize.

The reader may have noticed a seeming contradiction between this policy of separating potential deviants and the policy of segregation that was mentioned earlier as a source of stability. The problem is that segregating low-status people from the rest of society has two rather different effects. It reduces social comparison with high-status people and hence makes these people more content with their inferior rewards. Yet the enforced association of segregated people also makes it easier for them to find common cause and to organize for struggle, making conflict more likely under certain circumstances. It is not yet clear under which conditions these opposing effects prevail, but some insights into this issue can be gained by watching the behavior of successful ruling elites. Ruling groups usually segregate low-status people, distancing themselves from these people but allowing them free association with one another. However, when there is reason to believe that a struggle group is developing, a policy of divide and rule is often substituted. Known dissidents are jailed or exiled, and others of the disadvantaged are "co-opted," or brought into closer association with the ruling group. This often nips conflict in the bud.

This combination of tactics was employed by administrators on a university campus (the University of Chicago) that survived an undergraduate crisis of the late 1960s without the sort of serious conflict that engulfed many other schools. (One of the authors of this book conducted interviews at that school shortly after the incident.) At the start of the crisis, the undergraduates were heavily segregated from the faculty and administration in the usual dormitory and classroom configurations. The crisis was initiated by a student sit-in designed to reverse a decision to deny tenure to a leftist professor. The administration immediately organized a series of meetings between the faculty and all students who would participate with the aim of revising the curriculum to make it conform more closely to student wishes. This dramatic activity produced bonds between the faculty and the bulk of the student body, psychologically separating the latter from the students who were sitting in. At the same time, a student court began systematically expelling hard-core members of the sit-in. As a result, the sit-in diminished in numbers and finally ended with its leaders admitting defeat.

Group formation usually requires leadership. Some individual or small group must articulate and codify the interests of the larger group, formulate a program, and organize people behind it (Dahrendorf, 1959). In fact, whether a dissident movement can get off the ground is largely a function of whether leadership is available and able to operate. It follows that one method of containing the development of a struggle group is to remove potential leaders. Another method, which is effective in somewhat aroused situations, is for moderate and respected community members to speak against, and thus discredit, emerging radical leadership (Coleman, 1957).

The success of struggle groups often depends on support from outside their community. In recent years, much has been made of outside military support for guerrilla groups in countries like South Vietnam and El Salvador. But the issue is more complicated than this. Community dissent often grows out of a broad social movement at the national or even world-wide level. A case in point is the radical student movement of the late 1960s, which permeated the United States and had its counterparts in France, West Germany, Mexico, and many other countries. Some people thought that national or international leaders were pulling the strings in local communities, but this was

seldom the case. The leadership was usually local in origin, and the main contributions of the national and international movements were moral support
and examples that could be imitated. These demonstrations, which spread
rapidly in 1968 and 1969, often seemed to contain an element of "keeping up
with the Jones's." The news that students had started to demonstrate in one
location encouraged the belief that it was possible elsewhere. Pride in one's
own local movement depended in part on having a demonstration comparable
to those that had occurred on other campuses.

It follows that communities are less stable when there exists a national or
international movement consisting of struggle groups in other communities
(Coleman, 1957). Once such a movement gets started, it is hard to put the
genie back in the bottle. Each struggle action serves as an example to other
communities, which then serve as examples to still others in a chain reaction.

Critique of Stability as the Discouragement of Conflict

As mentioned in Chapter 1, conflict has a number of positive functions.
Hence, conditions that produce stability by discouraging conflict are a mixed
blessing. One problem with discouraging conflict is that archaic policies that
advance few people's interests may be preserved. Communities that are
averse to conflict typically fail to make needed changes, because there are almost always some proponents of the status quo, however unfavorable it may
be for the majority of citizens. In Coser's (1956) words, "Conflict prevents the
ossification of the social system by exerting pressure for innovation and
creativity" (p. 197). Another danger of putting a cap on conflict is that doing
so may encourage premature decision making. A group that is fearful of conflict among its members may adopt the first plausible suggestion in order to
close off debate among its members. Premature decisions are, of course, often
poor decisions. A third danger is that benign misunderstandings that serve nobody's interests may arise. Research (Fry, Firestone & Williams, 1983) suggests that such misunderstandings are sometimes found in courtship. Each
party is so afraid of antagonizing the other that neither pushes his or her
viewpoint sufficiently for the other to understand it.

Conflict is also often necessary to achieve justice. Many of the techniques
described in the previous section are used by tyrants and other unfeeling elite
groups to prevent agitation for the redress of legitimate grievances. A
seemingly tranquil situation may serve to mask gross inequities and interpersonal exploitation.

Nevertheless, there is a limit to the amount of conflict that society can tol-
erate, even conflict of the mildest and most productive sort. Conflict takes
time and energy away from other pursuits. A group, organization, or country
can become so embroiled in controversy that it is unable to cope with basic
environmental demands. Something like this appears to have happened in Po-
land during 1981 and 1982, when the struggle between the government and
the popular union Solidarity greatly diminished industrial productivity.

In conclusion, groups and societies must tread a fine line between too little and too much stability. Some element of stability is essential, because it is necessary to keep the total amount of conflict between their members within bounds. If most issues were under debate most of the time, there would be no time or energy for coping activities. But too much stability can be maladaptive because efforts to avert conflict run the risk of producing premature decisions and perpetuating outdated policies.

CONCLUSIONS

In this chapter, we have examined the causes of conflict and the conditions of stability that reduce the likelihood of conflict. Stability, in the sense of the absence of conflict, seems superficially attractive, but efforts to achieve this goal can easily be counterproductive. They may consign society to a state of affairs that is static, sometimes unjust, and often unworkable in the long run.

We turn now to strategic choice. Chapter 3 deals with the conditions that determine the decisions that parties to conflict make among the five basic strategies discussed earlier: contending, problem solving, yielding, inaction, and withdrawing.

CHAPTER 3

Strategic Choice

Peter Colger has to make a decision. For months he has been looking forward to taking his two weeks of vacation at a quiet mountain lodge where he can hunt, fish, and hike to lofty scenic overlooks. Now his wife Mary has rudely challenged this dream. She has told him that she finds the mountains boring and wants to go to Ocean City, Maryland, a busy seaside resort that Peter dislikes intensely. Peter must decide what strategy to employ in this controversy.

As we saw in Chapter 1, five general strategies are available to Peter. He can engage in *contentious behavior* and try to prevail—for example, by arguing for the merits of a mountain vacation, indicating that he had already made up his mind, threatening to take a separate vacation if Mary does not agree, or even making a large deposit on a room in a mountain hotel. He can take a *problem-solving* approach and try to find a way to go to both places or to a vacation spot that satisfies both sets of interests. He can *yield* to Mary's demands and agree to go to the seashore. He can be *inactive* (do nothing) in the hope that the issue will simply go away. Or he can *withdraw* from the controversy—for example, by deciding not to take a vacation.

The aim of this chapter is to examine the conditions that determine how Peter (and, more generally, anyone facing a conflict) decides among these basic strategies. We will focus mainly on the first three strategies (contending, problem solving, and yielding), which we call the "coping strategies" because, as we saw in Chapter 1, they involve active efforts to resolve the controversy.

NATURE OF THE STRATEGIES

Contending refers to any effort to resolve a conflict on one's own terms without regard to the other party's interests. Parties who employ this strategy maintain their own aspirations and try to persuade the other party to yield. Various tactics are available to parties who choose this strategy. They include making threats, imposing penalties with the understanding that they will be withdrawn if the other concedes, and taking preemptive actions designed to resolve the conflict without the other's consent (such as making a deposit at a mountain hotel in our example). If the parties are trying to reach a negotiated settlement of the controversy, contending may also involve presenting persuasive arguments, making demands that far exceed what is actually acceptable, committing oneself to an "unalterable" position, or imposing a deadline.

By contrast, *problem solving* entails an effort to identify the issues dividing the parties and to develop and move toward a solution that appeals to both sides. Parties who employ this strategy maintain their own aspirations and try to find a way of reconciling them with the other party's aspirations.

The agreement developed in problem solving can take the form of a compromise (an obvious alternative that stands part way between the two parties' preferred positions), or it can take the form of an integrative solution (a creative reconciliation of the two parties' basic interests). The difference between a compromise and an integrative solution is illustrated by two options that were discussed during the Camp David negotiations described in Chapter 1. A compromise proposal, in which Egypt and Israel would each get half the Sinai, was unacceptable to both sides. The key to settlement was an integrative solution, in which Egypt got the Sinai and Israel got diplomatic recognition and military guarantees.

Various tactics are available to implement the strategy of problem solving. These include risky moves such as conceding with the expectation of receiving a return concession, mentioning possible compromises as talking points, and revealing one's underlying interests. They also include cautious moves such as hinting at possible compromises, sending disavowable intermediaries to discuss the issues, communicating through back channels, and communicating through a mediator.

Although problem solving has been described so far as an individual activity, it can also be a joint enterprise involving both parties. For example, two people can exchange accurate information about their underlying interests, collectively identify new issues in light of this information, brainstorm to seek alternative ways of dealing with the issues, and sometimes even work together to evaluate these alternatives. Joint problem solving is an excellent way to locate mutually acceptable solutions, but it is sometimes impractical because one party is not ready for it or the parties do not trust each other. Hence, individual problem solving must at times be substituted.

Yielding, which involves lowering one's aspirations, need not imply the total capitulation that we saw in the vacation example. It can also imply a partial concession. For example, Peter Colger might decide to foresake his secondary goal of hiking to mountain overlooks in order to make it easier to find a mutually acceptable agreement. He could then engage in problem solving, seeking a quiet resort that permits fishing and hiking where his wife can also accomplish her major goals.

Withdrawing and *inaction* are similar to each other in that they involve termination of efforts to resolve the controversy. They differ in that withdrawing is a permanent termination, whereas inaction is a temporary move that leaves open the possibility of resuming efforts to cope with the controversy. Withdrawing is usually a distinct strategy, but it may at times be hard to distinguish from contending or yielding. For example, if I withdraw from a controversy with my son over the use of my car, I automatically win and thus gain a contentious advantage. If my son withdraws, he is essentially yielding to my viewpoint.

CHOOSING A STRATEGY

There are trade-offs among the five basic strategies, in the sense that choosing one of them makes selecting the others less likely. Inaction and withdrawing are totally incompatible with each other and with the three coping strategies. Though sometimes found in combination with each other, the coping strategies are also somewhat incompatible. There are three reasons for this latter incompatibility. First, the coping strategies are alternative means of moving toward the same end, agreement with the other party. If it is not possible to use one of them, a person is more likely to employ the others. Second, these strategies require different psychological orientations; for example, it does not seem quite right to try to push another party around while yielding to or working with that party. Third, these strategies tend to send out contradictory signals to the other party. Yielding often implies weakness, which is incompatible with putting effective pressure on the other. Contending can undermine the other party's trust, which is an important element of effective problem solving.

Because of these trade-offs, there are indirect as well as direct antecedents of all five strategies. Direct antecedents, as we would expect, directly affect the likelihood of adopting a strategy. Indirect antecedents affect this likelihood by encouraging or discouraging one of the other strategies.

Most of the rest of this chapter is devoted to two theoretical notions about the determinants of choice among the basic strategies. The first, which is summarized in a *dual concern model*, traces strategic choice to the relative strength of concern about own and other's outcomes. The second, which we call the *perceived feasibility perspective*, attributes this choice to the perceived likelihood of success and the cost of enacting the various strategies. These two theoretical notions are complementary in the sense that each deals with issues ignored by the other.

A good deal of evidence will be cited in support of these theoretical notions, most of it derived from laboratory experiments on simulated negotiation. *Negotiation*, a form of conflict behavior, occurs when two parties try to resolve a divergence of interest by means of conversation. Laboratory experiments on this phenomenon place subjects (usually undergraduates) in a simulated negotiation setting and manipulate theoretically relevant variables. Careful measurements of reactions to these variables are taken. A more detailed discussion of this kind of research can be found in Pruitt (1981) and Rubin and Brown (1975).

The chapter ends with a discussion of the forces that determine the vigor with which the three coping strategies are enacted.

THE DUAL CONCERN MODEL

The dual concern model appears in Figure 3.1. It postulates two types of concerns: *concern about own outcomes,* which is shown on the abscissa, and *concern about the other party's outcomes,* which is shown on the ordinate. These concerns are portrayed as ranging from indifference (at the zero point of the coordinate) to very great concern.

The two concerns in this model are defined as follows: Concern about own outcomes means placing importance on one's own interests—one's needs and values—in the realm under dispute. People with a strong concern about their own outcomes are highly resistant to yielding; in other words, their aspirations tend to be rigid and high.[1] Concern about the other's outcomes implies placing importance on the other's interests—feeling responsible for the quality of the other's outcomes. This concern is sometimes *genuine,* involving an intrinsic interest in the other's welfare. However, it is more often *instrumental,* being aimed at helping the other in order to advance one's own interests. Thus, for example, dependence on another person often encourages efforts to build a working relationship with that person by trying to satisfy his or her needs.

Although this is not shown in Figure 3.1, it is theoretically possible for people to have negative concerns about the other party's outcomes and even about their own outcomes. In other words, we might have extended the coordinates in the figure downward and to the left. A few points about negative concerns will be made in this chapter but not enough to warrant introducing further complexity into the formal statement of the model.

The dual concern model makes the following predictions about the antecedents of strategic choice: Problem solving is encouraged when there is a strong concern about both own and other's outcomes. Yielding is encouraged by a strong concern about only the other's outcomes. Contending is encouraged by a strong concern about only one's own outcomes. Inaction is encouraged when concern about both parties' outcomes is weak. The model makes no predictions about the antecedents of withdrawing.

The dual concern model has its origins in Blake and Mouton's (1964) managerial grid and has been adapted to the analysis of conflict by various authors (Blake & Mouton, 1979; Filley, 1975; Gladwin & Walter, 1980; Rahim, 1983; Ruble & Thomas, 1976; Thomas, 1976). Other labels are sometimes given to the dimensions in this model. For example, concern about own outcomes is sometimes called "assertiveness," and concern about other's outcomes is sometimes called "cooperativeness."

Other versions of the dual concern model (Filley, 1975; Thomas, 1976) postulate a fifth strategy called "compromising," which is ordinarily shown in the middle of the figure because it is viewed as due to a moderate concern about both self and other. We do not take this approach, because we see no need to postulate a separate strategy in order to explain the development of

---

[1]See Kelley, Beckman & Fischer (1967) for a sophisticated discussion of the concept of resistance to yielding.

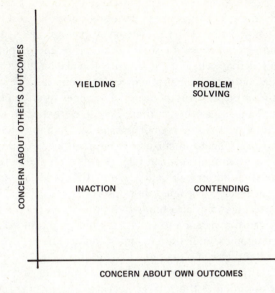

Figure 3.1   The dual concern model.

compromises. We see compromises as arising from one of two sources—either lazy problem solving involving a half-hearted attempt to satisfy the two parties' interests, or simple yielding by both parties.

Thomas (1976) notes that the two concerns in the dual concern model are often erroneously reduced to a single dimension, with selfishness (concern about own outcomes) on one end and cooperativeness (concern about other's outcomes) on the other. This is an improper simplification, because it is clear that both concerns can be strong at the same time. People can be both selfish and cooperative (leading them to engage in problem solving in an effort to reconcile both parties' interests). By postulating dual concerns, we are forced to distinguish between two ways of cooperating with the other party, yielding and problem solving. These were not sufficiently separated in a prior theory of strategic choice (Deutsch, 1973), which proposed only a single motivational dimension ranging from competition to cooperation. Postulating dual concerns also forces us to distinguish between two ways of advancing one's own interests, contending and problem solving.

Determinants of Concern about Own Outcomes

The strength of concern about own outcomes differs from situation to situation and from person to person. For example, person A may be relatively indifferent about the location and quality of his or her vacation, whereas this may be a matter of great concern for person B. Person A, on the other hand, may have a much deeper concern about the quality of his or her work on the job.

Concern about own outcomes can be traced to a number of determinants.

One is the importance of the values affected by these outcomes. Person B may have an extremely taxing job, which produces a great need for rest and relaxation during his or her vacation, whereas person A may not have such strong needs. When a spouse challenges these vacation preferences, person A is likely to yield or be inactive, whereas person B will make an effort to salvage these preferences via contentious or problem-solving activities.

Another determinant of concern about own outcomes in any one realm is the importance of outcomes in other realms. People do not have an infinite amount of time or energy, so they cannot pursue all of their interests with equal intensity. A strong concern about one issue often leads to a weak concern about others. For example, person A may be relatively indifferent to the issue of quality of vacation because of being wrapped up in his or her job, the campaign for a nuclear freeze, or some other absorbing activity.

Concern about own outcomes also tends to be low when people are afraid of conflict. This is because resistance to yielding, which is produced by a high concern about own outcomes, tends to engender conflict. Fear of conflict is a personality predisposition for some people. It is also produced by certain situations, such as being attracted to—or dependent on—another person but distrustful of the other's opinion of the self (Hancock & Sorrentino, 1980). Situations such as this, which are said to involve "false cohesiveness" (Longley & Pruitt, 1980), are especially common at the beginning of a relationship when people are feeling each other out. Research on newly formed romantic couples suggests that such sentiments can block all forms of assertiveness, including both contentious and problem-solving behavior (Fry, Firestone & Williams, 1983).

Concern about own group's outcomes. The forces mentioned so far affect individuals acting on their own behalf. But the parties to conflict are often groups. Hence we must inquire into the antecedents of the concern that is frequently felt by group members about the outcomes achieved by their group.

Especially strong concerns about the fate of the group tend to develop in cohesive groups whose members share a similar life situation and discuss their common fate with one another. This is particularly likely when the members of such groups regard themselves as part of a broader social movement, making common cause with similar groups in other locations (Kriesberg, 1982).

When the parties are groups or organizations, actual conflict behavior is usually carried out by representatives. Research on negotiation (Benton & Druckman, 1973) suggests that representatives are usually more reluctant to yield than are individuals bargaining on their own behalf. This is because they are trying to please their constituents and typically view their constituents as nonconciliatory. The effect disappears in those infrequent cases where the constituent is revealed to have a conciliatory bias (Benton & Druckman, 1974).

Other studies suggest that representatives are especially reluctant to yield under conditions that make them anxious to please their constituents, such as when they have low status in their groups (Kogan, Lamm & Trommsdorff,

1972), are distrusted by their constituents (Wall, 1975), wish to continue associating with their constituents (Klimoski, 1972), or have female as opposed to male constituents (Forcey, Van Slyck, Carnevale & Pruitt, 1983). All of these conditions can be viewed as enhancing concern about own side's outcomes.

Accountability to constituents has much the same effect. A representative is accountable to the extent that he or she must report the outcome of the negotiation to powerful constituents. Accountable representatives are especially reluctant to concede in negotiation (Bartunek, Benton & Keys, 1975), suggesting that they are particularly concerned about group outcomes. As a result, they are more likely to adopt a contentious or problem-solving approach than to yield (Ben-Yoav & Pruitt, 1984b).

Quite often, constituents instruct their representatives to achieve high outcomes and are dissatisfied when they come home with less. This also serves to bolster the concern felt by representatives for their side's outcomes.

Determinants of Concern about the Other Party's Outcomes

As mentioned earlier, concern about the other party's outcomes takes two basic forms: *genuine* concern, based on an intrinsic interest in the other's welfare, and *instrumental* concern, aimed at advancing one's own interests. There is an important difference between these two forms of concern. Because instrumental concern is aimed at impressing the other, it is stronger when the other is more concerned about his or her own outcomes. By contrast, genuine concern aims at serving the other regardless of the other's degree of self-interest.

Genuine concern about the other party's outcomes is fostered by various kinds of interpersonal *bonds*, including attraction (Clark & Mills, 1979), perceived similarity (Hornstein, 1976), and kinship or common group identity (Hatton, 1967). Genuine concern is also fostered by a positive mood (Isen & Levin, 1972) and by taking helpful actions toward someone (not necessarily the party with whom one is now in conflict) in the recent past, especially if there were no clear external incentives for this action (Freedman & Fraser, 1966; Uranowitz, 1975).

Instrumental concern about the other party's outcomes is common whenever one sees oneself as dependent on the other—when the other is seen as able to provide rewards and penalties. An example is the expectation of further negotiation in the future. Dependence leads to the conclusion that it is desirable to build a relationship with the other now. Hence one tries to impress the other with one's concern about his or her welfare.

Dependence is by no means a one-way street. Mutual dependence is quite common and can encourage either mutual yielding or mutual problem solving. The impact on mutual problem solving is illustrated by a case study of mediation between two managers in the same company (Walton, 1969). It was not until both men discovered that they could be hurt by one another that they began trying to solve the problems they were having with each other.

For people to be aware of their dependence on another party, it is often necessary for them to project themselves into the future. This point is important for understanding conflict, because people embroiled in escalating conflicts often lose awareness of the future. They concentrate so hard on winning in the present that they lose track of the importance of maintaining good relations with the other party. In such situations, future perspective can be regained in a number of ways. One is to take time out from the controversy—to become disengaged for a while. Research suggests that such a "cooling off period" enhances cooperativeness in settings where parties are basically interdependent (Pilisuk, Kiritz & Clampitt, 1971).

Although bonds and dependencies usually foster concern about the other party's outcomes, under certain conditions they can produce exactly the opposite reaction—antagonism toward the other and adoption of contentious tactics. This reaction occurs when people to whom we are bonded—friends, relatives, people we admire—fail to fulfill their minimum obligations or severely frustrate us. Our bonds to these people can actually encourage more anger and aggression than we would otherwise feel, because we believe they owe us preferential treatment. A similar reaction occurs when people on whom we are dependent are unresponsive to our needs (Gruder, 1971). The ordinary reaction to dependence is concern about the other party's needs. But if the other is perceived as taking advantage of this concern, it often seems necessary to reverse gears and retaliate in order to motivate the other to be more responsive. (These reactions are outside the scope of the dual concern model, which deals only with positive concern about the other's outcomes.)

Predictions from the Model

The dual concern model has received support in three recent studies. These studies made use of a laboratory simulation of negotiation in which two participants play the roles of buyer and seller in a wholesale market. Their task is to reach agreement on the prices of three appliances: typewriters, vacuum cleaners, and sewing machines. Each participant has a benefit schedule showing the profit that his or her firm will make at each price level. The participants are allowed to talk about their benefit schedules but not to show them to each other. The benefit schedules are constructed so that there are hidden solutions that provide much greater benefit to both parties than those that are obvious at first, but these solutions can be achieved only if one or both parties engage in problem solving. In all three studies, the two concerns specified in the dual concern model were manipulated independently of each other in a 2×2 design. Both subjects in a dyad always received the same combination of concerns.

In the first two studies, concern about own outcomes was manipulated by means of instructions about the lower limit of profit the subjects could achieve. High concern was produced by telling both subjects privately that their firms required them to achieve no less than a particular profit level ($4,600); low concern was produced by telling them nothing about a lower limit on profit. The researchers reasoned that the former condition would encourage more resistance to yielding than the latter.

The first study (Pruitt, Carnevale, Ben-Yoav, Nochajski & Van Slyck, 1983) involved a manipulation of genuine concern about the other's outcomes. High concern was produced by putting the participants in a good mood, which has been shown to induce a desire to be helpful (Isen & Levin, 1972). Just before the beginning of negotiation, both subjects received gifts from a confederate of the experimenter. There were no gifts in the low-concern condition. The second study (Ben-Yoav & Pruitt, 1984a) involved a manipulation of strategic concern. High concern was produced by giving the subjects an expectation of cooperative future interaction. They were told that they would have to work together toward a common goal on a task following the negotiation. The aim of this instruction was to make them feel dependent on each other and hence desirous of developing a working relationship. In the low-concern condition, they were told that they would be working alone on a subsequent task.

The average joint benefit (sum of the two parties' profits) achieved in the first two studies is shown in Figure 3.2. In both studies, a combination of high concern about own outcomes and high concern about the other's outcomes (shown in the upper right-hand cell) produced especially high joint benefit. This result is evidence of active problem-solving behavior, as predicted by the dual concern model. Other evidence of problem solving in this condition is the fact that the negotiators were especially likely to give each other information about the entries in their profit schedules. A combination of high concern about own outcomes and low concern about the other's outcomes (lower right-hand cell) produced moderately low joint benefit. Contentious statements such as persuasive arguments and threats were especially common in this condition, again supporting the dual concern model. A combination of low concern about own outcomes and high concern about the other's outcomes (upper left-hand cell) produced the lowest joint benefit of all, suggesting the yielding (aspiration collapse) predicted by the dual concern model.

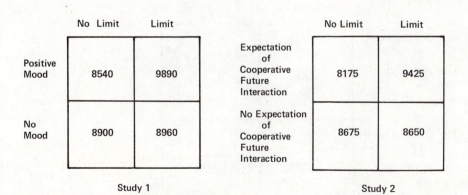

	No Limit	Limit		No Limit	Limit
Positive Mood	8540	9890	Expectation of Cooperative Future Interaction	8175	9425
No Mood	8900	8960	No Expectation of Cooperative Future Interaction	8675	8650
	Study 1			Study 2	

Figure 3.2   Joint benefit achieved in studies 1 and 2.

The results of these two studies show that, as predicted by the dual concern model, concern about the other party's outcomes is a two-edged sword. In conjunction with concern about own outcomes, it leads to problem solving and (when both parties share the same concerns) especially high joint benefit. But when concern about own outcomes is weak, concern about the other party's outcomes produces yielding and especially low joint benefit.

In the third study (Ben-Yoav & Pruitt, 1984b), concern about the other party's outcomes was again manipulated by the presence vs. absence of an expectation of cooperative future interaction. Concern about own outcomes was manipulated by means of high vs. low accountability to constituents. Under high accountability, the constituents (who were confederates) were able to divide the money earned in the negotiation and write an evaluation of the outcomes achieved by their negotiators. Under low accountability, the negotiators divided the money earned, and no evaluations were written.

The results for joint benefit are shown in Figure 3.3. As predicted by the dual concern model, high accountability in the absence of an expectation of cooperative future interaction encouraged heavy contentious verbalizations and low joint benefit (as shown in the lower right-hand cell). But the impact of accountability was completely reversed when there was an expectation of future interaction. In this condition (upper right-hand cell), accountability encouraged especially high joint benefit, presumably because it fostered heavy joint problem solving.

These results suggest that accountability, and hence concern about own outcomes, is also a two-edged sword. Under normal conditions, it fosters contentious behavior and low joint benefit. But under conditions that encourage a desire for good relations between the opposing parties, it fosters problem solving and high joint benefit.

	Accountability	
	Low	High
Expectation of Cooperative Future Interaction	8600	9770
No Expectation of Cooperative Future Interaction	8840	8300

Figure 3.3   Joint benefit achieved in study 3.

In summary, the dual concern model postulates that strategic choice is determined by the strength of two concerns: concern for own outcomes and concern for the other party's outcomes. When both concerns are strong, people prefer problem solving; when the former concern is strong, they prefer contending; when the latter concern is strong, they prefer yielding; and when both concerns are weak, inaction is likely to be found. Concern about own outcomes produces high, rigid aspirations. It tends to be strong when the interests at stake are important, when outcomes in other realms are unimportant, when there is low fear of conflict, when there is high accountability to constituents, and when constituents insist that their representative achieve a high level of benefit. Concern about the other party's outcomes can be either genuine or instrumental (strategic). Genuine concern is fostered by interpersonal bonds of all types and by good mood. Instrumental concern is fostered by a desire to develop a working relationship with a person on whom one is dependent. The predictive value of this model has been demonstrated in three studies.

THE PERCEIVED FEASIBILITY PERSPECTIVE

Choice among the five basic strategies is also a matter of perceived feasibility—the extent to which the strategy seems capable of achieving the concerns that give rise to it and the cost that is anticipated from enacting each strategy. Considerations of feasibility supplement those specified by the dual concern model. The dual concern model indicates the strategies preferred under various combinations of concern about own and other's outcomes. But for a strategy actually to be adopted, it must also be seen as minimally feasible. If not, another strategy will be chosen, even if it is less consistent with the current combination of concerns.

For example, take parties who are concerned about both their own and the other party's outcomes. Problem solving is their preferred strategy. But if this strategy seems infeasible or too risky, they are likely to shift to yielding or contending, their next best alternatives. Which of these is chosen is determined both by the relative strength of the two concerns and by other considerations of feasibility and cost. If the parties are more concerned about the other's outcomes than their own, they adopt a yielding approach, provided that this seems reasonably feasible. If they are more concerned about their own outcomes than the other's, they shift to contentious behavior, also provided that this seems reasonably feasible.

For another example, take parties who are concerned mainly about their own outcomes. Contending is their preferred strategy because it holds the promise of getting something for nothing. But problem solving is a close second if the contentious approach appears infeasible or costly. Indeed, problem solving often seems the most feasible way of pursuing one's own interests.

The next three sections deal with the perceived feasibility of three of the fundamental strategies under consideration in this chapter: problem solving, contending, and inaction.

Perceived Feasibility of Problem Solving

Problem solving seems more feasible the greater the *perceived common ground* (PCG). PCG is a party's assessment of the likelihood of finding an alternative that satisfies both parties' aspirations. The more likely it seems that such an alternative can be found, the more feasible problem solving appears to be. PCG is greater (1) the lower Party's own aspirations, (2) the lower Other's aspirations as perceived by Party, and (3) the greater the perceived integrative potential (PIP)—that is, Party's faith that alternatives favorable to both parties exist or can be devised.

This definition implies that PCG is the mirror image of perceived conflict. As PCG goes up, conflict, in the sense of perceived divergence of interest, goes down.

The reader may be surprised to learn that lower aspirations make problem solving seem more feasible. Superficially, this seems inconsistent with the point made earlier that lack of concern about one's own interests (which produces low aspirations) reduces the likelihood of problem solving. However, these two points are not contradictory. We are talking about two countervailing forces that are simultaneously activated when concern about own interests is low. The one makes problem solving seem more feasible, and the other (by permitting the strategy of yielding) makes problem solving seem less necessary.

Perceived integrative potential (PIP) (a component of PCG) needs further elaboration. At any given point in negotiation, some alternatives are known and the availability of others is suspected. PIP is high when there are known alternatives that provide high benefit to both parties. It is moderately high when it seems probable that such alternatives can be developed—the more definite the prospects for developing such an alternative, the higher is PIP. It is low when there seems little prospect of finding mutually beneficial alternatives.

Greater clarity about the concepts of PIP and PCG is provided by the graphs in Figure 3.4. The abscissa in these graphs maps Party's own benefits; the ordinate, Party's perception of Other's benefits. The heavy points in these graphs refer to known alternatives, the medium points to alternatives that seem potentially discoverable, and the light points to long shots. The location of a point in the space shows the perceived value of that alternative to the two parties. The vertical lines in these graphs refer to Party's own aspirations and the horizontal lines to Other's perceived aspirations.

PCG is greater the more points there are to the northeast (above and to the right) of the intersection of the aspiration lines and the darker these points are. PCG is greater in Figure 3.4B than in Figure 3.4A because Party's own aspirations are lower. It is greater in Figure 3.4C than in Figure 3.4B because Other's perceived aspirations are also lower. It is greater in Figure 3.4D than in Figure 3.4C because of greater PIP—that is, greater perceived likelihood that mutually beneficial alternatives can be developed (as shown by the fact that the darker points are farther from the origin in the northeast direction).

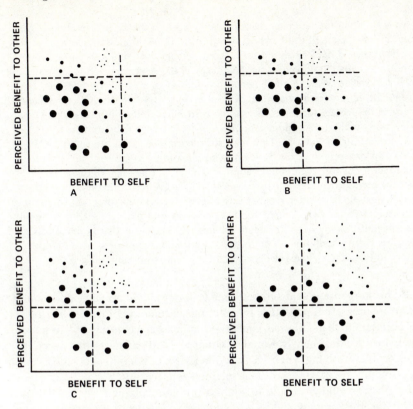

Figure 3.4   Four levels of perceived common ground.

Determinants of perceived integrative potential. A number of conditions contribute to PIP and hence to the likelihood that problem solving will be employed.

1. *Faith in own problem-solving ability.* Some people are good communicators and/or understand well how to devise mutually beneficial alternatives. Hence their experience leads them to see considerable integrative potential in almost any situation. Others, less well endowed, are likely to view conflict as more intractable and to adopt strategies of yielding or contending rather than problem solving.

2. *Momentum.* Momentum refers to prior success at reaching agreement in the current controversy. The more frequent and recent such successes have been, the greater will be Party's faith that these successes can be reproduced in the future and that problem solving is worthwhile. Momentum can sometimes be encouraged by scheduling easier issues earlier in a negotiation agenda, so that a solid foundation of success has been built by the time more difficult issues are encountered.

3. *Availability of a mediator.* Mediators often serve as communication links between the parties, coordinating movement toward compromise or helping to develop integrative solutions. Their availability should make problem solving seem more likely to be successful.

An example of the latter mechanism can be seen in the British reaction to the Argentine occupation of the Falkland Islands in 1982. Yielding was ruled out on the grounds of cost to the British image. Inaction seemed inadvisable because every day of the occupation enhanced the legitimacy of the Argentine action. In short, the choice was between contending and problem solving. At first it appeared that there might be integrative potential; American Secretary of State Alexander Haig was trying to mediate the crisis. Hence the British adopted a problem-solving strategy, working with Haig while defending their basic interests by moving their fleet slowly toward South America. However, PIP disappeared with the failure of Haig's mission, making problem solving seem quite infeasible. As a result, the British adopted an exclusively contentious approach, an all-out invasion of the islands.

4. *Other's perceived readiness for problem solving.* Problem solving seems more feasible to the extent that Other seems ready to participate in this process. There are two reasons for this. One is increased PIP, because joint problem solving is usually more efficient than unilateral problem solving. The second is that problem solving seems less risky when Other is not taking a contentious approach, because under those conditions there is less danger in allowing oneself to look weak.

Trust. The perception that Other is ready for problem solving, and hence that there is integrative potential, is sometimes a function of trust—that is, of Party's perception that Other is concerned about Party's interests. Research (Kimmel, Pruitt, Magenau & Konar-Goldband, 1980) suggests that trust encourages problem solving when Party is otherwise inclined to adopt this strategy, presumably by making problem solving seem feasible.

Although trust allows people to adopt a problem solving strategy, it is no guarantee that this strategy will be adopted. Indeed, trust can sometimes have quite the opposite effect, encouraging high, inflexible aspirations defended by contentious behavior.

Whether trust encourages problem solving or contending depends at least in part on Other's perceived resistance to yielding—that is, the apparent firmness of Other's aspirations. A trusted Other whose aspirations do not seem firm will be expected to give in to Party's demands. Hence contentious behavior seems especially feasible. But if Other's aspirations seem firm, trust implies instead that Other will cooperate if and only if Party cooperates. This encourages Party to adopt a problem-solving strategy.

Evidence that problem solving is encouraged by a combination of trust and perceived firmness comes from several bargaining experiments. All of these studies examined bargainer response to helpful actions from the other party, which actions presumably engendered trust. When the other party had been helpful, bargainers were more willing to cooperate if the other also (1) had high threat capacity (Lindskold & Bennett, 1973; Michener, Vaske, Schleifer, Plazewski & Chapman, 1975), (2) had a tough constituent (Wall, 1977), (3) had been unyielding or competitive in the past (Deutsch, 1973; Harford & Solomon, 1967), or (4) had been unwilling to make unilateral concessions in the past (Komorita & Esser, 1975; McGillicuddy, Pruitt & Syna, 1984). These four conditions presumably enhance Party's perception that Other has firm aspirations.

Trust develops in a number of ways. It is encouraged by a perception that the other party has a positive attitude toward us, is similar to us, or is dependent on us. As an example of the latter point, Solomon (1960) has shown that trust is greater when one sees oneself as having a capacity to punish the other for failing to cooperate.

Trust also tends to develop when one has been helpful toward the other party (Loomis, 1959). This prediction is implied by dissonance (Festinger, 1957) and self-perception (Bem, 1972) theories. It also follows from the assumption that the other will reciprocate one's helpful behavior.

We tend to trust people who have been helpful or cooperative, especially if their help is directed toward us (Cooper & Fazio, 1979) and has occurred recently (Kelley & Stahelski, 1970). Trust is an especially common response when the other's helpful behavior is seen as voluntary and not as a product of environmental forces. Hence we tend to trust others whose helpful behavior is not required by their role (Jones & Davis, 1965) or seems to be costly to them (Komorita, 1973). All of these circumstances encourage problem solving by enhancing perceived integrative potential.

Perceived Feasibility of Contending

Contending seems more feasible the lower the Other's apparent resistance to yielding. There is not much point in putting pressure on an opponent who has ultra-strong feelings, has powerful and resolute constituents, or has already yielded to the bare bone of need. Other tactics, such as yielding and problem solving, are more likely to be adopted. But if the other's aspirations (however high they may be) seem relatively easy to dislodge, contentious behavior gets a boost.

The points just made imply that contentious behavior is often self-liquidating, a victim of both failure and success. If it fails, this indicates that Other's resistance is greater than originally thought, so Party will abandon the tactic. If it succeeds and Other yields, Other's resistance to further yielding is likely to grow because Other will come closer and closer to his or her limit. Again, Party must eventually abandon the tactic.

The feasibility of contending is also a function of Party's apparent capacity to employ contentious tactics and of Other's apparent capacity to counter them. Does Party have good arguments? Does Other have counterarguments? Is Party adept at arguing his or her case? How effective is Other as a debater? Can Party reward or punish Other? How good are Other's defenses against such tactics? Does Party have ways to commit himself or herself credibly? Is Other capable of undoing these commitments?

Capacities such as these are sometimes lumped together under the familiar concepts of "power" and "counterpower." These concepts have some merit in that they allow us to make a few broad generalizations. For example, we can generalize that more powerful people have higher aspirations and make greater use of heavy contentious tactics, regardless of the source of their power. But there is a tendency to overuse these concepts in social science theory, making facile generalizations with little real meaning (see, for example, Morgenthau, 1967). The problem is that there are many kinds of power, each with a different set of properties (French & Raven, 1959).

In a stable long-term relationship, each party's capacity to employ contentious tactics tends to be matched by the other's level of resistance, so that there is relatively little advantage to either party in employing contentious tactics. Hence, on important issues where the parties cannot easily yield, joint problem solving is most likely to be the strategic choice. This is true even when threat capacity greatly favors one side, as in a relationship between master and slave. Joint problem solving is not uncommon in such relationships, though the outcome is likely to benefit the master far more than the slave. The slave's situation produces aspirations that are so low that his or her resistance to further yielding is strong enough to balance the master's superior threat capacity.

Perceived Cost.   Contentious behavior, particularly in its more severe forms, runs the risk of alienating the other party and starting a conflict spiral. There is also some danger of third-party censure. Such considerations can deter contentious behavior, particularly when one is dependent on the other party or on watchful third parties.

Costs are also associated with constituent *surveillance,* which has a complicated relationship to the use of contentious tactics. Surveillance must be distinguished from accountability to constituents. Representatives are accountable to the extent that they can be rewarded or punished on the basis of the outcomes they generate for their constituents. They are under surveillance when their actual conflict behavior (for example, how they negotiate) is being observed. Representatives who are being observed by their constituents usually fear getting out of line with these constituents' expectations. If they believe the constituents favor toughness, they will tend to adopt contentious behavior; if they see the constituents as conciliatory, they will avoid contending. These points are supported by a study of the joint effect of surveillance and sex of constituent (Forcey, Van Slyck, Carnevale & Pruitt, 1983) on strategic choice. Surveillance by male constituents was found to enhance negotiator contentiousness, whereas surveillance by female constituents was found to diminish contentiousness. This makes sense if we assume that the subjects subscribed to the usual stereotype that men favor a tough approach and women a conciliatory approach to interpersonal relations.

Perceived Feasibility of Inaction

Inaction is obviously the greatest time waster of the strategies. Hence *time pressure* should discourage use of this strategy and, if Party remains engaged in the controversy, encourage the three coping strategies.

There are two sources of time pressure: cost per unit time of engaging in the controversy and closeness to a deadline. In negotiation, time pressure can be due to any cost of continued negotiation, including time lost from other pursuits, the expense of maintaining negotiators in the field, or rapid deterioration of the object under dispute (such as fruits and vegetables). Deadlines are points in the future at which significant costs are likely to be experienced if the controversy has not been resolved. At a strike deadline, the union pulls the workers out of the factory; at a hiring deadline, the job offer is withdrawn. The closer one is to a deadline and the larger the penalty for passing that deadline without agreement, the greater the time pressure and hence the less likely one is to enact the strategy of inaction.

An example of the impact of time pressure on strategic choice can be seen in the 1968 student rebellion in Mexico City, which occurred just before the Olympic Games in that city. As the opening of the games approached, the Mexican government became increasingly concerned about the continuing student disorder. In effect, deadline pressures were increasing, and the existing impasse with the students seemed less and less tolerable. All three of the coping strategies were employed in quick succession. First, the government yielded to a few student demands and then entered into problem-solving discussions. Finding the latter unsuccessful, the government then took the contentious (to say the least) approach of shooting hundreds of students at a rally.

All three coping strategies are possible in the face of time pressure, but research (Pruitt & Drews, 1969) suggests that the favorite strategy is yielding. This is presumably because yielding is the fastest way to move toward agreement. It follows that contending and problem solving are adopted in the face of time pressure only when there is heavy resistance to yielding.

In summary, we have argued that perceived feasibility—assessment of effectiveness and cost—affects strategic choice. This consideration supplements the forces specified in the dual concern model. Thus, for example, problem solving is adopted when one is concerned about both own and other's outcomes provided that there is some perceived possibility of success at a reasonable cost. The perceived feasibility of problem solving is a function of perceived common ground (PCG), the perception that an alternative can be found that satisfies both parties' aspirations. PCG, in turn, is a function of own and perceived other's aspirations and of perceived integrative potential (PIP), the apparent likelihood of identifying mutually beneficial alternatives. Perceived feasibility of contending is a positive function of perceived power and an inverse function of Other's apparent resistance to yielding. Perceived feasibility of inaction diminishes with increased time pressure.

ANTECEDENTS OF WITHDRAWING

The dual concern model and the perceived feasibility perspective are not very useful in understanding the conditions under which people withdraw from a conflict. Hence, we must turn to other considerations.

People decide to withdraw when the benefit they expect from a controversy falls below their limit—that is, their minimal aspiration.

The benefit they expect is determined in part by how far they think the other party will concede. Thus I am unlikely to withdraw from negotiation with an auto dealer if he or she proposes a moderate price for an attractive car and seems willing to go lower. It is also determined in part by perceived integrative potential. If a jointly acceptable package of price, car, and accessories looks easy to devise, I am also unlikely to withdraw.

Logically speaking, the limit should be set at the level of benefit that can be achieved by withdrawing (Fisher & Ury, 1981), and this is often the case. For example, in negotiating with a car dealer, I should set my limit at the lowest price I would have to pay another dealer for a comparable car. However, in actual practice, people often get locked into unrealistic limits through a process of premature commitment. For example, before going to buy a car, I may tell my friends that I intend to pay no more than $6,250, and I may even announce this figure to the dealer as a contentious gambit. Unless I am willing to renege on this commitment, $6,250 becomes my effective limit, and I must withdraw if the dealer does not accept it. (It follows that the contentious strategy of positional commitment is risky unless one is fairly certain about what the other will accept.)

THE VIGOR OF STRATEGIC BEHAVIOR

Implementation of the three coping strategies can be more or less *vigorous*. In the case of contentious behavior, vigor refers to the heaviness of the actions taken. Shouts are more vigorous than persuasive communications, blows more vigorous than shouts, shots more vigorous than blows. In the case of problem solving, vigor refers to the creativity of the problem-solving effort. At the low end of vigor is a simple, dull effort to coordinate the making of concessions toward an obvious compromise. At the high end is an active effort to understand the other's interests and a thoughtful search for a way to reconcile these interests with one's own. In the case of yielding, vigor refers simply to how far one drops one's aspirations. Vigor has no meaning with respect to the strategies of inaction or withdrawing.

There are various determinants of how vigorous a strategy will be. One set of determinants is embodied in the dual concern model (Figure 3.1). The stronger the concerns specified by this model, the more vigorous will be the predicted strategy. Thus, if concern about own outcomes is weak, greater concern about the other party's outcomes will produce more profound yielding. If concern about the other's outcomes is weak, greater concern about own outcomes will encourage more extreme contentious behavior. If neither concern is weak, problem solving will be more vigorous and creative the stronger are the dual concerns.

It is common for parties who have adopted a coping strategy to begin less vigorously and move toward greater vigor if earlier efforts do not achieve agreement. Such gradualism ensures that no greater costs will be incurred than are necessary to achieve their goals. This point is most obvious in the realm of contentious behavior. Like the United States in the Vietnam War, parties usually begin cautiously and escalate only if they are unsuccessful.

Two of the coping strategies have a paradoxical feature: If they are adopted, the vigor with which they are enacted is a function of some of the same conditions that *discourage* their being adopted in the first place.

One of these strategies is contending. As mentioned earlier, the expectation of resistance from the other party discourages contentious behavior. But suppose that other conditions (such as being a highly accountable representative with no dependence on the other) predispose a party to contend. What is the effect of expected resistance then? Our hypothesis is that it promotes the use of heavier contentious tactics. If the other looks like a pushover, it should be easy to get a concession by simple stonewalling or persuasive argumentation. But if the other's position seems engraved in stone, heavier guns will be needed, in the form of threats or other coercive actions.

Problem solving is the other strategy that exhibits this paradoxical feature. Low PCG discourages problem solving. But it also encourages a creative form of problem solving when this strategy is adopted for other reasons. Suppose, for example, that there is a complete stalemate—both parties are totally unwilling to yield and contentious tactics seem useless. If withdrawing is infeasible and inaction also seems unattractive (perhaps because of time pressure), problem solving is the only possible approach. To the extent that PCG is low (whether because of high aspirations, a perception that the other party has high aspirations, or minimal PIP), it will seem necessary to employ a more creative effort in order to reach agreement.

The latter point can be illustrated by reference to Figure 2.2. PCG is lower in Figure 2.2a than in any of the other three cases in this figure. Hence problem solving seems infeasible and is unlikely to be elected. But suppose that problem solving *must* be employed despite its infeasibility. Then a greater creative effort will be needed to resolve the conflict in Figure 2.2a, because the viable options seem more remote.

CONCLUSIONS

Chapter 3 has presented a preliminary theory about the conditions that affect the choice people make among the five strategies available to them in conflict: contending, problem solving, yielding, inaction, and withdrawing. This theory consists mainly of a dual concern model, supplemented by some ideas about the effect of feasibility considerations. The theory also implies some paradoxical hypotheses about determinants of the vigor with which certain of the strategies are employed. Strangely, the same conditions that make contending and problem solving seem less feasible cause these strategies to be employed with greater vigor if they happen to be adopted. We turn in the next chapter to a detailed consideration of one of the five strategies, contending. The main tactical manifestations of this strategy are described, and information is presented about how each manifestation affects the party against whom it is directed.

CHAPTER 4

Contentious Tactics

Most exchanges and encounters between people do not result in conflict, let alone the use of the increasingly heavy contentious tactics that accompany conflict escalation. As we saw in Chapter 1, people are typically able to deal with others in the absence of conflict. Moreover, many (if not most) of the conflicts that arise can readily be addressed through the collaborative problem-solving efforts of the parties involved. On the other hand, when conflicts do arise, and when the parties employ contentious tactics that take them along the winding pathway of dispute escalation, powerful and destructive forces are often unleashed. This alone makes it important to understand these events better.

Although there are five primary strategies for dealing with conflict, we have already argued that only two of these strategies—problem solving and contending—depend for their effectiveness on social influence processes. I can do well at your expense (contending) or find a jointly satisfactory solution (problem solving) only if you allow me to do so or find such behavior acceptable. These two strategies, then, are of particular interest and will be the object of special attention in the rest of this book. The next four chapters examine the pathway of escalation. This chapter focuses on the nature and impressive variety of contentious tactics that people use in an effort to get their way at another's expense—how, in effect, Party persuades Other that "what's mine is mine, and what's yours is mine."

Contending is likely to be chosen, in preference to the other conflict strategies, when the following conditions obtain: Party is concerned about own outcomes but not Other's outcomes; Party is antagonistic toward Other; Party's aspirations are high and are resistant to lowering; Party views Other's aspirations as also high (though not so resistant); little integrative potential is believed to exist, such that alternatives cannot be developed that satisfy both parties' aspirations; Party has the capacity for contending; and Other's resistance to lowering aspirations is deemed to be low. Under these circumstances, Party is likely to make use of contentious behavior in an effort to lower Other's aspirations, while keeping his or her own aspirations at their currently high level.

The basic strategy of contending is rather straightforward and does not require much elaboration. Party wishes to lower Other's aspirations and resistance to yielding so as to find a solution at Other's expense. Of greater interest are the contentious *tactics* themselves—the detailed moves and counter-moves, the gestures, positions, and ploys—that each side uses in an effort to prevail. It is the things that each side actually does to the other, rather than merely contemplates, that are of interest.

The tactics to be explored here are an assortment of odd bedfellows ranging from ingratiation, gamesmanship, and persuasive argumentation to promises, threats, and irrevocable commitments. Our analysis of these various and sundry tactics is guided by the following set of premises:

First, there is nothing inherently destructive or baleful about contentious tactics. Rather, it is the end to which these tactics are used that renders them harmful. For example, although threats (involving an effort to impose one's will through the contingent statement of intention to use force) are most easily conceived of as instruments of destruction or malevolence, they may also be used to signal Party's unwillingness or inability to bend beyond some critical point in a generally collaborative arrangement. Similarly, promises may be used to extract something from an adversary in the interest of competitive advantage, but they may also be used to forge a mutually beneficial contractual arrangement between parties. In short, contentious tactics can often be used to advance the interest of collaboration as well.

Second, we assume that contentious tactics differ along a dimension of "lightness–heaviness" and that it is useful to consider them in relation to this dimension. We define "light" tactics as those whose consequences for Other are favorable or neutral. By contrast, "heavy" tactics impose, or threaten to impose, unfavorable or costly consequences on Other. Promises are thus lighter than threats, and threats are lighter than physical assaults.

Third, we assume that contentious tactics are more often than not deployed in an escalative sequence, moving from light to progressively heavy. Such a sequence serves notice on Other, and on any bystanders who may happen to be observing, that Party is a "reasonable" person, someone who is moved to heavy tactics only as a last resort. In effect, this transition from light to heavy suggests that Party has tried to prevail by utilizing carrots and has been dragged only reluctantly into the use of sticks as a result of Others intransigence. The light-to-heavy shift thus permits Party to place the locus of control for his or her own contentious behavior on the shoulders of Other.

One can better appreciate the general psychological sense of this light-to-heavy shift by considering the consequences of efforts to implement the reverse sequence. A Party who first makes use of heavy tactics (such as irreversible commitments to particular positions) and then subsequently uses light tactics (such as promises of reward) is in danger of conveying to Other and to any on-lookers the impression of being a bully who tries to force his or her will on others. Moreover, the eventual shift to lighter tactics may create an impression of weakness—the view that Party has been unable to prevail with heavy tactics and has been forced to adopt a more conciliatory stance. Under these circumstances, light tactics may even be seen as an attempted bribe, as when failed attempts to influence others lead people to try to "buy their way out."

To be sure, there are occasions when the light-to-heavy shift in tactics seems inappropriate. And it is not uncommon for negotiators to employ heavy tactics such as threats to "soften up" an adversary before resorting to light tactics such as promises. The light tactics seem so appealing by contrast to their heavier counterparts that they are likely to be quite effective. Such an effect is particularly compelling when different members of Party's team utilize the heavy and light contentious tactics, creating a "bad cop" and "good cop," respectively. However, we contend that the sequence from light to heavy tactics is more common.

In keeping with the preceding analysis, the order of presentation of contentious tactics in this chapter conforms roughly to the light-to-heavy sequence. We will look first at the tactics of ingratiation and "feather ruffling," both of which constitute relatively lightweight maneuvers that are designed to make subsequent moves more effective. Next we will look briefly at persuasive argumentation before turning to such heavier contentious tactics as threats and some promises and closing with an examination of coercive commitments that appear irrevocable.

INGRATIATION: THE ART OF RELATIONSHIP BUILDING

Some of the most effective contentious tactics involve little understanding by Other that he or she is the target of an influence attempt. Indeed, the effectiveness of a tactic such as ingratiation stems from Other's very ignorance of Party's ultimate designs. To the extent that Other is able to see through or "read" Party's true intentions, these tactics are likely to prove ineffectual and may even backfire.

As defined by Jones and Wortman (1973), ingratiation is "a class of strategic behaviors illicitly designed to influence a particular other person concerning the attractiveness of one's personal qualities" (p. 2). A successful ingratiator enhances his or her perceived attractiveness in an effort to prepare the target for subsequent exploitation.

Ingratiation is characterized by an interesting and important dilemma: It is easiest to achieve when it is least needed. It is precisely when Other's positive feelings are most in demand that these feelings are hardest to cultivate. Why? Because to the extent that Other is aware that Party has something to gain by creating a favorable impression, Other will be suspicious of any and all attempts in this direction. The more help Party needs from Other, the more likely it is that Other will interpret Party's ingratiating behavior as a sign of manipulative intent rather than as a genuine expression of liking and regard. Ingratiation can have some effect even when Other is suspicious or aware of Party's true intentions; but this effect is likely to be greatly attenuated.

How should ingratiators go about their business? Jones and Wortman (1973) make a number of tactical suggestions. First, they argue for the importance of flattery or "complimentary other-enhancement," a class of tactics that exaggerates Other's admirable qualities while soft-pedaling Other's weaknesses. This technique relies for its effectiveness on the assumption that people find it hard to dislike people who say kind things about them.

Flattery is clearly a useful tactic in settings that range from international diplomacy and business transactions to the most mundane everyday situations. To be effective, flattery must be accomplished without sacrificing Party's credibility. That is, it is entirely possible for flattery to be so excessive in view of the circumstances that the tactic simply fails to work. This point has been documented experimentally in studies by Dickoff (1961), Kleinke, Staneski, and Weaver (1972), and Lowe and Goldstein (1970). To avoid this problem, Jones and Wortman (1973) suggest a number of ways for an ingratiator to enhance the credibility of his or her flattering overtures. These include avoiding excessive compliments, picking attributes to admire that Other may be a bit insecure about (and therefore vulnerable to flattery), making sure that all compliments are plausible, and carefully mixing negative with positive comments (what Jones and Wortman describe as "a judicious blend of the bitter and the sweet," p. 9). Sound advice indeed, as attested to by the litany of successful flatterers in history and literature, such as Machiavelli and Iago.

The second major class of ingratiation tactics involve what Jones and Wortman describe as "opinion conformity." By expressing agreement with Other's opinions, Party attempts to create the impression of having attitudes that are similar to Other's—a state that social psychologists have found generally induces interpersonal attraction. There are at least two pitfalls, however, that Party must avoid in these efforts at opinion conformity. First, as before, Party should try to avoid the impression that his or her agreement is driven by some ulterior motive. To this end, on the basis of supportive research evidence (see Jones, Jones & Gergen, 1963), Jones and Wortman advise ingratiators to try to anticipate Other's views rather than merely react to them. They provide the following example:

> If the target person says he thinks there should be more "law and order" and you indicate your agreement with his position, he may infer that you are agreeing in order to impress him. But if you cleverly intuit from his short hair, his manner of dress, and his other attitudes that he feels this way, and then spontaneously mention how concerned you are about the problem of law and order, such an attribution on his part is probably less likely (p. 17).

Second, Party must avoid giving the impression that he or she is the kind of person who goes around blindly agreeing with everybody's point of view (Gerard & Greenbaum, 1962; Jones & Wein, 1972). This can be accomplished by systematically agreeing with some of Other's positions but not all—or, even better, by indicating disagreement with the views of people that Other can reasonably be assumed to disagree with.

A third set of ingratiation tactics involves the giving of favors, on the grounds that people tend to like those who do nice things for them (Greenberg & Frisch, 1972; Nemeth, 1970). Of course, if Other suspects Party of doing favors to get something in return, the tactic will surely backfire; Other must have no sense that "strings are attached." Jones and Wortman suggest two ways in which Party can successfuly avoid Other's suspicion in this regard: doing small rather than large favors, on the grounds that the latter will arouse the suspicion that something is desired in return; and performing favors that do not lead Other to feel constrained to respond in some particular way (Brehm & Cole, 1966)—for example, doing a favor in Other's absence that he or she will eventually learn about.

Finally, Jones and Wortman describe several tactics of "self-presentation" that may be adopted by the successful ingratiator. The idea here is for Party to present his or her own virtues in such a way that Other finds them attractive. Self-presentation is tricky business. Too forthright a description of one's virtues may lead Other to conclude that Party is conceited or has manipulative intentions; too subtle a description of one's virtues may dilute the intended effect to the vanishing point (Jones & Gordon, 1972). Jones and Wortman advise the ingratiator to address this dilemma by using indirect but clearcut methods of tooting his or her own horn, such as doing rather than merely saying self-aggrandizing things. "Rather than telling the target person that he is a good cook," they write, "an ingratiator can invite the target person to a gourmet dinner" (p. 23).

In summary, when used in a contentious exchange, ingratiation tactics soften Other up for later concessions not through coercion, assertion, or aggression, but through charm and guile. How much easier and less costly it is to persuade Other to surrender something of value to Party of Other's own volition than to extract it through the imposition of will.

As we have suggested throughout this analysis, it is important for successful ingratiation that Other not attribute Party's behavior to ulterior motives. Paradoxically, the greater Party's power relative to that of Other, the more effective Party's ingratiation tactics are apt to be (because Other is less likely to attribute Party's behavior to ulterior motives)—but the less necessary such tactics are in the first place. Conversely, it is when Party is in a position of relatively low power vis-à-vis Other that Party is most likely to be dependent on ingratiation tactics—and that these tactics are least effective. The more you need me, the more suspicious I am likely to be of your attempts to make a good impression.

GAMESMANSHIP: THE ART OF FEATHER RUFFLING

Another class of tactics entails inducing a state of upset or unrest that has the effect of lowering Other's resistance to yielding. This is the art of "feather ruffling." If ingratiation is like the gift of a Trojan horse, lowering Other's suspicions and resistance and allowing Party to penetrate the walled city, feather ruffling resembles a diversionary blaze outside the walls that becomes the focus of so much attention that the enemy can scale another part of the city walls and have its way.

Perhaps nowhere have the tactics of feather ruffling been articulated more elegantly and creatively than in the writings of the British author Stephen Potter. In his book *The Theory and Practice of Gamesmanship: The Art of Winning Games Without Actually Cheating* (1948), Potter describes several key tactics and maneuvers that can be used to get, and keep, an adversary off guard. Although his book is written largely tongue-in-cheek and all his examples are drawn from the British sporting world of rugby, tennis, and golf, his analysis reveals some important varieties of contentious behavior.

The key to effective gamesmanship, writes Potter, is finding a way of creating a state of "muddled fluster." One important technique for accomplishing this objective entails behaving in a manner that is antithetical to the actions of Other. Thus, by deliberately playing against the opponent's tempo—by speeding up when Other wishes to slow down, or taking one's sweet time when Other seems in a rush to proceed—Party can break Other's rhythm and induce distraction. Among Potter's many amusing examples of this maneuver:

> . . . tying up a shoe-lace in a prolonged manner, after the opponent at squash or lawn tennis had served two or three aces running; the extended noseblow, with subsequent mopping up not only of the nose and surrounding surfaces, but of imaginary sweat from the forehead and neck as well (p. 59).

Analogously, in *any* form of contentious encounter, it may make good sense for Party to break Other's rhythm by insisting, for example, on more time to review the facts or on a faster pace of decision making.

Although Potter advises the artful gamesman against spending too much time looking for his or her own "lost ball," it makes good sense to make "a great and irritatingly prolonged parade of spending extra time looking for his *opponent's* ball" (p. 35). More generally, gamesmanship requires deflecting Other's suspicions by behaving in ways that appear to be in the interest of helping Other. For example, a negotiator who wishes to use contentious tactics effectively, in the service of disrupting Other's momentum, might suggest, "Let's slow down a bit, so that I can understand better exactly what it is that you want and how I can provide you with what you need."

Potter's second general bit of advice to the artful gamesman is to behave in ways that are likely to lead Other to feel either irresponsible or incompetent. As before, the key is to induce these feelings without arousing Other's suspicion or encouraging Other to blame Party in any way. Two of Potter's examples may suffice to make this point. First, there is the art of "limpmanship": "the exact use of minor injury, not only for the purpose of getting out of, but for actually winning difficult contests" (p. 36). For example, Potter recommends intense and ferocious play by an inadequate tennis player. At some point the gamesman pauses momentarily, as if lost in thought. When the adversary makes inquiries, he or she confesses to having an "ancient ticker" that is "not supposed to be used full out at the moment . . . only a temporary thing." Rather than creating the sense that Party is searching for an inappropriate excuse, this ploy has the effect of laying the responsibility for Party's unhappy fate squarely on the shoulders of Other.

Second, Potter provides the example of the Party who, when Other arrives to pick him or her up by car, deliberately stalls by delaying answering the bell, not having things ready, and forgetting some necessary item of equipment. All of these moves are likely to increase Other's impatience, even agitation, and lead Other to feel incompetent—while lacking insight into the precise source of these feelings.

In the more general realm of contentious tactics, quite apart from the rarified atmosphere of Potter's sporting examples, one can see ploys like this being adopted by negotiators who subtly point out that their adversary seems to be having a bit of difficulty understanding the charts and statistical summaries of the issues in dispute.

When all is said and done, the key to successful gamesmanship (just like the key to ingratiation) is keeping Other blind to Party's true intentions. To this end, Potter advises that a gamesman whose tactics are successful should then "shield" himself or herself behind a set of situational circumstances. Thus it was a favorable wind or an unusually effective piece of equipment in a tennis game, or fortuitous timing and a lucky break in a hard-fought negotiation, that explains Party's success—not Party's talent, skill, or artifice. As Potter writes, "Let the gamesman's advantage over an opponent appear to be the result of luck, never of play" (p. 45). By so doing, Party can deflect the anger or determination that might otherwise lead Other to respond effectively.

PERSUASIVE ARGUMENTATION

Ingratiation and gamesmanship are preparatory tactics in the sense that they erode Other's resistance to lowering aspirations, rather than acting on these aspirations directly. In contrast are a number of contentious tactics that are applied in a direct effort to induce Other to reduce his or her aspirations. The lightest of these tactics is "persuasive argumentation," a technique whereby Party induces Other to lower his or her aspirations through a series of logical appeals.

The skill required for successful persuasive argumentation should not be underestimated. I must convince you to surrender something that you hold dear and that I covet—not through coercion or the lure of reward, but through persuasion. This is a tall order in a contentious encounter.

In another volume in this series (see Zimbardo, Ebbeson & Maslach, 1977) social psychological theory and research in the area of attitude change have been reviewed in great detail. Hence, rather than dwell on the issue of attitude change, we shall simply describe two general types of appeals that can be useful when there is conflict of interest.

First, Party may try to persuade Other that he or she has a legitimate right to a favorable outcome in the controversy. If I can persuade you that it is "your money or *my* life"—that is, I am in considerable jeopardy unless you grant my wish—I may be able to persuade you to lower your aspirations. Such is the case when negotiators argue that they are in danger of being fired, demoted, or replaced unless they can return a particularly favorable division of resources to their constituents. Prime Minister Begin of Israel and a number of his senior advisors managed to employ exactly such arguments with considerable success in the Mideast negotiations of the late seventies and early eighties.

A second major form of persuasive argumentation requires Party to convince Other that lower aspirations are in the latter's interest. This is really quite an extraordinary maneuver when one stops to think about it. I am persuading you that it is in your interests to permit me to prevail.

Consider the example of a failing business whose management persuades labor negotiators that, unless workers accept pay cuts and layoffs, the business will go down with all hands aboard. Sound farfetched? If so, recall the successful effort by Chrysler management to persuade auto workers to accept deep pay cuts in order to increase the chances of corporate survival. Or recall similar efforts in the early 1980s by commercial airlines and the Greyhound Bus Company. In each of these examples, Party convinced Other to embrace lower aspirations by pointing to a credible alternative that appeared to be even less attractive.

PROMISES AND THREATS

Promises and threats are messages of intention by Party to behave in ways that are either beneficial or detrimental to the interests of Other, depending on what the latter does or does not do. Our analysis of these forms of influence begins with a review of some general characteristics and issues that they have in common. We then appraise each tactic separately, considering both the potential advantages and the drawbacks of each. Finally, we comment on the reasons why threats, more than promises, seem to emerge as the predominant form of social influence in contentious exchanges.

General Characteristics of Promises and Threats

Imagine, for the purposes of the following general analysis, a world in which there are two people—Party and Other—and three possible behaviors that Other can perform: X, Y, and Z. Imagine further that Party wishes to induce Other to do X, whereas Other prefers Y and to a lesser extent Z. Obviously we are describing here an ideal case in that there are often more than two participants and more than three forms of available behavior. Still such situations do exist in reality, as when Other is a child (Johnny) who has a plate with three foods remaining—spinach (X), mashed potatoes (Y), and steak (Z)—and Party is Johnny's father.

Assuming that Party is able and willing to mete out rewards and punishments to get his or her way, how might Party proceed to influence Other to do X rather than Y or Z? One possible approach would be for Party to say, in effect, "If you do X (the thing I want), I will reward you." Translated into English, father says to Johnny, "If you eat your spinach now, I'll give you your favorite flavor of ice cream for dessert." Such a statement is a prototypical promise, providing a consequence (ice cream) that Other is believed to find desirable in exchange for compliance (eating the spinach now).

By contrast, Party might instead attempt to induce the performance of X by saying, "Unless you do X, I will punish you" ("Unless you eat your spinach now, I will send you to your room"). In this, a prototypical threat, Party is proffering a consequence that is presumed to be undesirable to Other (being sent to his room) contingent on Other's failure to comply with Party's wishes.

Both the promise and the threat are designed to have the same effect, but one involves the lure of a carrot, the other the menace of a stick. This difference—in the positive or negative consequence implied—is the most important and obvious feature separating promises and threats. Less obvious, perhaps, is the fact that *threats ordinarily provide more information about how Party intends to behave than do promises*. To understand why this is so, take a look at Figure 4.1.

The typical promise designed to compel or induce the performance of some behavior (X) indicates what will happen if Other does the thing desired, but it leaves uncertain the consequence of noncompliance (doing Y or Z). By contrast, the corresponding threat makes abundantly clear the negative consequences of not doing X and leaves uncertain the consequence of compliance with the threat. In the example of Johnny and the three remaining foods on his plate, his father's threat actually conveys twice as much unequivocal information about consequences (a minus sign for Y and for Z) than the corresponding promise (a plus sign for X). Extended to a more extreme case, we might imagine 1,000 things that poor Johnny can do, only one of which is the thing desired by his autocratic father. Whereas the promise informs Johnny about the consequences of doing only the one thing his father prefers, the threat clearly implies that Johnny is to be punished for doing any of 999 things![1]

---

[1]Note that our informational analysis has been based on compellent promises and threats (those designed to induce some desired behavior), primarily because these are the promises and threats that are typically used in most conflictual encounters. The same analysis can reasonably be applied to their deterrent counterparts (designed to deter the performance of some undesirable behavior), so long as the aim of these threats is to deter everything other than X. However, in the case of a deterrent promise or threat that aims to prevent the performance of X while tolerating Y and Z, the preceding informational analysis changes. The deterrent promise, "If you do anything other than X, I will reward you," clearly contains more informational clarity than the corresponding threat, "If you do X, I will punish you." Note, however, that this deterrent promise may fail to work because it resembles a bribe. It is a bit like the Lord's promise in the Garden of Eden: "Eat the fruit of any tree but the Tree of Knowledge and all will go well with you." Such a promise invites the temptation to explore the one alternative for which reward is not forthcoming.

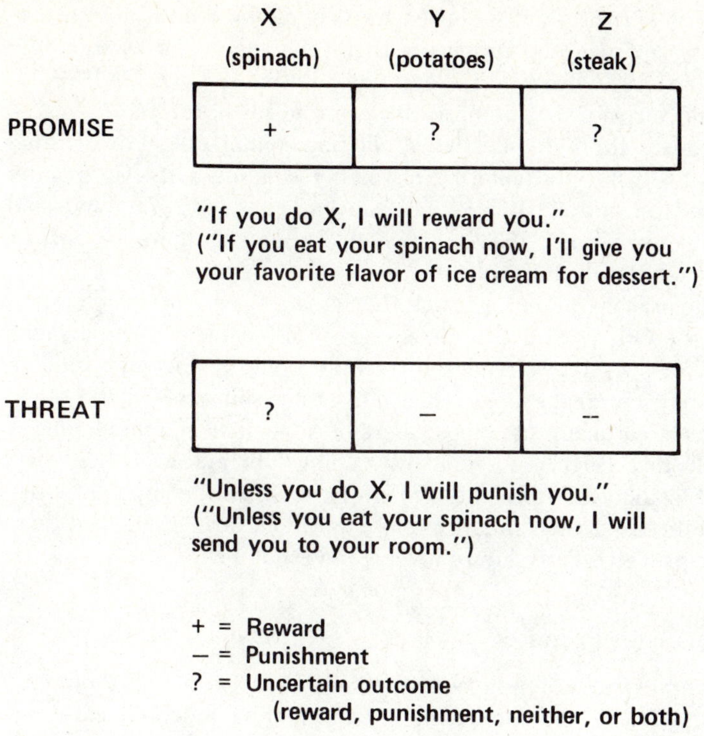

	X (spinach)	Y (potatoes)	Z (steak)
PROMISE	+	?	?

"If you do X, I will reward you."
("If you eat your spinach now, I'll give you
your favorite flavor of ice cream for dessert.")

THREAT	?	–	–

"Unless you do X, I will punish you."
("Unless you eat your spinach now, I will
send you to your room.")

+ = Reward
– = Punishment
? = Uncertain outcome
   (reward, punishment, neither, or both)

Figure 4.1   Information conveyed by a typical promise and a typical threat.

Research by Lewicki and Rubin (1973), Rubin and Lewicki (1973), and Rubin, Lewicki, and Dunn (1973) has consistently pointed to the potential importance of differences in the informational clarity of promises and threats. This work indicates that, the greater the apparent information conveyed by a promise or threat, the more likely Party is to be rated by Other as powerful and in control of the interaction. As a result, compliance is rated as more likely in response to threats than to promises. This sort of analysis also reveals why Party, given a choice, might well prefer to make use of threats. They help to foster the impression that Party is fully in control of the interaction— more so than would be implied by use of the corresponding promise.

The Good News about Promises

Despite the preceding observation, a promise has much to recommend it in a contentious encounter. First of all, unlike most threats, most promises are relatively "nice" (light) tactics. They offer something that is presumed to be attractive to Other in exchange for Other's compliance. Promises don't just take, they give in return. Indeed, as Schelling (1960) has pointed out, promises are at the heart of all contractual relations: In exchange for your giving me something I want, I will give you something you want. In keeping with these observations, it is no surprise that promises are generally rated as more attractive than threats and that the promisors themselves are seen as friendlier (Lewicki & Rubin, 1973; Ring & Kelley, 1963; Rubin & Lewicki, 1973). It should also be no surprise that promises beget promises in return.

Second, promises are quite effective at eliciting compliance, provided that the promisor has a history of honoring his or her commitments (Gahagan & Tedeschi, 1968; Horai et al., 1969; Lindskold & Tedeschi, 1971; Lindskold et al., 1972; Schlenker et al., 1973). (As we shall soon see, however, threats are *even more* likely to elicit compliance.)

A third virtue of many promises is that they create a sense of indebtedness in the mind of the Other. Not all promises have this characteristic; payment for merchandise or for services rendered does not typically engender indebtedness, nor would ice cream in exchange for eating spinach. On the other hand, there are a great many situations wherein the making and fulfillment of a promise imply that Party is in some way doing Other a favor—and that Other has an obligation to return the favor to Party. Like the apparently benevolent acts of the Godfather, promises often have long strings attached that, at least in principle, give Party future leverage over Other.

Some Problems with Promises

Given these several virtues of promises—their apparent "niceness," their ability to elicit compliance, and the possibility of creating indebtedness—one might expect promises to be used with greater frequency and greater success in contentious encounters than in fact turns out to be the case. There are several problems with promises that are not apparent at first blush.

First, and of paramount importance, an effective promise costs Party whatever reward was promised. By contrast, a threat that works as intended costs Party nothing. Hence, if Party is optimistic about success, promises look more expensive than threats.

A second problem is that the fulfillment of a promise may, paradoxically, make it less likely to work in the future. Other may tire of the carrots that Party has available to dole out in exchange for compliance. Ice cream in exchange for eating spinach works only so long as Other is not tired of ice cream. Having sampled the best that Party has to offer, Other may be tempted either not to comply in the future or to try to extract increasing rewards in exchange for such compliance ("What else will you give me, Dad?").

A third problem is that the repeated tender and fulfillment of promises may create the problem not of satiation but of undue dependence. Other may come to expect Party to deliver continued benefits in the future, which may prove quite costly for Party in the long run. A good example of this can be seen in the increasing dependence of certain nations in the Middle East on the infusion of various resources by wealthy nations such as the United States and Saudi Arabia.

Because of the problems just described, it might appear sensible for Party to make promises but not to keep them. Unfortunately, this creates a fourth problem: Promises are often costly to break. To renege on a promise is to create a situation in which Party is almost certain to be disliked and distrusted and in which Other may feel duty-bound to respond punitively. Moreover, Party is not likely to be believed if and when he or she tenders promises in the future.

A fifth problem with promises is that it is often difficult to decide how much to promise. For Party to offer Other too paltry or measly a reward is to run the risk of failing to elicit the desired behavior and even of antagonizing Other with an insulting offer. For this reason, Party would be well advised to offer large rewards in exchange for Other's compliance. However, rewards that are too attractive may be regarded by Other as a bribe. Other may come to view Party as having far more to gain from Other's compliance than he or she is willing to reveal. Under these circumstances, Other may be tempted either to avoid compliance, in an effort to discover what has motivated Party to make so lavish a promise, or to blackmail Party, arguing, in effect, that if compliance is important enough to Party to justify so lavish a reward, then perhaps Party should pay even more in order to have his or her way.

As an illustration of the latter risk, consider again the role of the United States in the Middle East negotiations of the last several years. American willingness, even eagerness, to support movement toward agreement by Israel, Egypt, and the other principals in the region—through offers of lavish economic and military assistance—appears to have whetted the appetite of the Middle East nations for even more extravagant tenders of American aid.

Some Good News about Threats

Threats may not be so nice as promises, but they are more tempting to use and are more effective at eliciting compliance. Why should this be so?

First, as we have already observed, the threat that works costs Party nothing; there is no reward to be doled out *and* no punishment to be imposed. It is the leverage provided by the desire to avoid a cost—rather than the cost itself—that makes the threat work. As Schelling (1966) observes, where brute force often fails because it increases Other's resistance and pluck, the *threat* of such force may well succeed.

Second, threats are often highly effective; their value has been demonstrated repeatedly and consistently (for example, Black & Higbee, 1973; Bonoma et al., 1970; Bonoma & Tedeschi, 1973; Gahagan, et al., 1970; Lindskold, et al., 1969; Mogy & Pruitt, 1974). Indeed, it can be argued that threats are, on the whole, more effective at motivating Other to comply than are promises. This is in part because threateners usually seem more powerful and controlling than promisors, due to the fact that their messages provide more information about what is likely to happen. It is also in part because people are ordinarily more highly motivated to avoid a possible loss than to obtain a possible reward. Hence they are more likely to yield when confronted with a threat than with a promise.

A third potential "virtue" of threats is that threateners can benefit even when they renege on them. If Party elects *not* to enforce the terms of a threat when Other fails to comply, this choice may be regarded by Other not as particularly weak or foolish, but as humane. Whereas a reneging promisor is almost certain to be seen by Other as a person who cannot be trusted to do what he or she says, a reneging threatener may be regarded as powerful but compassionate—the sort of person (like a kindly parent) who understands the wisdom of forbearance. To be sure, one who reneges on either a threat or a promise runs the risk of reduced credibility in the eyes of Other. But the potential cost for Party associated with reneging on a threat may be offset, at least in part, by the possibility of a charitable interpretation of Party's actions.

A fourth virtue of threats, causing them to be used with considerable frequency by people in conflict, is that they are consistent with the sense of justice and rectitude that often accompanies the exchange of influence attempts. People in contentious encounters often believe, or act as though they believe, that they have God and Right on their side. Under these circumstances, what better way of exerting influence than by means of a threat? If Other does what Party demands, this is only right and proper and deserves no special reward. But if Other fails to do what Party requests, then punishment is the appropriate response to this wrong. ("If Johnny doesn't have the good sense and respect to do what I asked him to do, then he deserves his medicine. He knew what was coming to him.")

A Major Difficulty with Threats

The single most serious problem associated with the use of threats is that they tend to beget similar behavior from Other. Threats lead to counterthreats, so the effect of using them is often to escalate the controversy at a precipitously rapid rate. Deutsch and Krauss (1960) and others have amply demonstrated that threats often lead to increased suspicion and dislike by Other for Party, which in turn makes it more likely that Other will respond with threats of his or her own. In this way, a negative spiral of intensifying hostility is set in motion, creating a pattern that is described in more detail in Chapters 6 and 7.

To restate the preceding observations, threats are used because they are cheap, they often seem justified, and they may appear to be the only tactic that will work. However, the resentment and hostility engendered by threats often motivate a response in kind from Other, creating an escalative spiral.

IRREVOCABLE COMMITMENTS

Promises and threats are "if-then" messages, assertions by Party of the following form: "If you do (don't do) X, then I will reward (punish) you." By contrast, the coercive tactics that we are about to examine do not appear to contain this element of contingency. Instead, these threat tactics typically assume the following form: "I have started doing something that requires adjustment from you and will continue doing it despite your best efforts to stop me."

Party guarantees to continue behaving a certain way, and the coercive commitment that has been made is—or appears to be—an irrevocable one. In order to understand better the nature of these irrevocable commitments, let us briefly consider two rather different examples, the first drawn from the fabled game of Chicken, the second from the world of nonviolent resistance.

As it was played in old James Dean, Sal Mineo, and Marlon Brando movies, Chicken involves two participants who are driving their cars at breakneck speed on a direct collision course with each other. The loser in this game (the "chicken") is the first person to turn aside, thereby averting a head-on collision and almost certain death for both players. Researchers (such as Deutsch & Lewicki, 1970) and theorists (such as Schelling, 1960) have studied the game of Chicken with interest because of its structural similarity to the contests of will that are occasionally played out in such international settings as the Cuban missile crisis and the U. S.–Iran hostage negotiations. More generally, the game of Chicken can be observed whenever two or more parties lock into contest of wills in which neither side is willing to concede first and both sides stand to lose a great deal through joint intransigence. Thus a divorcing couple in the throes of a nasty custody dispute and the affected sides in a costly labor strike are also good candidates for a Chicken analysis.

Because the game of Chicken is a quintessential example of a test of grit and determination, the usual threats and promises are not likely to work very well. Why should Other give in on a vitally important issue simply because Party has tendered some statement of contingency that may or may not be honored? No, more powerful influence medicine is required here, in the form of a (seemingly) irrevocable commitment. For instance, in the driving example already mentioned, Party could fling his or her steering wheel out the window in full view of Other (Schelling, 1960). The message conveyed through this commitment is that now only Other has control over what will happen. Party has irrevocably committed himself or herself to a threatening and costly course of action. As a result, the locus of control over the outcome of the exchange has been shifted from the shoulders of Party to those of Other, who is now the only one capable of preventing mutual disaster.

As a dramatically different illustration of irrevocable commitment, let us consider some of the basic tactics of nonviolent resistance. By nonviolent resistance we mean such events as Mohandas K. Gandhi's fasts in order to secure concessions from the British forces that occupied India, the boycotts and sit-down strikes by courageous blacks in the American South of the 1950s and early 1960s, and refusal to register for the draft or to move out of the way of approaching tanks as a means of protesting a national war effort. Although many of us may admire the courage, determination, and moral conviction that has characterized such examples of nonviolent resistance, let us not lose sight of the essentially contentious tactics at work here, which are designed to prevail in an intensely conflictual exchange.

Nonviolent resistance is probably best thought of as a class of tactics rather than a monolithic entity; indeed Sharp (1971) has distinguished nine different types of nonviolence. Nevertheless, there are certain central features that are found in virtually every use of this approach. The most important of these is Party's apparently irrevocable commitment to a set of demands and a nonviolent course of action. If effectively conveyed to Other, such commitment shifts the locus of responsibility for what happens squarely onto Other's shoulders. In announcing his intention to begin fasting in protest of continuing British policies in India, Gandhi served notice on the British that they now had exclusive responsibility for determining the outcome of the crisis. Nothing would budge Gandhi from this stance other than British surrender to his wishes, and it fell entirely to the British to decide whether to accede to the Mahatma's demands or let him die. As is well known, on virtually every occasion in which nonviolence was tried in India—both by Gandhi alone and as a form of mass, collective action—the tactic worked as intended.

Some Advantages of Irrevocable Commitment

We have looked at two very different examples of irrevocable commitment at work. The first, deliberately stripping oneself of control in the game of Chicken, serves notice on Other of Party's commitment to a belligerent course of action. The second example, nonviolent resistance, is a demonstration of similar unswerving commitment—although typically to a moral stance rather than to outright belligerency. What the two examples have in common is that they place the onus for escaping mutual disaster squarely on the shoulders of Other. Let us now consider some of the several "virtues" of this tactic.

If used successfully, irrevocable commitments force Other to do the work of bringing about agreement, and hence they elicit concessions from Other. If you and I are approaching an intersection in our respective automobiles, and you believe (because I am staring straight ahead of me) that I am unaware of your presence, the responsibility for what happens to the two of us is not mine but yours; it is you who must do the work of jamming on your brakes to prevent a collision. Many a Boston driver has put this very tactic to good use in an effort to slip through a busy intersection (Rubin, Steinberg, & Gerrein, 1974).

A second virtue of irrevocable commitments is that they do not require Party to hold power that is equal to or greater than that of Other. For a promise or threat to work as intended, Party must be able to present himself or herself as being in a position, even temporarily, of doling out rewards and costs that matter to Other. In the case of irrevocable commitment, however, the basis for imposition of cost on Other is not some greater pool of resources but the ability to commit oneself in ways that appear irreversible. Gandhi's power to compel the British to modify their policies in India stemmed not from superior physical resources but from his very weakness. Commitment of his frail body to a fast that it could not endure for very long was a powerful lever to force the mighty British to yield. Weakness can thus paradoxically be a source of strength in irrevocable commitments—provided, of course, that this commitment is highly credible.

A third virtue of irrevocable commitments is that they often work without Party or Other ever witnessing the commitment's ultimate consequences. Gandhi did not actually have to fast to the death to prevail; it was sufficient for the British to believe that he would continue fasting as long as necessary. When Party has a history of "honoring" commitments of various kinds, this history may be sufficient for Party to prevail without carrying through to the bitter end.

Some Problems with Irrevocable Commitment

The other side of the coin is that, because of their irreversibility or apparent irreversibility, commitment tactics often entail considerable risk. Party's fate is placed in the hands of another who may *or may not* be ready to make the concessions necessary to avoid disaster. If Other is not ready to make these concessions, the disaster is often mutual: Both Chicken players are killed, or Gandhi starves to death and India is thrown into massive communal disorder. A risky tactic indeed.

There are several reasons why Other may fail to make the concessions this tactic is designed to evoke. For one thing, there is always the possibility that Other has failed to understand or fully acknowledge the consequences of the commitment that has been made. If you cannot see me behind the wheel of my car, and hence do not know that I am unaware that we are both approaching the same intersection, the two of us have a serious problem. Similarly, if one Chicken driver is unaware that the other has sent the steering wheel hurtling out the window, a genuine disaster is in the making. Second, Other may want to comply with Party's wishes but may be genuinely unable to do so— as when the other driver in the Chicken game has lost control of his or her brakes and is therefore unable to stop in time, or when a kidnap victim has no access to ransom money. Third, and most important, Party may misjudge the relative value to Other of the options that he is forcing Other to choose between. Party may believe Other will prefer capitulation to mutual disaster, but Other may actually prefer disaster. In his fasts, Gandhi always ran the risk that the British would prefer massive communal disorder to the concessions he was asking them to make; they might decide that it was better to try to weather a political storm than to give in to yet another of Gandhi's demands. To minimize this latter danger, it is important for the strategist to have a thorough knowledge of the opponent's perceptions and values. For a newcomer to a relationship, making an irrevocable commitment can be playing with fire.

Because of these three risks, it is desirable for Party's apparently irrevocable commitments to be reversible if necessary. A Chicken player, for example, would be well advised—before flinging the steering wheel out the window— to engineer a tiny steering wheel, unseen by the other person, that can be used to avert a last-minute disaster in the event that the tactic fails to work. Similarly, it might make good sense for a faster to arrange for a bit of sustenance to be squirreled in, unbeknownst to the other side. Under most circumstances it is better to be seen as a fool or a trickster than to die. The most effective unilateral commitment may thus be one that Other believes to be irreversible but that can be modified if absolutely necessary.

If a first general problem with irrevocable commitments is that they may prove too risky to actually implement, a second difficulty stems from the fact that they must be used preemptively. It is the *first* player to strip himself or herself of control in the game of Chicken who is likely to prevail. To throw one's own steering wheel out the window at the same moment as, or immediately after, one's opponent does the same thing is to be both terribly brave and terribly foolhardy. It only makes sense to surrender control over events if one can count on the other person's retention of control. Unfortunately, it is precisely in those contentious encounters where irrevocable coercive commitments are most likely to occur that *both* sides are likely to resort to this tactic—often to their mutual detriment.

Because there are costs and uncertainties associated with the use of irrevocable commitments, Other may quite correctly suspect Party of not wishing to carry such commitments through to completion. Therefore, a third major problem with this tactic is that of credibility: how to get Other to believe that Party means what he or she has said and should therefore be taken seriously. There are also risks involved with credibility. Party may think he or she is committed to take the stated action, but Other may doubt this commitment. Such a misunderstanding has the makings of tragedy.

Enhancing the Credibility of Irrevocable Commitments

There are several things that Party can do in an effort to bolster the credibility of an irrevocable commitment. First, Party may wish to make use of the services of some third person who has been given instructions that are virtually impossible to change, such as a messenger sent to deliver a message by a person who cannot subsequently be contacted in any way. Schelling (1960) observes in this general regard, "At many universities the faculty is protected by a rule that denies instructors the power to change a course grade once it has been recorded" (p. 38). This places the registrar in the position of a messenger conveying information that Party is now unable to change.

A second way to enhance the credibility of this tactic is to pledge commitment in public rather than in private, thereby laying on the line one's reputation for consistency in word and deed. Writes Schelling, "If national representatives can arrange to be charged with appeasement for every small concession, they place concession visibly beyond their own reach" (p. 29).

A third way of enhancing credibility is to demonstrate that one has a constituency looking on that will hold one responsible for anything surrendered. In effect, one attempts to argue that one's neck is in a noose that is about to be drawn tight by intransigent constituents who are watching every move that is made.

A fourth technique for enhancing the credibility of a seemingly irrevocable commitment involves confronting Other with evidence of Party's resolve. Indeed, such evidence contributes immeasurably to the effectiveness of nonviolent resistance. There is nothing like an eyeball-to-eyeball exchange for letting Other know full well the depth and intensity of Party's commitment to a position. In the absence of such direct interpersonal confrontation, Party's forcefulness cannot truly be grasped, and this tactic is less likely to work as intended.[2] As Gandhi (1949) wrote, perhaps surprisingly, "Non-violence . . . does not mean meek submission to the will of the evil-doer, but it means putting one's whole soul against the will of the tyrant" (p. 4). In Gandhi's nonviolent resistance campaigns and those of Martin Luther King's civil rights activists and boycotters, the forcefulness of the commitment was buttressed even further by the presence of ideology—a set of organizing beliefs that the resisters used to explain and justify their behavior.

We have seen that irrevocable commitments carry with them potential problems of risk and credibility. The most serious problem of all, however, stems from the contributions to escalation often made by such coercive commitments. These tactics tend to beget responses in kind that, instead of bringing an end to the contentious exchange, are likely to cause each side to dig in its heels, to take positions from which it feels it cannot budge without losing face, and thereby to exacerbate an already difficult situation.

CONCLUSIONS

In this chapter we have tried to outline several of the more important contentious tactics that people use in an effort to prevail. As reflected in the general organizational sequence of the topics presented, we believe there is a general tendency for lighter contentious tactics to be utilized before people resort to their heavier counterparts. Mind you, this light-to-heavy sequence is not always followed, as when Party moves away from an initially tough posture in order to seem cooperative by comparison or when the ingroup eventually capitulates. But this sequence is very common, and it is a major source of escalation, the topic of the next three chapters.

We have also portrayed one party as the initiator of contentious moves and the other as their recipient and reactor. This portrayal is something of a distortion. The interactions of antagonists are often more like a minuet in which the steps of *each* side are matched quite precisely by corresponding moves on the part of the other. Each side takes, in turn, the stance of the aggressor and that of the defender, and escalation is as much (or more) the product of a vicious circle or conflict spiral as of a sequence of tactical initiatives on the part of only one side. Such conflict spirals will be closely examined in the next few chapters.

[2]Noteworthy in this regard is the repeated demonstration by Zimbardo and his co-workers (Zimbardo, 1970; Zimbardo, et al., 1973) that the anonymity afforded by a Klansman's white sheet or a police officer's reflecting sunglasses fosters an illusion of safety and security that may help make room for subsequent aggression.

CHAPTER 5

Escalation and Stability

The term "escalation" brings most prominently to mind the realm of international relations, such as the events that led up to the First World War or the deterioration in U.S.–Soviet relations in the years immediately after the Second World War. However, conflict can escalate in any kind of relationship, including marriage, labor–management relations, and the relations between students and administrators in a university. This chapter introduces the concept of escalation, using a campus crisis as an example, and discusses a number of conditions that affect the likelihood that conflicts will escalate. Part of the latter discussion is devoted to the antecedents of *stability*, which is defined in this part of the book as resistance to escalation.

THE CRISIS AT UB[1]

The years from 1964 to 1969 saw the growth of a national student movement aroused about such issues as racial discrimination and U.S. involvement in the Vietnam War. This movement touched many campuses, including the State University of New York at Buffalo (known locally by its former initials "UB"). UB began the 1969–1970 school year with a large number of students who were concerned about such issues and a sizable contingent of campus radicals who were ready to provide any emerging student action with the necessary leadership.

The crisis began on a cold winter night in late February with the appearance of city police on campus at the time of a demonstration by black athletes against the Physical Education Department (the black athletes played no further part in the demonstrations after this incident). The next night 40 to 50 white students, including many of the campus radicals, proceeded to the acting president's office to demand an explanation for the police appearance. The acting president, who was in a meeting about the black athlete problem, refused to talk with the students whereupon some of them threw rocks at his windows. The campus police arrived in riot gear, and the acting president instructed them to arrest the window breakers. Moving to the student union, the police apprehended two of the radicals, beating one of them in front of an excited crowd of student onlookers. The police officers were then chased

---

[1] The chronology given here is adapted from Pruitt and Gahagan (1974).

across the campus by parts of this crowd, and one officer was badly injured when a metal trash barrel was thrown at him. Someone called for city police reinforcements, who confronted a crowd of about 500 enraged students and arrested several dozen of them.

During the next two days, rallies were organized by the Student Government and the radical student leadership to decide upon a student response to these incidents. The thousands of students who attended these rallies clearly rejected the student government proposal for communication with the administration and endorsed a plan developed by the radical leadership to organize a strike on class attendance. A set of nine demands was endorsed, including the barring of city police from campus, the resignation of the acting president, and the abolition of ROTC and of research supported by the Defense Department. By the end of the second evening, it became clear that the Student Government was no longer respected by the bulk of the politically active students. As a result, this government essentially collapsed. It was replaced by a radically led Strike Committee, which even took over the student government office suite. During the first of these two nights, the library was fire-bombed by enraged students.

The Strike Committee, consisting of about 400 active members, put together a well-organized campaign to discourage students from going to class. But the strike was only partly successful, class attendance being curtailed by about 30 to 40 percent. The Strike Committee then moved to heavier tactics, occupying the Administration Building and turning on its fire hoses. In an effort to defend itself, the administration suspended a group of radical leaders and eventually summoned the Buffalo police back onto the campus. Early on a Sunday morning, 11 days into the crisis, 400 Buffalo policemen quietly moved into position.

The student response was initially a series of symbolic events, such as a mock funeral for the university. Eventually an ultimatum was issued to the administration, and a "War Council" was held to decide on appropriate action. The night of the War Council, a large group of students began taunting and throwing objects at the police, who were massed in front of the Administration Building, presumably to defend it. The police finally broke ranks and charged into the crowd with clubs swinging, injuring and arresting a number of students.

The next day, 45 faculty members held a sit-in at the acting president's office and were removed from the building and arrested by the police. No more student demonstrations were held after this time, but, angered by the arrest of their fellows, the Faculty Senate passed a motion of no confidence in the administration.

The rest of the semester witnessed a moderately successful effort to reunite the campus. As part of this effort, a committee made up of student, faculty, and administration representatives was organized to discuss the demands made by the Strike Committee and related matters. This committee made a number of recommendations that were adopted as campus policy, including the abolition of ROTC.

TRANSFORMATIONS THAT OCCUR DURING ESCALATION

As conflicts escalate, they go through certain incremental transformations. Although these transformations occur separately on each side, they affect the conflict as a whole because they are usually mirrored by the other side. As a result of these transformations, the conflict is intensified in ways that persist and are often exceedingly difficult to undo. The aim of this chapter is to understand the nature of these transformations and the conditions under which they are most likely to take place.

At least five types of transformations commonly occur during conflict escalation. All may not occur in a single conflict, but all are very common. The five transformations are as follows:

1. *Light→heavy.* As we observed in Chapter 4, efforts to get one's way in a competitive exchange typically begin with light influence attempts: ingratiation overtures, gamesmanship, persuasive arguments, promises. In many cases, these gentle tactics are eventually supplanted by their heavier counterparts: threats, irrevocable commitments, and so on. Eventually even violence may erupt. The second day of the UB crisis illustrates this kind of transformation. Student tactics moved from efforts to lodge a protest with the acting president, to stoning his windows, to chasing and throwing objects at campus policemen, to firebombing the library. The administration and its allies in the city police also moved rapidly from rebuffing protesters to clubbing and arresting them.

2. *Small→large.* As conflict escalates, there is a tendency for issues to proliferate. There is also a tendency for the parties to become more and more absorbed in the struggle and to commit ever-increasing resources to it in an effort to prevail. Both tendencies can be seen in the UB crisis. On the student side, the initial concern about police on campus immediately mushroomed into a set of nine demands. Still other demands, such as reinstatement of the students who had been suspended, were added to this list as events unfolded. On the administration side, new issues appeared at every turn in the student strategy: punishing the students who threw stones at the windows, punishing the students who fire-bombed the library, saving the Administration Building from vandalism and possible destruction, and so on. An escalation of resources occurred early on both sides, with a massive infusion of time and attention. Eleven days into the crisis, the administration increased its allocation of resources still further by bringing a large contingent of city police to the campus.

3. *Specific→general.* In escalating conflict, specific issues tend to give way to general issues, and there is movement toward a general deterioration in the relationship between the parties. What starts out as a small, concrete concern tends, over the painful history of an escalating exchange, to be supplanted by grandiose and all-encompassing positions and by a general intolerance of the other party. This point is illustrated by the student concerns in the UB crisis. Having started narrowly with protest over a single incident of city police on campus, these blossomed into general disaffection with the administration and demands that the university divorce itself from complicity with the national war effort, admit large numbers of black and third-world students, and fire the acting president.

4. *Doing well→winning→hurting the other.* In the early stages of many conflicts, the parties are simply out to do as well as they can for themselves, without regard for

how well or poorly the other is doing. This outlook has been described by Deutsch (1958) as an "individualistic orientation," an outlook characterized by self-interest that is quite independent of the other's fate. As conflict escalates, however, this simple interest in doing well is supplanted by a clearly competitive objective. Now "doing well" means outdoing the other. Finally, as escalation continues and the costs for both parties begin to mount, each party's goals tend to shift again. The objective now is to hurt the other and, if one is experiencing cost, to hurt the other more than oneself. For every drop of blood that Party has shed, a far more terrible blood-letting must be forced on Other. This is competition in the extreme. Such a transformation can be seen in the UB crisis, where student goals escalated from protesting an isolated instance of police on campus to making it impossible for the administration to govern and ousting the president. The administration's goals also escalated from containing the radicals to ejecting them from the campus.

5. *Few→many.* Conflicts that begin with the agitation of a small number of partici- pants often grow, in the face of failure of any party to prevail, into collective efforts. If you won't do what I insist that you do—and I am unable to get my way by threatening, promising, or in some other way manipulating you—then it is in my best interest to find other people who are willing to band together with me. What I cannot accomplish on my own, I may well be able to achieve with the increased support and muscle of my associates. The point is clearly illustrated on both sides of the UB crisis. Student radicals, acting alone at first, were able to recruit thousands of allies as time went on. (A student survey estimated that as many as 70 percent of the students eventually participated in the protest activities in one way or another. Many faculty members also allied themselves with the student effort, as they became increasingly upset about the way the administration handled the crisis.) Similarly, the administration brought in increasingly larger numbers of city police.

ESCALATION VS. STABILITY

When conflicts escalate, they tend to remain escalated, at least for a while. Hence a typical path in the development of escalated conflict might look like curve A in Figure 5.1. Time is on the abscissa in this figure. The variable of intensity on the ordinate refers to the degree to which any or all of the trans- formations just described have taken place.

By no means do all conflicts escalate. Indeed, those that do are in the mi- nority, though they are often quite noteworthy because of the problem they create for the parties involved and for the surrounding community. Curve B shows the path taken by conflict in relationships that are not plagued by esca- lation. Conflict intensity is not at a zero level in such relationships. Rather, it rises and falls over time like a sine wave. As each new issue arises, there is a period of rising tensions and augmented tactics. But then the conflict is re- solved or abandoned, and the relationship returns to harmony until the next issue arises.

Relationships in which conflicts do not easily escalate are said to be high in *stability*. This is a different kind of stability from that discussed in Chapter 2. It involves resistance to escalation, not to conflict as a whole. Stability as

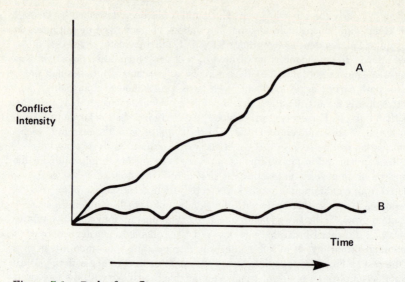

Figure 5.1. Path of conflict intensity over time. Curve A represents an escalating relationship; Curve B, a nonescalating (stable) relationship.

resistance to escalation is usually beneficial to a relationship, whereas stability as reluctance to engage in any conflict tends to be detrimental.

The rest of this chapter is devoted to a discussion of the conditions that affect whether conflicts escalate or not—whether they take path A or path B. The first section reviews some of the circumstances that foster escalation by encouraging people to choose a contentious strategy. The other five sections examine several conditions that promote stability—including conflict-limiting norms and institutions, the fear of escalation, social bonds, and various threat-related configurations such as the balance of power. The latter sections focus on stability rather than escalation, because the literature on which they are based is organized around this concept. But we have a broader purpose, so at times we will draw conclusions about the antecedents of escalation by reversing the points made about the antecedents of stability.

CONDITIONS ENCOURAGING CONTENTIOUS BEHAVIOR

In Chapter 3, we discussed many individual mechanisms that affect the choice between contending and the other strategies for dealing with conflict. The use of heavy contentious tactics is a major aspect of escalation. Hence we can deduce that conflict escalation is especially likely when:

- The parties see themselves as having the power to substantially alter one another's current aspirations. This should encourage each party's hope that it can resolve its problems with the other by using contentious tactics.
- The parties do not see integrative capacity in the situation. That is, they do not see the possibility of finding a mutually beneficial solution to the controversy. This

should discourage problem-solving behavior and hence encourage contending. It implies, for example, that relationships between people who have discovered that they have little to offer each other should be particularly unstable.
• The parties have, and view each other as having, relatively high aspirations. High aspirations diminish the perceived likelihood that a mutually acceptable solution can be devised, and hence encourage contentious behavior.

CONFLICT-LIMITING NORMS AND INSTITUTIONS

Social norms often contribute to stability, prohibiting the use of harsh contentious tactics and prescribing problem solving as the proper approach to conflict between group members. "Don't let the sun set on your anger" and "Love thy neighbor as thyself" are but a few examples of maxims that may also serve as guiding norms in the regulation of conflict. Note that norms such as these must be distinguished from substantive norms and norms about who makes what decisions. As mentioned in Chapter 2, the latter types of norms tend to diminish the likelihood of conflict arising at all, rather than the likelihood that conflict will escalate.

Like all norms, conflict-limiting norms are effective with people who are well socialized and with those who do not have major grievances. They are also effective with other types of people to the extent that society has the capacity for enforcement—that is, for learning about and punishing norm violation. Escalation is common in societies that lack adequate social controls of this kind.

Societies also generally provide forums and third-party institutions for helping their members resolve conflict peacefully. These include legislative bodies (such as committees of representatives from different agencies), arbitral services (such as courts and formal arbitrators), and mediation services (see Chapter 10 for a discussion of mediation). Formal judicial and mediation services are sometimes established by law, such as the services provided by the Public Employee Relations Board in the State of New York. This board has a set of steps for dealing with impasse in negotiations between public-employee unions and government agencies. In the case of police and firefighter disputes, a mediator (a person who tries to help the principals find a mutually acceptable agreement) is first sent. If mediation is not successful, a fact-finder (a person who looks into the issues and renders an advisory judgment) is dispatched. If fact-finding does not produce agreement, the controversy must go before an arbitrator for a binding judgment. More commonly, third-party intervention is informal and relatively unstructured. A mother resolves an argument over a toy in favor of one of her children. A mutual friend suggests a way to resolve a dispute between neighbors about a noisy dog. A middle ground between the formal and the informal is occupied by the various community, marital, and divorce mediation services that have sprung up recently around the country (Dugan, 1982).

Forums and third-party institutions contribute to stability by giving people a nonviolent and face-saving way to resolve their disputes. For such institutions to be effective, they must be seen as legitimate and relatively unbiased. It is also essential that they be seen as giving a full hearing and careful consideration to user grievances, even if the ultimate decision or recommendation favors the opponent (Thibaut & Walker, 1975).

In the absence of legitimate and trusted forums or third-party institutions, people often "take the law into their own hands," employing harsh contentious tactics in an effort to settle controversies in their own favor, and thus escalating these controversies. This tendency can be seen in frontier regions, where blood feuds are common, and in the results of an interview study of black residents of Los Angeles after the Watts riots of 1965 (Ransford, 1968). This study showed that those who felt that it was not possible for the average citizen to influence government decisions were especially likely to endorse the use of violence in pursuit of racial justice.

THE FEAR OF ESCALATION

As will be explained in the next chapter, escalation is often the result of a conflict spiral (a form of vicious circle) in which each party reacts contentiously to the other party's recent contentious action. In his classic treatise on arms races, Richardson (1967) argues that conflict spirals, and hence escalation, are less likely to occur when people are aware of the potential for such spirals and concerned about the consequences of escalation. When such is the case, they are likely to tone down their reactions to the other party's aggressive actions. The fear of escalation may underlie in part the tendency noted in nondistressed marriages (Gottman, 1979) and successful roommate relationships (Sillars, 1981) for people to respond in a conciliatory fashion to contentious challenges from their partners. We find in such cases a stillborn spiral; Party is racing toward the brink but Other is not trying to catch up.

Sometimes fear of escalation arises as a result of a frightening prior episode of controversy with the other party. If the parties manage to continue their relationship beyond such an incident, one or both of them is often chastened and wary of overreacting. This presumably happened at the time of the Cuban missile crisis of 1963, when the United States and the Soviet Union came close to war. Shortly after this crisis, a period of détente emerged, in which both sides made efforts to de-escalate the controversy between them. In essence, these two nations looked over a precipice together and then drew back in an effort to avoid disaster. The fear of escalation resulting from this crisis has largely worn off over the ensuing years, which may explain why the forces of escalation are once more in the ascendant.

SOCIAL BONDS

As pointed out in Chapter 3, social bonds tend to encourage yielding and problem solving and to discourage the use of contentious tactics, especially those of the harsher variety. Hence bonds are a source of stability in relationships; they reduce the likelihood of escalation. The bonds in question include positive attitudes, respect, friendship, kinship, perceived similarity, common group membership, and future dependence. As an example of the impact of friendship on social conflict, Ransford (1968) found that blacks who had socialized with whites were less willing to endorse the use of violence in pursuit of racial justice than were those who had not. The importance of common group membership is reflected in Coleman's (1957) contention that identification with one's community tends to moderate the tactics used for pursuing disagreements with other community members.

Most bonds cut in both directions. That is, when Party feels bonded to Other, Other feels bonded to Party. This is inevitably true of kinship and common group membership and is usually true of perceived similarity. Also positive attitudes and respect are usually reciprocal (Berscheid & Walster, 1978), and friendship is usually a two-way street. The only kind of bond that is not typically reciprocal is dependence on the other party. Dependence sometimes, though by no means always, cuts only one way.

The stabilizing impact of bonding is often masked by the fact that people who are more securely bonded to each other feel less constrained by the canons of politeness. They are likely to raise more issues with one another and argue more vigorously, at least for a time. Still, if conflict persists, they are more likely to engage in problem solving and less likely to employ harsh contentious tactics. This paradox was observed in a laboratory study of dyads by Back (1951). When a difference of opinion arose, more cohesive dyads argued more vigorously but also eventually reached fuller agreement.

The opposite of bonding is antagonism. Antagonism tends to encourage the use of harsh contentious tactics and hence to encourage conflict escalation. Antagonism can take the form of anger, negative attitudes, grievances of all kinds, perceived dissimilarity, membership in an opposing group, or an expectation of frustration at the other's hands. Past contentious interchanges tend to foster antagonism, making the parties especially likely to overreact when a new conflict arises. This is particularly likely to happen if the prior issues remain unresolved. Antagonism, like bonding, tends to be reciprocated.

Conflict per se, in the sense of perceived divergence of interest, can be a source of mild antagonism even in the absence of struggle and of frustrating incidents. This is because one feels alienated from people whose interests seem to be opposed to one's own. Accordingly, unless there are bonds or social norms to balance this phenomenon, conflicts have an inherent tendency to gravitate toward a contentious expression and hence toward escalation.

We shall now examine the impact on stability and escalation of two important types of bonds: common group membership and dependence.

Common Group Membership

One of the most important sources of bonding is common group membership—the perception that Other is a member of a group to which one also belongs. A good deal of experimental research has been conducted on the relationship between this phenomenon and *ethnocentrism*, the tendency to favor the ingroup over the outgroup (Brewer, 1979; Tajfel, 1970). Even the most minimal common group membership—being classified by outsiders with some people and not with others—is sufficient to produce ethnocentrism. People like better, think more highly of, and discriminate in favor of other people with whom they are classed, regardless of the basis for the classification. This is the social categorization effect. It helps to explain why ethnocentrism is so universal a human characteristic (Sumner, 1906).

The link between ethnocentrism and stability has not yet been examined empirically. But the research just cited suggests that escalation may be more common in relations between groups than in relations between individuals, and more common in relations between individuals who do not see themselves as sharing a common group membership than in relations between those who do. Evidence favoring the first of these two generalizations (more escalation between groups than between individuals) has been found in two studies (Komorita & Lapworth, 1982; McCallum, et al., 1984).

What mechanism can account for the social categorization effect? There are two popular explanations: Allen and Wilder (1975) propose that common group identity produces perceived similarity with other members of one's group, which leads to positive sentiments toward these people. Turner (1981) postulates that social categorization produces competition for status between the ingroup and the outgroup, which is motivated by the fact that people's own self-concepts are very much wrapped up in their social identities.

The latter, status-competition explanation is supported by three recent findings. One is that personal failure leads people to voice more positive images of their own group and more negative images of rival groups (Cialdini & Richardson, 1980). This finding can be deduced from the status-competition explanation, because personal failure threatens the self-concept. The second is that there is more bias against groups that are more similar in status to one's own (Turner, 1981). This finding can also be deduced from the status-competition explanation, because groups that are roughly equal in status are more likely to compete for status. The third finding is that there is more bias against an outgroup of a different status from one's own to the extent that there is uncertainty about one's own or the other group's status (Turner, 1981). This can be deduced by the same reasoning.

These findings suggest three conditions under which intergroup conflict may be especially likely to escalate: when many group members have insecure self-images, when the groups are similar in status, and when status differences between the groups are uncertain or changeable.

Dependence

Dependence is the most complicated source of bonding. Party is dependent on Other to the extent that Other has control over certain of Party's outcomes and can reward Party for desired behavior and/or punish Party for undesired behavior. Dependence usually encourages yielding and problem solving and discourages the use of heavy contentious tactics. The more Other can help or harm Party, the more careful Party must be not to annoy Other by pressing petty claims or employing harsh tactics. Hence dependence ordinarily contributes to stability, especially if it is bilateral. An example is the high level of cooperation and absence of escalated conflict in relations between the United States and the Soviet Union during the Second World War, when they were dependent on each other for support in the common war against Germany and her allies. This relationship deteriorated drastically as soon as the war was over, a topic that will be explored in depth in Chapter 6.

Dependence is, however, a two-edged sword. There is a potential divergence of interest when one party relies on another for rewards. If I ever rely on you for rides to work and it is costly for you to provide them, our interests are divergent. If you are haphazard in providing this service and I cannot find another source of rides, I am likely to try to improve your performance by employing contentious tactics. The more dependent I am on you, the harsher the tactics I am likely to employ so as to teach you an enduring lesson. This is why conflicts between friends and family members are sometimes especially prone to escalation. Because such people are interdependent, each has a large stake in gaining conformity from the other. In short, dependence on an unreliable Other is a source of conflict and encourages escalation rather than stability.

There is also a complicated association between breadth of dependence—that is, the number of realms in which one depends on another party—and stability. The more realms in which Party relies on Other, the less likely is Party to use harsh tactics in any one realm, for fear of losing Other's cooperation in alternative realms. Hence the less likely is escalation. Paradoxically, however, broader dependence means more potential for conflict. If something goes wrong in the U.S. relationship with Ecuador, we are more likely to employ sanctions than if a comparable problem arises in our relationship with Britain. This is because our country is more dependent on Britain. However, this very dependence means that there will be more frequent conflict with Britain than with Ecuador. Month after month and year after year, more issues arise in the former relationship than in the latter. In short, breadth of dependence reduces the likelihood that conflict will escalate but increases the number of issues over which there will be conflict.

This last generalization must be qualified in that there are diminishing returns for stability when dependence becomes too broad. Indeed, extreme dependence can actually foster conflict escalation. The problem is that no party can satisfy all of another's needs. Suppose I rely on you for food, money, affection, respect, decisions about my clothes, haircuts, advice on presents to relatives, and so on and on. Unless you are a superman or supermom, some of my needs will go unfulfilled and I will be frustrated. Hence I am likely to become angry and to employ harsh tactics in dealing with you. This happens, for example, to some older people who become overdependent on a relative or nurse and, as a result, very crabby. Their relationships would be more stable, in the sense of producing fewer quarrels, if they were involved with more people so that they could rely on each person for the benefits he or she was most capable of providing.

There are two other ways in which heavy involvement outside a relationship reduces the likelihood that conflict will escalate within that relationship. First, heavy conflict takes time and resources. If one is engaged in many outside pursuits, one must avoid escalation unless the issues are of considerable importance. Second, issues loom larger the more attention is paid to them. When life is rich with many activities, one gains a certain perspective. It is unnecessary to achieve all of one's aspirations—one can afford to lose a few because one is winning many. Under these conditions, one is less likely to push the other for maximal concessions, and escalation is less likely.

The Destruction of Bonds

Bonds tend to restrict conflict escalation, discouraging retaliation and the use of heavy contentious tactics. But they are no absolute guarantee against escalation. Even strong bonds cannot protect a relationship when conflict of interest is multiple and profound.

When controversies escalate, bonds tend to disintegrate. Relationships are severed, love turns to hate, people shift their dependencies to other, less difficult partners. Such developments account partly for the one-way street so often seen in conflict escalation. A little bit of escalation partially destroys interparty bonds, making further escalation possible, which further destroys bonds, etc., etc. Thus escalation becomes a self-perpetuating process.

In summary, social bonding tends to protect relationships from escalation. Two of the most important types of bonds are common group membership and dependence. The sense of common group membership can be produced by any classification scheme that divides people into two or more groups. Within such groups, stability tends to be high. Between them, there is a tendency toward escalation if conflict arises. Dependence tends to be a two-edged sword. Ordinarily it contributes to stability, but it can flip-flop and contribute to escalation if the party on whom we are dependent turns out to be grossly unreliable. There is a curvilinear relationship between breadth of dependence and escalation. The potential for escalation diminishes as Party becomes increasingly dependent on Other until the point of overdependence is reached, at which Other cannot adequately serve Party's needs. Beyond this point, the probability of escalation increases. When a controversy escalates, bonds tend to disintegrate, making the next controversy even more likely to escalate. We turn now to an extension of the theory of bonds to the multiple-party setting—a topic that we refer to as the "geography of social bonds."

THE GEOGRAPHY OF SOCIAL BONDS

So far we have focused only on the relations between the parties themselves. But it is also possible to examine how these parties are related to members of the broader community in which they reside and how these members are related to each other. All bonding and antagonism anywhere in a community tend to affect the stability of relations between particular subsegments of that community, though the influence is smaller the greater the social distance from these subsegments. The entire configuration of bonding and antagonism among members of a community can be called the "geography of social bonds." To understand how this geography contributes to stability and escalation, we must start with three-party systems and then move systematically to larger configurations.

Three-Party Systems

In the three-party case, the critical question is how conflict between two parties (A and B) is affected by their relationship with a third party (X). Three situations or "cases" can be distinguished. These are shown schematically in Figure 5.2.

In case I, parties A and B both have bonds to the third party X; for example, husband and wife have a strong common friendship with the wife's father or two nations have a common ally. This should strengthen the bonds between A and B, and hence the stability of their relationship, encouraging resolution rather than escalation of their controversies. There are two reasons for predicting this. One is perceived similarity; following balance theory (Heider, 1958), we can predict that A and B will have positive attitudes toward each other as a result of their similar relationship to X. The other, perhaps more important, reason is that X will often become active in trying to reconcile any differences that develop between A and B, putting pressure on both sides not to escalate their controversies and providing an avenue of communication between them.

Third parties who are sympathetic to both sides do not always attempt to mediate controversy. Sometimes, as Coleman (1957) points out, they find the conflict distasteful and simply withdraw. But controversies between friends, relatives, or allies are frequently seen as a threat to a third party. They disturb the peace and endanger group unity and effectiveness. There is also an ever-present danger that both antagonists will try to draw the third party into the conflict on their side and become resentful about any unwillingness to join them. Hence third parties are often active in trying to resolve conflict between adversaries with whom they are associated. Illustrative of this point are the constant efforts by the United States to mediate controversies between the nations in its orbit, such as those between Israel and Egypt.

In case II, parties A and B are both antagonistic to party X—they share a common antipathy toward the third party. This should also increase the stability of the A–B relationship. There are two reasons for this. One is the point made earlier that perceived similarity encourages the development of psychological bonds. The other is the need that may well arise for a common effort against X. When two parties work together on a common cause or anticipate that they may have to do so, they must be careful not to become involved in escalated conflict with each other.

In case III, there is a bond between parties A and X and antagonism be-

tween parties B and X. In this case, we can predict the development of antagonism and consequent potential for escalation in the A–B relationship. This is
partly because A and B perceive dissimilarity in their attitudes toward X. It
is also partly because X will often try to recruit A into the campaign against
B. In other words, A's bonds with X are likely to draw A into a coalition
against B.

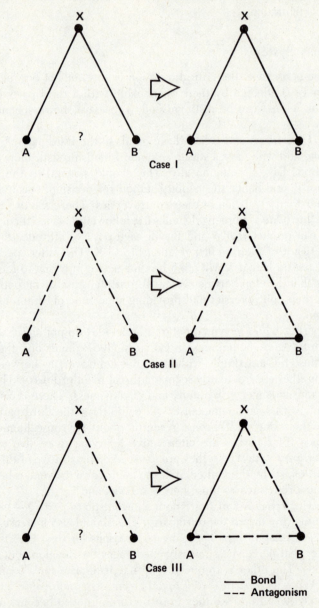

Figure 5.2.   Predictions for some three-party systems. (The figure on the right
shows the bond or antagonism between parties A and B that is predicted from the
figure on the left.)

Four-Party Systems

Several further predictions are possible if we add a fourth party (Y) to the system just described. Excluding the relationship between A and B (whose nature is the item to be predicted), there are six possible configurations of bonds and antagonisms in such a four-party system. We shall examine only two of these configurations (Figure 5.3), leaving the others for the reader to figure out. Both involve a bond between A and X and a similar bond between B and Y. In other words, A and X are friends or allies, as are B and Y. The question is how the X–Y relationship will affect the stability of the relationship between A and B.

The answer to this question is straightforward. In case IV, where the A–X, X–Y, and Y–B relationships all involve bonds, we can predict stability in the A–B relationship (Rubin, 1971). There are two reasons for this. One is the simple psychological phenomenon of balance: A friend of my friend's friend is my friend. The other resides in the activities of X and Y, who will often urge

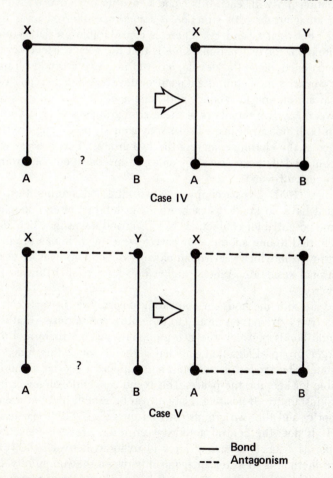

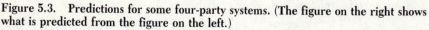

Figure 5.3. Predictions for some four-party systems. (The figure on the right shows what is predicted from the figure on the left.)

moderation on A and B or act as a mediation chain between these parties in order to take the strain off their own relationship.

In case V, where X and Y are antagonistic, we can predict instability in the A–B relationship and hence a tendency to escalate if conflicts develop. This is partly because of balance and partly because X and Y can be expected to try to split up the A–B relationship in order to have more reliable allies in their struggle with one another.

Stability in Larger Communities

The points we have just made about three- and four-party systems can be used to understand stability in larger communities consisting of two or more groups.

Consider first the case of two groups (G and H) whose members have little or no relationship with each other and hence no objective basis for forming bonds or antagonisms (this situation is sometimes referred to as involving a "cleavage" between G and H). There is considerable escalation potential in such a situation, for two reasons. One is that the very existence of discriminable groups encourages the development of negative attitudes (Tajfel, 1970). In other words, a modicum of antagonism develops between any two groups that are aware of, and lack bonds with, one another. The other is that a conflict between any two members of these rival groups is likely to be joined by others on both sides (because of case V dynamics), producing multiple antagonisms across the chasm separating the two groups. This process will be further encouraged if there are prior antagonisms between the groups arising from earlier controversies.

Coleman (1957) gives examples of two kinds of communities containing groups that have no bonds to each other but interact often enough for there to be some potential for conflict: (1) New England towns in which old Yankees are closely tied to one another but have few ties with Italian immigrants and (2) resort towns in which year-round citizens view themselves as a group apart from seasonal residents. When conflict develops in such towns, it is often quite severe.

There are four methods for combating polarization in such communities. One is to try to strengthen loyalty to the entire community—that is, to forge sentimental bonds between the two groups by making them feel part of the same larger group. Flags and national anthems serve this function in the nation–state. The second is to install and support a central authority that is responsible for keeping the peace. This is the conventional governmental approach to instability. If positive relations can be established between the central authority and the two groups, this encourages stability via the dynamics of case I. If not, the central authority can often prevent escalation by enforcing norms against the use of force in relations between the two groups. The third method is to foster antagonism between the community as a whole and an outside enemy, making use of case II dynamics. An example is the

Argentine occupation of the Falkland Islands in 1982, which appears to have been at least partly designed to unify a divided domestic polity around a patriotic issue.

The fourth way to combat polarization is to encourage bonds between individuals on both sides, making use of case IV dynamics in an effort to reduce tensions between the groups as a whole. This method is used whenever ruling groups incorporate ("co-opt") members of agitating factions into their decision making. Likert (1961) recommends the use of this method in organizations, urging that interdepartmental committees be formed in which representatives of potentially adversarial departments get to know each other and engage in problem solving about matters of common concern. Such representatives are called "linking pins." A similar method was used by royal families in the past when, in an effort to achieve peace, they arranged for their daughters to marry foreign princes. Such procedures produce a small cadre in both groups whose members are ready to question the use of heavy contentious behavior and to serve as mediators when conflict arises between other members of the two groups.

Crosscutting Group Memberships

If one linking pin on each side can contribute to community stability, two should be better and 200 even better. This brings us to the theory of *crosscutting* (interlocking) *group memberships* (see, for example, Coleman, 1957). A diagram of a crosscutting system is shown in Figure 5.4. Four groups are depicted, but the analysis can easily be extended to many more groups. Two of the groups in the diagram crosscut the other two groups, in the sense of having overlapping membership. Such a situation is stable because there are

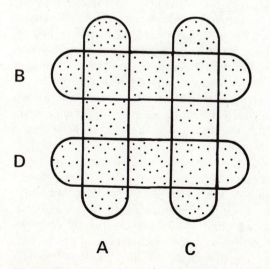

Figure 5.4. **Four groups with crosscutting memberships.**

many people in each group with bonds to one or more of the other groups. These people are reluctant to use heavy tactics in intergroup controversies, are likely to discourage fellow group members from using such tactics, and often serve as mediators between the groups.

The most interesting cases are the groups that are opposite each other in the diagram (A and C, B and D) and have no members in common. The relations between these groups tend to be stable because some members of each group are tied to one another by their common membership in crosscutting groups. This linkage provides bonds of perceived similarity and common group identity between these individuals, as well as ties to other individuals in the crosscutting groups who may be motivated to mediate controversies. Stability in such systems cuts both ways: Conflicts between groups A and C are held in check by crosscutting memberships in groups B and D, and conflicts between B and D are held in check by crosscutting memberships in A and C.

Gluckman (1955) provides two anthropological examples of crosscutting. He found that when a Nuer man moves away from his male relatives to the region of another group, he exerts a calming force on his relatives in their quarrels with this group. There are probably two mechanisms at work. One is that fear of retribution causes the man to urge his kin to compromise the affair. The other is that, "he is likely to urge his kin to offer compensation, since he has many interests in the place where he resides" (p. 12). Gluckman also points out that marriage produces stability in those African societies in which the wife must move to her husband's village. Thereafter she exerts a calming influence whenever there is conflict between her original village and that to which she has moved. Both examples illustrate crosscutting because the person who has moved becomes a member of both groups.

Closer to home, the United States today can be regarded as a heavily crosscutting system. For example, regional rivalries are held in check by the fact that there are thousands of strong nationwide organizations as divergent as IBM and the Catholic Church. Classes, too, are crosscut by political party. And so on and on. In such a system, few subsets of people can form an unambivalent alliance against any other subset. A possible exception is alignment of blacks against whites in our society, because there are relatively few bonds between these groups. The civil rights movement, with its effort to introduce blacks into every institution of our society, can be seen as a massive program to develop such bonds and the stability that goes with them, though most of its members would deny that this is their aim.

There is one other wrinkle to the theory of crosscutting group memberships—a paradoxical one. In a crosscutting situation, mild conflict between social groups can actually contribute to the overall stability of the community, making severe conflict less likely. Imagine a community of Yankees and Italians in which some people from each ethnic group consider themselves management (and belong to management associations and clubs) and others consider themselves labor (and belong to unions). A little conflict between management and labor should make it more difficult for Yankee–Italian antagonisms to escalate, because Yankees and Italians have served together on both sides of the battle line and recognize that they may need to do so again. Likewise, a little conflict between Yankees and Italians tends to diminish the intensity of future conflict between labor and management. Hence, and this is the crucial point, if there has been a little conflict in both sets of groupings, severe controversy is likely to be avoided in both. Almost everybody in the community recognizes almost everybody else as a past or potential future ally.

In addition, mild controversy sometimes contributes to the development of institutions (such as representative committees and mediation services) that stand ready to resolve more serious future controversies.

Stability through crosscutting group memberships is also found in the Congress of the United States. Coalitions change from issue to issue in this body, so antagonisms usually do not run very deep. Members maintain decorous relations with one another and observe many informal conflict-limiting norms in order to be able to work together in future coalitions. Today it may be the farm states against the manufacturing states, tomorrow North against South, the next day pro-military budget against anti-military budget. One never knows whose help one may need in a future controversy, so it is "politic" not to let current conflicts get out of hand.

Although crosscutting memberships reduce the likelihood of heavy contentious behavior between the groups, they are not always beneficial to society as a whole. Sometimes society needs active competition between groups. Consider interlocking directorates among corporations producing the same kind of product. This phenomenon has the capacity to undermine the kind of competition that is necessary for optimal performance of a capitalist economy (Schoorman, Bazerman & Atkin, 1981).

Crosscutting systems like those described are highly resistant to escalation. But no system is completely escalation-proof. A really severe conflict of interest between two groups can break through any bonds, however secure, producing a runaway escalation and a set of antagonisms that may take years to repair.

Community Size and Social Geography

In the 1960s, at the height of the black and student movements, statistical evidence showed that there were more racial blowups in large cities than in small, and more severe campus demonstrations on large campuses (such as UB) than on small. This can be explained in terms of social geography. More people know each other in small than in large communities, so bonds are closer and bond chains shorter. There is more opportunity for communication and problem solving and less temptation to employ heavy contentious tactics.

To summarize, we have extended the analysis of bonding to communities involving more than two members. Our theory predicts the development of bonding between two parties who are mutually bonded or mutually antagonistic to a third party; antagonism when one party is bound to, and the other antagonistic to, a third party; bonding when there are bonds between a third and a fourth party to which the two parties are respectively bound; and antagonism when there is antagonism between a third and a fourth party to which the two parties are respectively bound. Bonds are assumed to foster stability in a relationship, and antagonism is assumed to foster the potential for escalation. Stability in larger communities is encouraged by crosscutting group memberships, in which everyone is linked in some way to everyone else. Paradoxically, a certain amount of conflict in such a system can strengthen the bonds among its members. Bonds tend to be weaker in larger communities, making such communities more prone to escalated conflict.

STABILITY THROUGH THREATS

The mechanisms discussed so far (conflict-limiting norms and institutions, fear of escalation, and social bonds) ordinarily have tremendous force, accounting for the quiet way in which most conflicts are pursued and the high rate of peaceful conflict resolution ordinarily found in human affairs. However, there are limits to the effectiveness of these mechanisms in averting escalation. They can go wrong in a variety of ways.

• There may be so little perceived common ground and the issues involved may be so important that the temptation to take harsh contentious action may overwhelm all such constraints.
• The people involved may be poorly socialized, making norms ineffective.
• The institutions for third-party conflict resolution may be weak, as in frontier areas where courts have little enforcement capability or are nonexistent.
• The people involved may have had no recent experience with a frightening crisis that would make them fear new escalation.
• Social bonds may be weak between the potential antagonists or between them and broader communities that have a stake in the conflict.

Under such circumstances, it may seem necessary to use threats and punitive actions to deter the other from employing harsh tactics. Dramatic forms of threat and punishment can be seen in the apprehension and incarceration of violent criminals. Even more dramatic are the actions of nations to protect themselves against external aggression. Most nations arm themselves against potential enemies, threaten if there is apparent danger of attack, and go to war if they or their allies are attacked.

Less obvious, but nevertheless of vast social significance, are the subtle threats and small penalties that all human interactions exhibit. All people have means of imposing costs on those around them. Children can cry, servants and workers can move slowly, wives can get angry, and husbands can come home late. Most people are also adept at subtly signaling their discontent: the slow response to a statement, the lapse of attention, the lifted eyebrow, the frown, the sigh. These are often tantamount to stating a full-blown threat, in that the recipients realize that punitive action will be forthcoming if they are not careful. In short, threats and penalties are omnipresent in social relationships, potentially deterring others from taking hostile or bothersome action.

As we saw in Chapter 4, for a threat to be effective, the punishment threatened must be large enough to outweigh the benefits of noncompliance. The threat must also be credible—that is, believable. There are two kinds of credibility: credibility of capability and credibility of intent (Pruitt and Snyder, 1969). The former can be defined as the extent to which a party seems capable of carrying out its threats; the latter, as the extent to which it seems willing to carry them out. A threat need not always be 100 percent credible to be effective. The larger the damage that can be done to the adversary if the threat *is* carried out, the less credible the threat need be, because the adversary will be less likely to take chances. Thus it can be argued that a likelihood as low as 10 percent of American retaliation against a Russian nuclear attack should be enough to deter such an attack.

Balance of Power

Several theories of threat-induced stability have been developed for international affairs. The oldest and most famous of these is balance-of-power theory. This theory can be adapted so that it is broadly applicable to the use of threats in all social situations.

In one interpretation of this theory, a balance of power exists when all nations in a system are deterred for military reasons from attacking all others. Assuming conventional weapons, deterrence is a function of the existence of natural and artificial barriers to attack, the military capability of the target of a potential attack, and the assistance it can recruit from other nations. These deterrents are effective either by making it impossible for aggression to succeed or by imposing potential costs on an aggressor.

There are several mechanisms by which a balance of power can be achieved. Collective security is the ideal mechanism. According to this ideal, all other nations come to the rescue of a nation under attack. Such a mechanism was built into the charter of the League of Nations and that of the United Nations. But it is usually difficult to activate because, in most controversies, some nations sympathize with one side and some with the other.

Barring collective security, nations that are faced with a militarily capable opponent try to maintain or restore the balance of power by arming themselves and seeking allies. Some analysts argue that the most stable situation of this kind is one in which all potential opponents are equal in military strength; others argue that the least aggressive nations must have a preponderance of military strength (Claude, 1962). The existence of balancer nations contributes to both kinds of stability. Balancers are nations that change alliances from time to time in order to side with the underdog. In earlier times, England played the role of balancer in the European system of nations.

A number of conditions can be cited that probably contribute to the international balance of power:

1. Having a large number of nations in a system. The argument usually given for this assertion (Deutsch & Singer, 1964; Kaplan, 1957) is that, with more nations, a

greater variety of coalitions can be formed. Hence the system is more flexible for developing a coalition against any would-be aggressor.

2. Freedom of action among statesmen. Statesmen must have considerable autonomy to be able to execute the fine maneuvers involved in shifting alliances in order to restore the balance (Gulick, 1955). The greatest departure from freedom comes when the nations in a system are linked together in two tight alliances, and no way exists for any of them to change sides in order to right an imbalance or to mediate a controversy between two other nations (Kaplan, 1957). This is a condition of severe community polarization.

3. The absence of extreme hostility between nations. If hostility is too great, it is not possible to join one's old enemies in an alliance against an emerging aggressor.

4. Measurability of military capacity. When military capacity can be measured accurately in terms that are understood by all, it is possible to estimate the strength of arms and the size of a coalition that will deter a would-be aggressor (Lasswell, 1950). But when this measurement is not possible, as when different sorts of weapons systems are found on each side, defensive coalitions may prove inadequate, or potential aggressors may launch an attack on the basis of an erroneous assessment of their own strength.

Regardless of which mechanism is involved (collective security, equality, preponderance of peace-loving nations, or alliance shifts by balancers), a balance of power is more likely to be effective when the military advantage lies with the defender rather than the aggressor. The greatest chance of escalation is found when there is an advantage to be gained by striking first. Such a situation existed just before the start of the First World War, when the first nation to mobilize could gain a major advantage over its neighbor by loading its troops onto trains and rushing them to the border for a massive assault. Such conditions are unstable for two reasons: there is a temptation to strike first, and fear that the other is about to strike first can motivate a pre-emptive first strike. The beginning of the First World War can be explained as due to a pre-emptive action. The first military move, a mobilization along the border, was made by Russia in an effort to deter an attack by Austria on Serbia. Fearing that this mobilization would put it at a military disadvantage, Germany then launched a pre-emptive attack against Russia's ally France, striking through Belgium.

Balance-of-power theory can be translated into other arenas of human interaction. For example, small groups, such as interdepartmental committees or families, must deter overly aggressive members who attack others or try to dominate discussions. Collective security is not uncommon in such situations, all other group members forming a temporary coalition against the aggressor. Barring this, smaller coalitions of like-minded individuals often form, and the members of each coalition rise to one another's defense so that no individual can be overwhelmed. If two tight alliances form within such a group, escalative processes may be encouraged and the situation will be relatively unstable. It will be more stable if a few people act as balancers, forever shifting to the defense of the underdog. The role of balancer is frequently played by the group leader.

Balance of Power in the Nuclear Age

The development of nuclear weapons has forced some changes in thinking about balance of power. These weapons are fantastically destructive, of course, and there is no defense against them. The only way to protect oneself militarily is to threaten to retaliate in the hope of deterring the other side from using them. Such retaliation is called a "second strike." It follows that the critical issue for stability is second-strike credibility: how believable it is that an aggressor will be destroyed.

Efforts to establish credibility must take somewhat different forms, depending on whether the nation attacked is a nuclear nation itself or the ally of a nuclear nation (Kahn, 1960). It is ordinarily assumed that a nuclear nation under nuclear attack will retaliate in kind if it can. Hence, only second-strike capability is at issue—that is, whether the nation can retaliate after suffering a nuclear first strike. By contrast, in the deterrence of an attack against an ally, *intentions* are the main issue. Will the nuclear nation run the risk of a devastating counterattack from the aggressor by actually retaliating? Willingness to come to the defense of an ally has always been an issue, even in strictly conventional contests, but it is more difficult to establish the credibility of intent in the age of nuclear weapons, because the cost of retaliation is so much greater.

Protecting Oneself. Second-strike capability depends on the security of the carriers (missiles and planes) of nuclear weapons and on their capacity to penetrate the adversary's defenses. The security of weapons carriers can be achieved in a variety of ways, including increasing their numbers, dispersing them, moving them frequently, concealing them, shielding them in bunkers, and protecting them by means of anti-aircraft and anti-missile weapons. For example, the United States has built a large number of missiles and dispersed them throughout the globe. A large number of our nuclear weapons are constantly on the move, in airplanes and submarines. (A proposal to move land-based missiles around on railroad tracks was only narrowly defeated a few years ago.) Heavy shielding is also a prominent feature of the bunkers in which our land-based missiles are stored, and the sea provides both shielding and concealment for the submarines that carry nuclear weapons. Some believe that the capacity of American airplanes to penetrate adversary defense is in jeopardy. Hence the United States is developing a new generation of bombers (the "stealth" fleet) that are capable of flying low enough to elude detection.

Provided that its second-strike capability is secure, a nation can afford to have dramatically less capability than its adversary and still be secure within its borders. The Soviet Union would not be "ahead" of the United States if we could destroy them ten times over and they could destroy us a hundred times over. In principle, then, a stable nuclear "balance of terror" should be a lot easier to achieve than a stable conventional balance of power. It follows that it should be easier to put a cap on the nuclear arms race than on conventional races, where both sides often feel it is essential to be slightly stronger than the adversary. In practice, however, the nuclear arms race grinds on.

This is partly because of exaggerated doubts about the vulnerability of second-strike capability. (Despite the panoply of safeguards for our planes and missiles, some Americans still worry about the security of these systems and urge the building and arming of substantially larger fleets.) It is also partly because of the supposed political disadvantage of having fewer planes, missiles, or warheads than the adversary. It is not clear that such a political disadvantage actually exists, because the adversary's weapons are unusable if one maintains a secure second-strike capacity. But some people still worry about this issue, presumably because they are afraid that other people (such as the adversary) believe that superiority in nuclear weapons carries the same advantages as superiority in conventional weapons.

Protecting Allies. In a nuclear age, nations without nuclear weapons often feel that they must rely on other, better-armed nations for protection. The United States has extended what is sometimes called a "nuclear umbrella" over dozens of other nations. The situation is even more complicated in Europe because of a belief in the West that the Soviet Union could prevail in a conventional attack on Western Europe. This concern has led to an American pledge to use nuclear weapons in response to a conventional attack in that theater. Earlier this pledge took the form of the "massive retaliation" doctrine, whereby the United States threatened to launch an all-out nuclear attack in response to a conventional attack against Western Europe. However, when the Soviet Union became capable of devastating our country with nuclear weapons, the credibility of the massive retaliation doctrine came into question. It was replaced by a policy of employing "tactical" (as opposed to "strategic") nuclear weapons in the battlefield against soldiers. It was believed that the threat to use these weapons would be more credible than the threat of massive retaliation, because the Soviet Union would be less likely to employ strategic weapons in retaliation.

More recently, the Soviet Union has put into place a large number of nuclear-tipped missiles (the SS-20's) aimed at Western Europe. In an effort to deter the use of these weapons, NATO has arranged with the United States to station a new fleet of missiles (the Pershing II's and cruise missiles) in Europe. This is assumed to be a more credible deterrent against Russian attack than missiles housed on the American mainland or in American submarines, because the second strike would actually originate from the territory under attack. Whether Russian decision makers actually reason in this way is a matter of conjecture.

Problems with Basing Stability on Threats

There are many problems with efforts to base stability on threats and hence with reliance on balance-of-power approaches. Such approaches assume that it is possble to clearly communicate one's resolve to a potential aggressor, yet history reveals many failures in this regard (Lebow, Jervis & Stein, 1984). Such approaches also assume that a would-be aggressor will be rational and able to predict accurately and hence will avoid taking action if the risks are too high or the probability of success too low. It follows that threat-based deterrents are likely to fail and escalation to materialize when the responsible decision makers (1) are mentally or emotionally incapacitated, making them unable to use the information available to them; (2) regard the military future as so bleak or the military balance as changing so fast against them that they feel they have little to lose by aggressing; or (3) are impelled by foreign or domestic political interests of such gravity that they are willing to take large risks in a military adventure. Lebow, Jervis, and Stein (1984) argue that the latter condition often arises in international affairs, citing the Japanese attack on Pearl Harbor and the two most recent Egyptian attacks on Israel as examples of occasions in which potent threats failed to deter a nation from launching a war. What happens, they contend, is that, under the pressure of compelling political considerations, political leaders often engage in wishful thinking about the likelihood of winning a war.

Another problem with the use of threat-based deterrents is their escalative potential. They involve fighting fire with fire, so they run the risk of contributing to a conflict spiral. As a result, they are capable of producing the very problem they are designed to avoid. There are three reasons for this. One is that the targets of threats tend to resent them and retaliate against them. This is less likely to happen when the threats are consistent with social norms and hence at least moderately legitimate, as in the case of most threats of retaliation. Yet even such threats signal Party's suspicion of Other and place limits on Other's freedom, producing some degree of resentment.

A second reason for escalation is that deterrent threats are often misinterpreted by Other (Jervis, 1976). An army mobilized to resist invasion may be misconstrued as an instrument of potential aggression. Missiles designed only for a second strike may be seen as a first-strike capability. (Such is the apparent Soviet reaction to some of the recent American nuclear armament programs.) A boys' gang organized to protect its members may be seen as threatening another gang's "turf." Such perceptions produce defensive counterreactions that tend to start (or continue) a conflict spiral.

The third reason for escalation is that, even if it is clear that Party's military preparations have defensive motives, Other must still be cautious lest these motives change. An army may be raised and equipped and alliances forged for strictly defensive reasons, yet the result may be such a formidable war machine that there is a temptation to use it for aggressive purposes. Other nations must be wary of preparations that can be used for aggression, even if they are clearly being made for defensive reasons.

What can be done to avoid such interpretations and misinterpretations of defensive preparations? Careful explanation of one's actions can help, along with an effort to tie them action-by-action to the other's behavior, so that they are seen as essentially reactive. Furthermore, some types of preparation are clearly defensive and cannot be converted to offensive use. Examples include building walls and installing ground-to-air missiles, which can be used only to shoot down attacking airplanes. It may also be possible to couple the carrot with the stick, offering punishment for aggression and reward for cooperation. This works because the "carrot" provides the other party an avenue for goal achievement that does not require aggression and makes it harder to believe that one is preparing for aggression oneself. (More will be said about this approach in Chapter 9 on problem solving.) Efforts to diminish tensions in other realms are also in order, so as to reduce the likelihood that the adversary will view one's military efforts through the prism of anger and indignation (White, 1984).

Such procedures are sometimes effective, but threats are so often problematic that it seems preferable to avoid them as much as possible and to substitute other forms of conflict management, such as positive bonds and the building of social norms.

In summary, by threatening to retaliate, it is sometimes possible to deter an adversary from employing harsh contentious tactics and thus to reduce the likelihood of escalation. Part of the success of this tactic depends on the credibility of such a threat. Extending this notion, it can be argued that two or more parties are safe from conflict escalation when a balance of power exists, so that every party is able to retaliate effectively in the face of aggression. The problem with this reasoning is that it assumes that (1) threats will be adequately communicated; (2) decision makers will be perceptive and rational, and not so impelled by other considerations as to lose sight of the risks they are facing; and (3) threats will not produce the very escalation they are designed to avoid. Hence, if they are available, other methods for discouraging escalation are preferable to the use of threats.

CONCLUSIONS

Events as dramatic as the UB crisis and the development of the Cold War (to be described in the next chapter) are unusual. But escalation is all around us, because any conflict is capable of intensifying. Conflicts are said to escalate when any of the following changes take place: heavier contentious tactics are employed, issues proliferate, increased resources are devoted to the struggle, issues become more general, relationships deteriorate, a goal of hurting the other party develops, and additional participants enter the struggle. Such changes can take place in any controversy.

A number of conditions have been described that increase or reduce the likelihood of escalation during conflict. The likelihood of escalation is increased by high perceived power, low perceived integrative potential, and high aspirations, particularly if these conditions exist on both sides. The likelihood of escalation is reduced (and hence the situation tends toward stability) in the presence of conflict-limiting norms and institutions, fear of escalation, bonds between potential antagonists, and bonds to third and fourth parties who can be expected to oppose the conflict. A balance of power can also be stable, though there are a number of problems with this approach. All of these sources of stability have their value, but none of them is totally reliable. If conflict becomes sufficiently profound, escalation occurs in even the most stable relationship.

The next two chapters probe the mechanisms of escalation. Chapter 6 examines the events that occur when conflict breaks through its restraints and begins to escalate—the processes that encourage greater severity of tactics, increased deployment of resources, and so on. Chapter 7 focuses on the persistence of escalation—the processes that cause conflict so often to stay at a given level of intensity once this level has been attained.

Processes that Produce Escalation

Chapter 5 described the transformations that occur during escalation and proposed sets of conditions under which conflict is most and least likely to escalate. In this and the next chapter, we look at the processes of escalation—the chains of events that produce and maintain these transformations when conflict occurs under conditions favorable to escalation. To put it another way, when the situation is unstable and the parties fall into conflict, what actually happens that pushes them in the direction of escalation?

The present chapter focuses mainly on the *production* of escalation: the processes that encourage the use of heavier tactics, cause issues to proliferate, and produce increasing absorption in the struggle. Chapter 7 examines the *persistence* of escalation once it has occurred: the processes that encourage the continued use of heavy tactics and a consistently deep absorption in the struggle.

We now introduce a second example of escalating conflict to supplement the case study of a campus crisis presented in the last chapter. This is the sequence of events that took place during the development of the Cold War between the United States and the Soviet Union. The fact that both of these cases involve conflict between collectives (groups, organizations, or nations) does not imply that escalation is found only in such relationships. Much of our theory also applies to the escalation of interpersonal conflict, such as conflict between spouses, neighbors, business associates, and the like.

DEVELOPMENT OF THE COLD WAR

The development of the Cold War between the United States and the Soviet Union immediately after 1945 is a prime example of conflict escalation. These two major nations were allies during the Second World War, which ended with high hopes for continued cooperation. But the Soviets emerged from the war with deep suspicions of the West. This led them to adopt a goal of controlling the nations adjoining their territory, making it difficult to maintain East–West cooperation. They built a communist satellite system in Eastern Europe, supported communist guerrillas in Greece, and put political pressure on Turkey. In 1947 the United States responded to these actions in three ways: It gave military aid to Greece and Turkey. It created the Marshall Plan, which was designed to revitalize the economy of Western Europe and weaken communist parties in Western European countries. And (in conjunction with Britain and later with France) it began the slow process of unifying West Germany and rebuilding its economy, as a further bulwark against Soviet expansion.

The latter move was viewed with considerable alarm by the Soviet Union, which had been at war twice with Germany in the prior 30 years. The Soviets responded at first with protests. Then, in 1948, they tried sporadically interrupting communications between Berlin (which was under joint control but was an enclave surrounded by the Russian-controlled portion of Germany) and West Germany. Finally, after the West introduced a currency reform in West Germany, they installed a full blockade of Berlin, claiming that they were repairing the routes to the city. The United States and its allies responded by launching a successful airlift between Berlin and West Germany and by beginning negotiations that led to the formation of the North Atlantic Treaty Organization (NATO), a military alliance involving the United States and most of the Western European nations. This latter development led eventually to the rearmament of West Germany, which caused considerable further alarm in the Soviet Union.

The story of this conflict continues to the present day, but we stop it at this point because we have said enough to give a massive and extremely significant example of conflict escalation. This escalation illustrates most of the transformations described in the last chapter: tactics went from light (protests) to heavy (blockading a city, forming a military alliance); issues proliferated; the parties became increasingly absorbed in the struggle; more and more elements of the relationship between the superpowers were affected; and goals changed from self-advancement to subverting the adversary.

We look now at the processes that encourage such transformations, especially those that foster the use of increasingly heavy tactics, a key transformation in most escalative episodes.

THREE CONFLICT MODELS

Most theories of escalation can be classified under one of three broad conflict models (Pruitt & Gahagan, 1974): the aggressor–defender model, the conflict spiral model, and the structural change model. Though all three models have some value (they all account well for some episodes of escalation), the first model has generally been overemphasized and the last underemphasized.

The Aggressor–Defender Model

The *aggressor–defender model* draws a distinction between the two parties. One party, the "aggressor," is viewed as having a goal or set of goals that places it in conflict with the other, the "defender." The aggressor ordinarily starts with mild contentious tactics because of the costs involved in escalation. But if these do not work, he or she moves on to heavier tactics, continuing to escalate until the goals are attained or a point is reached at which the value of goal attainment is outweighed by the anticipated cost of continued escalation. The defender merely reacts, escalating his or her efforts in response to the aggressor's escalation. Escalation persists until the aggressor either wins or gives up trying.

The terms "aggressor" and "defender" in this model are not intended to be evaluative. In other words, they do not imply that one side is wrong and the other right in the controversy. The aggressor is simply a party who sees an opportunity to change things in the direction of his or her interests; the defender, a party who tries to resist this change.

The aggressor–defender model helps to explain one of the stages in the development of the Cold War. This is the point at which the Soviet Union adopted the goal of blocking the unification of West Germany. At first the Soviets employed the mild tactic of protest. When this did not work, they moved to a heavier tactic of sporadically interrupting communications between Berlin and West Germany. When this was unsuccessful, and the West introduced a currency reform that contributed further to German unification, they employed an extremely heavy tactic, a full blockade of the city. This explanation is cogent, but despite its popularity, the aggressor–defender model is incapable of interpreting many other stages in the development of the Cold War—and indeed in most conflict escalation. In other words, this model provides a useful but incomplete account of the processes underlying escalation.

The Conflict Spiral Model

The *conflict spiral model* of escalation is found in the writings of many theorists (North, Brody & Holsti, 1964; Osgood, 1962, 1966; Richardson, 1967). This model holds that escalation results from a vicious circle of action and reaction. Party's contentious tactics encourage a contentious response from Other, which contributes to further contentious behavior from Party, completing the circle and starting it on its next iteration.

Two broad classes of conflict spirals can be distinguished. In a *retaliatory* spiral, each party punishes the other for actions that it finds aversive. An example is an argument followed by a shouting match followed by a fist fight. In a *defensive* spiral, each party reacts so as to protect itself from a threat it finds in the other's self-protective actions. An example is an arms race. In a defensive spiral, each party can be thought of as alternately the aggressor and the defender.

Conflict spirals produce escalation of tactics when, as is often the case, each reaction is more severe and intense than the action it follows. They also contribute to the perpetuation of tactical escalation—that is, to the fact that heavy tactics continue to be used on both sides once they are first employed. If I hit you, you will often hit me back, which leads me to hit you once again, and so on.

In addition to explaining the escalation of tactics, the conflict spiral model helps us understand the growing size of an escalating conflict, the proliferation of issues, and increased attention to the conflict. The point is that each retaliatory or defensive action in the spiral provides a new issue—a new grievance—for the target of this action, producing a growing sense of crisis in the mind of this party.

The conflict spiral model provides further insight into the dynamics of Cold War escalation. In response to Soviet moves in Eastern Europe and in Greece and Turkey, the United States and its allies began to establish a West German state. In response to this action, the Soviet Union instituted a blockade of Berlin. In response to this blockade and all that had come before, the United States and its allies formed NATO and began to arm West Germany. And so on. The sequence of actions in the UB campus crisis, which started with stones thrown at the president's window and ended with an ugly confrontation between a mob of students and a number of city police officers, also illustrates such a spiral.

The aggressor–defender and conflict spiral models are compared diagramatically in Figure 6.1. In the aggressor–defender analysis, causation flows in only one direction; the aggressor acts and the defender reacts. In the conflict spiral analysis, causation flows in both directions; each party reacts to the other party's actions. The conflict spiral diagram involves an oversimplification (which is necessary to help us distinguish the forest from the trees) in that it pictures each party's action as a response to the other's immediately preceding action. In reality, each action is a "result of the cumulative impression from all the previous actions by the other side" (White, 1984, p. 95), though more recent actions are usually given greater weight than earlier actions.

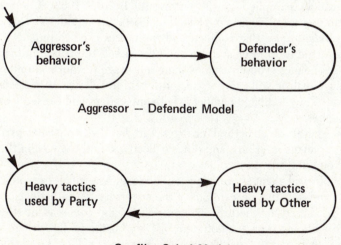

Figure 6.1 Aggressor–defender and conflict spiral models of conflict escalation.

The conflict spiral model should not be seen as an improved version of, or a replacement for, the aggressor–defender model of escalation. The latter is useful whenever one party develops a goal that places it at odds with another party and pursues this goal through an escalating sequence of actions. Many cases of escalation exhibit this form. However, even in controversies where an aggressor–defender analysis is useful, the conflict spiral model frequently provides additional insights. Quite often the goal that impels the aggressor is, at least in part, a reaction to the defender's prior actions. This point is often missed by participants in conflict, who attribute the cause of the conflict exclusively to their adversary's aggression. It is also often missed by involved observers, who assign the cause of the confict to actions of the side with which they have weaker relations or the side that has employed the heavier, less defensible tactics. But a careful analysis usually reveals that causation has flowed in both directions.

A case in point is the Soviet effort to prevent the unification and ascendancy of West Germany, which took the form of an escalating series of protest actions that were progressively resisted by the West. Even though these actions are properly labeled "aggression" (in the nonevaluative sense of the term used here), they can also be seen as a reaction to Western efforts to strengthen Germany. Hence they are also part of a larger conflict spiral. Likewise, German efforts to conquer Europe in the 1940s, which were surely aggression by any definition of the term, can also be seen in part as reactions to the humiliation of Germany after the First World War—and thus as part of a conflict spiral lasting many years.

The Structural Change Model

Our picture of the forces producing escalation is rounded out by a third model, which is implied by the writings of Burton (1962), Coleman (1957), and Schumpeter (1955, first published in 1919), among others. This *structural change model* argues that conflict, and the tactics used to pursue it, produce *residues* in the form of changes in the parties and the communities to which the parties belong. These residues then encourage further contentious behavior, at an equal or still more escalated level, and diminish efforts at conflict resolution. Thus escalated conflict is both antecedent and consequent of structural changes.

Three kinds of structural changes can be distinguished: psychological changes, changes in groups and other collectives, and changes in the community surrounding the parties.

Psychological changes are many and diverse. As conflict escalates, negative attitudes and negative perceptions of the adversary typically develop. The adversary is blamed for the growing controversy and comes to be distrusted in the sense of being seen as indifferent or even hostile to our welfare. Negative traits are attributed to the adversary, such as being self-centered, morally unfit, or (in extreme cases) a diabolical enemy. The adversary is dehumanized and deindividuated. Anger, fear, and wounded pride become the dominant emotions. Zero-sum thinking develops—it's either victory for them or victory for us. New goals come to the fore: to look better than, punish, discredit, defeat, or even destroy the adversary. The capacity for empathy with the adversary is eroded. There are also changes in the approach taken to joint decision making: Positions become rigid, there is little room for compromise, and there is a dearth of imagination and creativity. Emphasis is placed on proving how tough and unyielding one is, so as to persuade the adversary that one cannot be pushed around. Coupled with this is an exaggerated fear of small losses, which are seen as diminishing one's status vis-à-vis the other and possibly encouraging the other to take advantage of one. There is also a tendency to break contact with the adversary—to be unwilling to communicate with him or her. All of these changes typically occur on both sides of the dispute.

These psychological changes occur in all escalated conflicts, whether the actors are individuals or collectives. When collectives (groups, organizations, or nations) are involved in a controversy, structural changes also occur at the collective level. The psychological reactions just described are accentuated by collective discussion and tend to become collective norms. Collective goals of defeating the enemy tend to develop, and subgroups are set up to implement these goals. Increased cohesiveness, resulting from having an outside enemy, contributes to the force of these norms and to the dedication of individuals in the collective to the newly found goals and the means of implementing them. New, more militant leadership often emerges, contributing further to the collective orientation toward struggle. In other words, doves are replaced by hawks. If one of the parties is an unorganized set of individuals, conflict sometimes encourages the development of a struggle group—precipitated out of the mix of strong individual emotions—which then takes up the cudgel against the adversary.

Structural changes may also take the form of polarization in the broader community of which the antagonists are a part. Third parties join one or the other antagonist, forsaking the constructive neutral role they might otherwise play.

The important point about all of these changes is that they contribute to the cycle of escalation: They result from the use of escalated tactics and encourage further escalation. This contribution takes three forms: One is that psychological and collective changes are the mechanisms at work in conflict spirals. As can be seen in the top part of Figure 6.2 (model I), heavy tactics used by Party tend to produce structural changes in Other, which motivate similar heavy tactics from Other, provoking structural changes in Party, which start the spiral around once more. For example, Party's yelling at Other (a contentious tactic) causes Other to think of Party as an unpleasant person (structural change), making it easier for Other to yell back (more contentious tactics), encouraging Party to develop the goal of punishing Other (another structural change), motivating Party to make a fist (still more contentious tactics), and so on. Any or all of the changes described earlier, except community polarization, can be written into the boxes marked "structural changes" in this figure.

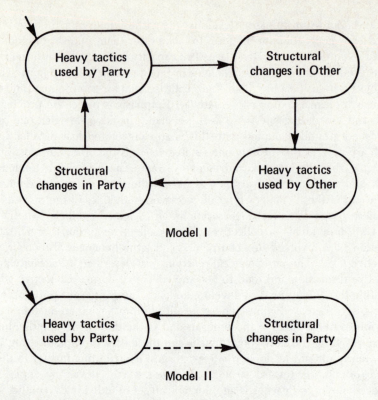

Figure 6.2   Structural change models of conflict escalation.

The second way in which structural changes contribute to the cycle of escalation is illustrated in the bottom part of Figure 6.2 (model II). These changes often result from Party's own use of heavy tactics and contribute to further use of these tactics. For example, by a dissonance theory (Festinger, 1957) analysis of attitude change, the very fact of defending one's nation against another nation is likely to create more negative attitudes toward the adversary, encouraging further defensive efforts.

The third impact of structural changes is to erode some of the safeguards against escalating conflict that were describe in the last chapter: positive attitudes, respect, friendship, perceived similarity, common group membership, and future dependence. Crosscutting relationships also tend to disappear as communities polarize, and the effectiveness of conflict-limiting institutions in the broader community (such as legislatures and courts) may be adversely affected. The result is not only to encourage further escalation in the current situation but also to make escalation more likely in future conflicts involving the same parties. Thus escalated conflict often weakens a community's capacity to deal effectively with further conflict.

In addition to reinforcing escalation, those changes involving the development of hostile goals actually increase the divergence of interest between the parties. New issues come to the fore, resulting from the desire each party has to defeat the other. Such developments confirm each party's distrust of the other. Distrust of this kind involves no misunderstanding; as a result of the development of hostile goals, each party has become an *actual enemy* of the other.

The short, diagonal arrows at the top left of the diagrams in Figure 6.2 are meant to suggest that the initial impulse for these circular processes has its impact on behavior rather than on structural change. We believe that this is the way such circles ordinarily arise. In response to a perceived divergence of interest (or in response to some stimulus entirely outside the relationship between the two parties), one of the parties engages in contentious behavior. This produces structural changes that start the system on the road to escalation. However, it is possible for escalation to start with a structural change. A conversation with a third party may turn me against my neighbor and kick off an escalative process. A radical leader may urge a crowd of students to stage a sit-in, producing a cohesive struggle group that is capable of mounting a concerted campaign against the university administration. (This was the sequence of events in the 1968 Columbia University student crisis.)

Structural changes help to account for the escalation that led to the Cold War and for the flinty persistence of this escalation. Such psychological changes as anger, hostility, profound distrust, blackened images, and an inability to empathize took root in the United States during the early period of the Cold War and persist today. Zero-sum thinking ("What is good for them is bad for us, and vice versa") set in and is still noteworthy in the modern era. Considerations of national pride and face-saving gripped every American president from Truman onward—none wanted to be in office when another country fell to communism. Most Americans became unable to empathize with the genuine Soviet security needs that underlay a large proportion of their actions. For a period of time in the late 1940s and early 1950s, most communication with the Soviet Union was broken off, and today it is at an uncomfortably low level again.

Collective changes also took place. At the depth of the Cold War, hostile norms were so strong that people who had a good word for the Soviet Union were made to feel uncomfortable and were sometimes hauled up before congressional committees. The country even flirted for a time in the 1950s with highly militant leadership, in the person of Senator Joseph McCarthy, a virulent anti-communist with a large political following. Fortunately, some of these collective excesses were overcome by the 1960s. But the establishment of a semi-autonomous military machine, with political support from technological sectors dependent on it, provides constant input into the still-festering controversy.

We have described these changes as we have seen them in the United States, because we know our own society better than that of the Soviet Union. However, there is good reason to believe that comparable changes have taken place and have been perpetuated in the Soviet Union (see White, 1984).

In addition to these psychological and collective changes, there has also been some polarization in the international community, with many other na-

tions choosing up sides between the two giants. This trend has abated somewhat in recent years.

In summary, we have described three models of conflict escalation that are
commonly found in the literature: the aggressor–defender, conflict spiral, and
structural change models. These models are not mutually exclusive. Rather,
each helps us understand certain aspects of escalation. The most complicated
model, by far, is the structural change model, because there are so many possible residues of escalation that keep escalation going. We shall devote most
of the rest of the chapter to a further elaboration of this model, examining in
more detail selected psychological, collective, and community changes. The
concluding comment looks at the impact on escalation of the models that the
parties themselves use in analyzing their conflict.

PSYCHOLOGICAL CHANGES

This section deals only with psychological changes that have been subject to
careful research: the desire to punish (aggress against) the other, negative attitudes and perceptions, and deindividuation.

The Desire to Punish (Aggress Against) the Other

A great deal of research has been conducted on the sources of "aggression"
(see Baron, 1977; Berkowitz, 1962; Zillmann, 1979). Because aggression is defined in this research as intentionally hurting another person, this research
sheds light on the antecedents of the desire to punish the other party.

Research on this topic indicates that aggression arises mainly from aversive
(unpleasant) experiences: deprivation, failure to achieve aspirations, inequita-
ble treatment, pain and suffering, and the like. Such experiences are, of
course, quite frequent when Other is engaged in contentious behavior. Hence
the desire to punish Other can be seen as one link between Other's contentious behavior and Party's subsequent contentious behavior.

Blaming Other.   Aggression is more likely when the perceived source of an
aversive experience can be blamed for his or her actions—that is, when these
actions seem to be Other's fault. Blame has a number of sources. For example, Other is more likely to be blamed for actions that seem voluntary than
those that seem involuntary (Schneider, Hastorf & Ellsworth, 1979). Actions
that seem freely taken are more likely to evoke blame than those apparently
resulting from heavy environmental pressures, unless Other is clearly responsible for resisting such pressures. Actions that appear contrary to the norms
of society are also especially enraging (Mallick & McCandless, 1966).

The implication of these points is that conflict is especially likely to escalate when the parties see each other's contentious behavior as arbitrary and
not attributable to extenuating circumstances, because under these conditions
the parties are especially likely to develop a desire to punish one another.

To forgive Other because of extenuating circumstances requires a high level of cognitive activity. Party must analyze Other's circumstances and motivation and hold them up to standards of reasonable conduct. It is clear that this is socially learned behavior. Small children do not behave this way, being much more likely than adults to hold people responsible for their actions regardless of why these actions were taken (Shaw & Sulzer, 1964). Furthermore, Party pays less attention to extenuating circumstances when he or she is autonomically aroused, as might be expected with any complex cognitive behavior (Zillmann, Bryant, Cantor & Day, 1975).

The Role of Anger. Theorists differ on the role of anger in aggression, but it seems reasonable to assume that anger is often at work when aversive experiences lead to aggression.

Like other emotions, anger can be interpreted as resulting from cognitive labeling of an undifferentiated state of autonomic arousal. According to Schachter (1964), the first stage in emotional experience is arousal—activation of the autonomic nervous system. The second stage is interpretation of this arousal. To make this interpretation, people employ whatever information is available. Not all interpretations lead to emotion; for example, if they have recently taken a new medicine or exercised, people may assume that this is the cause. But there are certain standard interpretations that produce emotion. If people see danger, they are likely to interpret their arousal as fear and feel fear; if they are aware of a recent aversive experience, their reaction is likely to be anger. When such interpretations are made, greater arousal leads to stronger emotion and more extreme emotional behavior.[1]

It follows that people become particularly emotional when they are aroused by other stimuli in addition to those that produce the emotional interpretation. Such an effect has been found in the case of anger leading to aggression. For example, Zillmann (1979) has shown in a controlled experiment that people who exercise and then have an aversive experience aggress more vigorously against the source of the aversive experience than they do if they have not exercised. This result is particularly apparent when the exercise comes somewhat earlier than the aversive experience so that people lose track of why they are aroused and attribute it entirely to the aversive experience. In addition, it has been shown that emotion can be destroyed by encouraging people to attribute their arousal to a neutral experience such as taking a pill. This "misattribution" effect is also found with anger (Loftis, 1974).

The ideas just presented imply that heavily contentious behavior and hence escalation are most likely to occur when people approach conflict in an aroused state. The arousal can be due to any source, including physical exercise (folklore to the contrary, a fast game of basketball is more likely to exacerbate controversies than to cure them) and listening to loud or complex music

---

[1]Schachter's theory has recently come under attack because some of his earliest research could not be replicated (Marshall & Zimbardo, 1979; Maslach, 1979). However, it still provides the best available theoretical account of the body of research results cited in this section.

(Konecȟni, 1975). The chances of escalation are diminished when people's emotions are subdued—for example, as a result of listening to soft, sweet music (Konecȟni, 1975)—or when they believe their state of arousal originates outside the controversy, in concern about health, tensions at home, or the like.

Inhibition of Aggression. The desire to punish another person is by no means always expressed in actual behavior. Indeed, aggressive impulses are usually inhibited. Inhibition may be due to a number of sources, including social condemnation of aggression, conscience, ability to empathize with the target's potential suffering, fear of punishment by the target, and ties with the target.

If social condemnation of aggression contributes to its inhibition, social endorsement should be disinhibiting. Thus, if Party is angry against Other and a third party acts aggressively, this should make it easier for Party to actually aggress. There is ample research support for this conclusion. The model for Party's aggression can be a fellow group member (Wheeler & Caggiula, 1966), a character in a movie (Berkowitz & Geen, 1966), or even a football player in a game Party is watching (Goldstein & Arms, 1971). It follows that, to help avoid escalation in a difficult controversy, the disputants should shun aggressively tinged entertainment and that people who are in contact with them should try to behave peacefully.

People who have difficulty projecting ahead are especially likely to act aggressively when they are tempted to do so. This is because they are not deterred by fear of punishment from the target or third parties. For this reason, people who are under the influence of high emotion (Zillmann, 1979) or alcohol (Mulvihill & Tumin, 1969) are particularly likely to get involved in escalating controversies.

Displacement. The preferred target for the expression of aggression is the party who is blamed for the aversive experience. However, it is not always possible to indulge this preference. The source of annoyance may be well protected, or there may be extenuating circumstances that reduce his or her culpability, or it may be impossible to identify the source. Under these circumstances, the desire to punish is sometimes displaced onto another target. If one cannot hit an offending boss, one can yell at one's spouse or kick the cat.

Evidence of displacement can be seen in a historical study by Hovland and Sears (1940), who found an inverse correlation between the price of cotton in the South and the number of blacks lynched over a 49-year period. The lower the price of cotton, the more lynchings. What presumably happened is that white farmers were frustrated by the decline in the cotton market but could not legitimately aggress against the cotton merchants who were paying less. Hence, they took it out on a handy displacement object, the black man. More recently, Berkowitz, Cochran, and Embree (1981) has shown that subjects who are forced to hold their hand in very cold water (another aversive experience) are more aggressive toward fellow subjects than are those who hold their hand in moderately cold water, another demonstration of displacement.

The phenomenon of displacement suggests that people who have had earlier aversive experiences in settings that do not permit aggressive behavior are especially likely to choose escalated tactics in the current conflict.

Negative Attitudes and Perceptions

An attitude is a positive or negative feeling toward some person or object. A perception is a belief about, or way of viewing, that person or object. Like all structural changes, negative attitudes and perceptions are both cause and effect of the use of contentious tactics. Accordingly, they are way stations in the escalation of conflict.

Attitudes and perceptions tend to be consistent in valence in the sense that, if I have negative (positive) feelings toward somebody, I tend also to have predominantly negative (positive) perceptions of that person. However, they are not 100 percent consistent. I may dislike a man and generally think ill of him but nevertheless trust him, because I have had a positive experience whenever I have relied on him. Hence, we must, to some extent, deal separately with these two psychological elements.

The following kinds of perceptions are particularly characteristic of escalated conflict. Adversaries tend to be seen as deficient in moral virtue—as dishonest, unfriendly, or warlike. They also tend to be distrusted; we believe them to be hostile to our welfare. In addition, they are sometimes seen as lacking in ability or achievement (Blake & Mouton, 1962), though this kind of perceptual distortion is less likely because of the greater availability of sound evidence about these characteristics (Brewer, 1979). By contrast, one's own side is seen often as more moral and sometimes as more able (White, 1984).

When groups are in conflict, a variant of these perceptions is sometimes found, which White (1984) has called the "evil-ruler enemy image." This is the perception that ordinary members of the other group feel neutral or even positive toward us but that their leaders are hideous monsters. In this view, aggressive actions taken by ordinary members of the other group are attributed to the fact that they are misled by their leaders, rather than to their moral degeneracy. Such images can be seen in American views of the Soviet Union and in Soviet views of America. They were also found in the UB campus crisis described in the last chapter. In the midst of the crisis, the university president went on the air to denounce a small group of "vicious vandals" who were misleading the larger body of normally reasonable students. The evil-ruler enemy image appears to permit a decidedly negative view of the opponent while realistically acknowledging that not all members of any group can be evil.

Attitudes and the perceptions that accompany them tend to be similar on both sides of a controversy. This is the so-called "mirror image" hypothesis (Bronfenbrenner, 1961; Frank, 1982). For example, the profound distrust felt by most Americans toward the Soviet Union is mirrored in Soviet attitudes toward the United States.

Unfortunately, the existence of a mirror image is often not recognized by the parties involved in a conflict, who tend to distrust the adversary without realizing that the adversary also distrusts them. This lack of insight can contribute to the conflict spiral in the following way: If Other is behaving in a contentious fashion and we do not recognize that Other fears us, we assume that Other's behavior is aggressively motivated and therefore feel the need to escalate our response further.

Effects on Behavior. Negative attitudes and perceptions encourage escalation and discourage the settlement of conflict in at least seven ways.

The first is by encouraging a tendency to blame the object of the attitude for one's unpleasant experiences. People who have aversive experiences commonly seek a culprit to blame. However, the evidence about who is to blame is often ambiguous. Even when another party is clearly the source of the aversive experience, there may be extenuating circumstances. When evidence is ambiguous, attitudes tend to structure perceptions. This means that disliked parties are blamed and that liked parties are given the benefit of the doubt.

A finding by Blumenthal, et al. (1972) illustrates the impact of attitudes and perceptions on blame. During a period of political turmoil in the United States, in the summer of 1969, people were found to blame the conflict on groups whose views they did not like. Liberals blamed the police, whereas conservatives blamed the demonstrators. Both tended to use the term "violence" to describe the behavior of groups they disliked and the term "justified force" to describe the behavior of groups whose views they favored. People were also more sympathetic to the use of force against the groups they blamed.

A second, and related, mechanism leading to escalation is that parties who are distrusted tend to be seen as threatening when their actions are ambiguous (Pruitt, 1965). They are given little benefit of the doubt or credit for good intentions. This produces an escalation of defensive and deterrent moves, and it often creates new issues for conflict.

Examples of this process are seen regularly in relations between the United States and the Soviet Union. Take, for example, American interpretations of the Soviet invasion of Afghanistan. This invasion is commonly seen as a sign of expansionist intent—as evidence that the Soviet Union is ready to invade other Middle Eastern countries such as Saudi Arabia. The United States has invested billions of dollars in additional armaments as a result of this perceived threat. Yet the evidence of this threat is ambiguous in the sense that there are other highly plausible interpretations of the Soviet invasion. Most notable is the view that the Soviet Union was simply trying to protect a beleaguered communist government from disintegrating and being reabsorbed into the Western community of nations. Under the latter interpretation, the Soviet invasion probably would still be labeled "aggression." But it would not be evidence of a major threat to the West, because Soviet intentions would be seen as strictly limited (White, 1984).

The point of all this is that American distrust of the Soviet Union has led many Americans to choose, from the various possible interpretations of the

Soviet invasion, the one that forbodes the greatest future danger. In a strictly parallel fashion, recent increases in the American arms budget have apparently been misunderstood in the Soviet Union as evidence of increased military threat. As in the case of the United States, distrust serves to shape Soviet perceptions of this inherently ambiguous evidence.

A third way in which negative attitudes and perceptions encourage escalation is by diminishing inhibitions against aggression among people who have been provoked. People are reluctant to aggress against parties they like and respect, even when these parties can clearly be blamed for unpleasant experiences, but they are quite willing to aggress against parties they do not like or respect. The finding that southern white students (many of whom can be assumed to have been prejudiced) retaliated more vigorously when insulted by a black than by a white (Rogers & Prentice-Dunn, 1981) supports these generalizations.

When negative attitudes lead to name-calling, inhibitions against aggression are particularly likely to fall away. Name-calling strengthens the impression that the other is morally inadequate and dissimilar to oneself. Some names (such as the epithet "pig," which was hurled at policemen by student demonstrators in the 1960s) even make the other seem subhuman. Hence they tend to erode normal inhibitions against aggression.

A fourth way in which negative attitudes and perceptions encourage escalation is by interfering with communication. People tend to avoid those toward whom they are hostile. The point is well put by Coleman (1957): "As controversy develops, associations . . . wither between persons on opposing sides" (p. 11). This contributes to misunderstandings and hence to the proliferation of conflict issues. It also makes it difficult to reach a peaceful settlement of the controversy.

The reasons for this common development are not altogether clear. Why stop meeting and talking when one becomes hostile toward another party? Conceivably, people view association as implying friendship and endorsement. If so, contact with an opponent might send out false signals that one accepts the opponent's position. This is part of the reason for mutual nonrecognition between Israel and the Palestine Liberation Organization. Or, conceivably, the phenomenon has deeper emotional roots. According to balance theory (Heider, 1958), negative attitudes toward any object psychologically imply a negative relationship with that object—and a desire to put psychological distance between oneself and that object.

A fifth mechanism is that negative attitudes and perceptions tend to make it difficult to empathize with the adversary (White, 1984). Adversaries seem so different from us that it is hard to put ourselves in their shoes. Furthermore, there is an easy explanation for all of their actions which makes empathy seem unnecessary: these actions stem from evil motives. Absence of empathy is like absence of communication in that it fosters misunderstandings. It also encourages escalation by blocking insight into the conflict spiral. Awareness that the adversary's hostile behavior is a reaction to our own hostile behavior causes us to limit our escalation as a matter of self-protection.

But if we lack empathy into the adversary's motives, we are unaware of our own role in encouraging the other to aggress and are likely to escalate unthinkingly.

A sixth point is that negative attitudes and perceptions foster "zero-sum thinking"—the belief that what is good for you is bad for me, and vice versa. This happens partly because of distrust. If I believe you are hostile toward my interests, I will tend to doubt that you can endorse any alternative that helps me. Zero-sum thinking also arises from negative feelings toward the other party. Why should I help you if I don't like or respect you? An example of this phenomenon can be seen in the results of a study by Sillars (1981), in which it was found that students who blamed their roommates for past conflict tended not to take a problem-solving approach in dealing with their roommates. Syna (1984) has found a similar effect with married couples.

Zero-sum thinking is the antithesis of perceived integrative potential (PIP), a concept introduced in Chapter 2. Hence it tends to diminish perceived common ground (PCG), which makes problem solving an unlikely alternative. To resolve the controversy, Party must either yield or contend, and the latter is the more common approach because there so often are constraints against yielding. Thus zero-sum thinking often leads to conflict escalation.

The seventh and final point is that, when negative attitudes and perceptions grow severe, the adversary comes to be viewed as a "diabolical enemy" (White, 1984) and the conflict is seen as a war between light (our side) and darkness (their side). We are the chosen people; they are the "evil empire" (to quote President Reagan's statement about the Soviet Union). In such circumstances, we are ready to blame them for all that goes wrong, communication often takes a nose dive, empathy is especially weak, and problem solving is extraordinarily hard to sustain. Heavy tactics tend to become the rule and new controversies develop regularly, confirming our view of them and theirs of us.

Sources of Negative Attitudes and Perceptions. Like all structural changes, negative attitudes and perceptions result from escalation as well as contributing further to it. More precisely, they are affected both by Other's escalated actions and by Party's own escalated actions.

Aversive behavior that is blamed on Other tends to produce an initial angry reaction characterized by a state of autonomic arousal. This is often followed by a cooler, longer-lasting residue, which serves to goad people toward aggression and hence toward escalation. The latter state is sometimes an active goal to punish Other, leading directly to escalation. But more often it is simply a negative attitude toward Other, which acts in the seven ways we have described.

An alternative reaction to Other's contentious behavior is sometimes found. Instead of blaming Other, one might instead blame oneself as the source of behavior to which Other is reacting or blame both parties equally on the assumption that a conflict spiral is at work. However, this is less likely to happen, especially if there are multiple conflicts between oneself and Other

(Syna, 1984). There are two reasons for the tendency to blame Other for controversy. One is ego-defensive: Finding fault with oneself is more painful than finding fault with another person. The other is perceptual: We are much more aware of other peoples' contributions to controversy than of our own, because their contribution is more apparent to the senses. In Heider's (1958) terminology, their contribution "engulfs the field." For these reasons we tend to see Other as more causally central to the controversy.

The perceptions of other people or groups that have the greatest effect on our conflict behavior are the inferences we draw about their stable dispositions—their basic traits and motives and their attitudes toward us. If these dispositions seem negative, we are more likely to escalate our tactics; if they seem positive, we are less likely to do so. To understand the origins of such perceptions, we turn to two principles of attribution theory: the discounting principle and the augmentation principle (Kelley, 1973; Schneider, Hastorf & Ellsworth, 1979).

According to the *discounting principle*, Other's actions are more likely to be attributed to an underlying disposition when alternative causes can be confidently ruled out. Thus role-related behavior is less likely to be seen as due to underlying attitudes or personality traits than is behavior that departs from Other's role (Jones & Davis, 1965). For example, a bank employee who forecloses on our loan is less likely to be viewed as morally destitute than is a friend who takes the same action, because the bank employee can be seen as simply doing his or her job.

According to the *augmentation principle*, Other's actions are viewed as expressing an underlying disposition to the extent that he or she incurs risks or costs in enacting them. This implies that a person who jeopardizes his or her job to harm our interests is especially likely to be seen as having negative dispositions. If a porter should refuse to carry our bags for no apparent reason, we are likely to view him or her in particularly negative terms, because his or her behavior can only be explained by assuming hostility toward us or toward people in our category.

It is no surprise to learn that Other's behavior affects Party's attitudes toward Other. But many people are astonished to learn that there is evidence (Bem, 1972; Festinger, 1957) that Party's *own* behavior toward Other also affects these attitudes and perceptions. Through a process of rationalization, people's feelings and beliefs tend to become consistent with their behavior.

There is no inconsistency between regarding behavior as a source of attitudes and regarding attitudes as a source of behavior. When people can choose among several courses of action, attitudes often influence their choice. But when environmental pressures push them in a particular direction, attitudes tend to fall in line.

We can conclude from these generalizations that Party's hostile behavior toward Other causes Party to dislike Other and see him or her in a negative light, whereas friendly behavior tends to erode such attitudes and images. (Evidence favoring the latter point can be seen in the experimental finding that people tend to trust others to whom they have directed promises of cooperation [Loomis, 1959].) This implies, in turn, another mechanism that can generate conflict escalation: Party takes contentious action toward Other, which encourages negative feelings and perceptions about Other, motivating heavier contentious tactics in the next time period.

Behavior affects attitudes only when the actor believes that it was freely taken and was not due to external pressures. If I call a policeman a pig and believe I did so of my own free will, I shall probably develop a negative attitude toward that policeman or all policemen. But if I believe that I was coerced into taking this action or (and this is rare) acknowledge that I was trying to impress somebody, my attitude will not be affected. The issue is not whether the behavior is actually freely taken (the authors of this volume take no stand on the question of whether people ultimately have free will) but whether the actor believes his or her behavior was freely taken. Because people usually believe that their actions are freely taken, behavior usually has a considerable impact on attitudes.

Deindividuation

Another person is *deindividuated* when he or she is perceived as a member of a category or group rather than as an individual. This perception has no valence and hence cannot be viewed as a negative attitude or perception. But it nevertheless encourages contentious behavior, apparently by eroding inhibitions against acting aggressively. What may happen is that people who are deindividuated seem less human than those who are individuated, and hence seem less protected by social norms against aggression.

Deindividuation was probably at work in an experiment by Milgram (1974) in which subjects in the role of "teacher" gave especially severe shocks to others in the role of "learner" when the latter were at a distance or out of sight. Deindividuation of the enemy may be what makes it easier for fliers to drop bombs on people they cannot see than for foot soldiers to shoot those they can see. Deindividuation is countered by receipt of information about others that makes them seem unique. Hence, guards in Nazi prison camps are said to have treated prisoners more leniently when they knew their names (Zimbardo, 1970).

Another way to discover that outgroup members are individuals is to have friendly relations with them over a period of time. It follows that residential settings that foster interracial friendships should lead to a reduction of white prejudice against blacks, an effect that has been demonstrated in two survey studies (Deutsch & Collins, 1951; Hamilton & Bishop, 1976). It is said that, before he led a protest demonstration, Gandhi would ask for hospitality from the local English governor and thus make friends with him. This was presumably a way of individuating himself—and his movement by association with him—in the eyes of the authorities, thereby reducing the aggressiveness of tactics used against his followers.

Similar reasoning suggests that aggressive or discriminatory impulses should lead to deindividuation of the prospective target. In this way, people will feel more comfortable about their hostile behavior. Evidence favoring this prediction emerges from a study by Worchel and Andreoli (1978). It was found that subjects who were angry with, or were expected to shock, another person were especially likely to forget individuating information about that person (such as his or her name) and to remember deindividuating information (such as his or her race). Name-calling during conflict may in part reflect this effect. An epithet such as "nigger" or "pig" reduces the individuality of the other, making it easier to aggress.

This finding implies that deindividuation is another way station in the circle of conflict escalation. Each participant deindividuates the other in order to rationalize his or her initial contentious moves. This state of mind then makes it easier to take more severe measures against the other.

In addition to viewing others as deindividuated, it is possible to see *oneself* in this way—in other words, to lose awareness of one's own distinct identity. This also facilitates aggression. Among the sources of self-deindividuation are acting in concert with others, wearing nondistinctive clothing, emotional arousal, and lack of sleep. In a study of the effect of clothing on aggression, Zimbardo (1970) found that college women playing the role of punitive teachers were especially likely to give shocks when they were wearing a hood. Such apparel reduces one's distinctiveness and, presumably, one's inhibitions. Military and police uniforms probably have a similar effect.

CHANGES IN COLLECTIVES

When groups, organizations, or nations become involved in contentious conflict, these collectives tend to change in at least six ways that contribute to escalation of the conflict. In describing these changes, we shall speak only of groups, because groups have been mainly studied in this context. But there is good reason to believe that these changes are found in all collectives.

First, group discussions often cause individual group members to become more extreme in their hostile attitudes and perceptions. This is due to the *group polarization* mechanism (Moscovici & Zavalloni, 1969). When group members share any view and discuss it with one another, this view tends to become stronger. Two main mechanisms apparently account for this phenomenon (Lamm & Myers, 1978). One is that the group members hear one another's views and the arguments underlying them. Finding that others agree with them, they feel their views are validated and also learn new arguments favoring them. The other is that a sort of competition develops among the group members, in which each strives to hold an opinion that is at least as extreme in the direction favored by the group as that advocated by the average group member. As a result, at least half of the members shift in the direction favored by the group.

In the context of social conflict, this means that psychological changes such as hostility and distrust are magnified when groups are involved. We see this phenomenon most clearly in mob action; a group of people who are upset about some incident gather and, through discussion, strengthen one another's sentiments to the point of angry action. But the phenomenon is not limited to mobs. It can occur in perfectly stable and respected groups and organizations, including the United States Senate and the Soviet Politburo.

A second kind of change is the development of *runaway norms* supporting a contentious approach to the controversy (Raven & Rubin, 1983). A norm is any attitude, perception, goal, or behavior pattern that is shared by the dominant segment of a collective. Norms come to be seen as "right thinking" by most members of the group and are taught to new members and imposed on old members who appear to question them. Most of the psychological changes mentioned earlier in this chapter—including negative attitudes, distrust, zero-sum thinking, and a reluctance to communicate with the other party—can become the subject of norms. When this happens, they gain more strength and stability than they would have if they belonged to a single individual or to a set of individuals who did not share a common group membership. Hence, escalation becomes more likely.

The development of *contentious group goals* is a third common outcome of conflict. Such goals include defeating or even destroying the adversary. Goals such as these arise from the conflict experience and fuel it. In addition, groups are capable of acting on their goals in ways that are not available to individuals. The activities of a number of individuals can be coordinated. Furthermore, a division of labor is possible, permitting highly complicated contentious routines, such as the recruitment and outfitting of an army. Hence groups are particularly efficient at conflict escalation if their members are so inclined.

A fourth kind of change that can contribute to escalation is the development of group *cohesiveness* or "solidarity," as it is commonly called. Groups are cohesive to the extent that their members find them attractive.

Cohesiveness affects group behavior in three important ways. It encourages conformity to group norms (Festinger, Schachter & Back, 1950). This conformity is due in part to enhanced communication within the group (Back, 1951), in part to member fear of being ostracized (Festinger, 1950), and in part to social pressure, which is especially strong in cohesive groups (Schachter, 1951). Cohesive groups are also capable of especially vigorous action in pursuit of their goals. And there is reason to believe that members of cohesive groups are particularly convinced of the rightness of their cause and the effectiveness of their intended actions (Janis, 1972; Kriesberg, 1982).

For all of these reasons, we can expect group cohesiveness to augment or multiply the effect of the psychological states discussed earlier in this chapter. If the attitudes toward an outgroup are generally negative, they should be particularly strong in a cohesive group. If the other group is distrusted or seen as a threat, cohesiveness should strengthen these perceptions. If a goal of defeating the adversary is adopted and contentious tactics for achieving this goal are developed, a cohesive group mounts a particularly vigorous campaign against the adversary. In making these points, we do not intend to say that cohesiveness per se encourages antagonism or escalation. Research evidence (Dion, 1973) does not support such a position. The point is simply that cohesive groups are likely to be particularly militant in contentious conflict.

Contentious conflict has been repeatedly shown to enhance group cohesiveness (Dion, 1979; Harvey, 1956; Ryen & Kahn, 1975; Worchell & Norvell, 1980).[2] It follows that enhanced cohesiveness is still another mechanism that results from and encourages conflict escalation.

The fifth type of change that often occurs in groups engaged in heavy conflict is that they take on *militant leadership* (Sherif, et al., 1961). Every group has its leaders. Some are formally designated as such; others can be called leaders because group members are influenced by what they say. Groups ordinarily choose as their leaders people who resonate with the dominant sentiments of the members and are good at the activities to which the group is dedicated (Hollander, 1978). This is as true of groups in conflict as of groups engaged in any other kind of activity. If conflict involves negotiation, people with bargaining skills are likely to gain status. If it involves heavy contentious activity, leadership is more likely to fall into the hands of militants, who can mirror the anger of the membership and build a fighting force. Such leaders have particularly strong negative attitudes and perceptions of the adversary and are especially rigid in the demands they make. Accordingly, they tend to reinforce and augment the group's commitment to extreme tactics.

Leadership changes of this kind occurred on both sides in the UB campus crisis. The heaviest part of the controversy began when the campus police clubbed several demonstrators in the Student Union. At first, officers of the Student Government tried to exercise leadership over the campus, promising to negotiate with the university administration. But the students were so angry at the administration that they shunted these officers aside in favor of a group of radicals who had not previously exerted much influence. Similar changes occurred in the university administration. A vice-president who wanted to mediate the controversy was excluded from decision making, while other officers who advocated sterner measures came to the fore.

In addition to devising tactics for dealing with the opponent, leaders of groups that are in conflict often try to strengthen their members' dedication to the struggle, for example, by blackening the image of the adversary (Bowers & Ochs, 1971).

The sixth and last type of collective change that often occurs in escalating conflict is the development of *new and more militant groupings*. Sometimes this involves the organization of a new subgroup in a well established collective—a committee or department to deal with the emerging struggle. At other times, it involves the development of an entirely new struggle group. The latter phenomenon will be discussed in some detail.

When a party in a conflict is an unorganized collection of people, a struggle group is sometimes born, which takes responsibility for defending that party's interests. The development of such a group is particularly likely to encourage further escalation, because, in addition to having all the other attributes of a group in conflict, a struggle group exists for the primary purpose of

---

[2]Rabbie and Wilkens (1971) were not able to replicate this common finding, but it appears that the subjects in their study lacked faith in the ability of their group and hence may have expected to fail in the competition.

prevailing over the adversary. Such a development is often a turning point in the conflict.

Many community conflicts have developed in this way (Coleman, 1957), including the UB campus controversy, in which student radicals organized a Strike Committee that kept the campus in turmoil for the next six weeks. What happens is that people who have not previously communicated with each other gradually become aware of their common interests and collective identity. A sense of ingroup and outgroup begins to develop, often in conjunction with growing pride about (Apfelbaum, 1979), and favoritism toward, the ingroup. Radical spokespeople now emerge, whose pronouncements help crystalize the developing consciousness. An organized group is then formed, at first in miniature but often growing to a sizable membership with a large following of sympathetic nonmembers. This group has the dual function of defeating the opponent and fostering its own further growth.

At the end of the controversy, most struggle groups simply wither away. A few, however, go on to assume a permanent, legitimate place in the community as advocates of the interests of the people who gave them their origin. Several American social movements have followed such a line of development, most notably the labor movement.

COMMUNITY POLARIZATION

When two groups come into heavy conflict with each other, it is often hard for other community members to remain neutral. One reason is that the participants in the controversy frequently seek support from others and demand that they decide whether they are "with us or agin' us." Another is that the use of escalated tactics is often annoying or frightening to the broader community. It is hard to remain indifferent when people are yelling at each other, hurting each other, or damaging each other's property. There is a tendency to cast blame in such circumstances, causing many third parties to join the side of the party to which they were initially closer or which seems to have escalated less and hence to be more properly considered the defender. This is the process of *community polarization*.

When communities polarize, their conflicts tend to escalate further. This is because of the destruction of crosscutting group memberships and the disappearance of neutral third parties who would otherwise urge moderation and mediate the controversy.

CONCLUSIONS: CONFLICT MODELS EMPLOYED BY THE PARTICIPANTS

The three conflict models (aggressor–defender, conflict spiral, and structural change) were presented earlier as aids to a scholarly analysis of conflict. But they can also be seen as models of participant thought—concepts that describe the way the parties in an escalating conflict understand what is happening to them. Each model has implications with respect to action, so we can sometimes make predictions about the direction taken by a conflict if we know what models the participants in the conflict subscribe to.

A firm belief in the aggressor–defender interpretation often serves to exacerbate the conflict spiral. This is because parties who interpret their conflict in this way usually see themselves as the defender and the adversary as the aggressor. If surrender is out of the question, they must redouble their efforts at deterrence and defense to prove to their adversary that aggression does not pay. Seeing this, the other is likely to redouble its efforts as well, spawning a new round of contentious activity. The result is a conflict spiral. Thus the pace of the current arms race between the United States and the Soviet Union is bound to be accelerated by President Reagan's belief that "There is no arms race; they are racing and we are just trying to catch up."

On the other hand, belief that one is in a conflict spiral can serve to dampen this spiral. Parties who make such an analysis of their conflict are likely to avoid overly contentious actions in order not to antagonize the other, and to be conciliatory on the grounds that the other party will probably reciprocate (Tetlock, 1983). These are the "doves," by contrast to the "hawks" who make an aggressor–defender analysis. If the doves are right about the nature of the conflict (as they often are), this stance can contribute to de-escalation. For example, in 1977 President Sadat of Egypt, concluding that his country was involved in a conflict spiral with Israel, made a gesture of good will in the form of a personal journey to Jerusalem. This started a de-escalatory spiral in relations between these countries that resulted in the eventual resumption of diplomatic relations. If the doves are wrong (as they sometimes are), a soft conciliatory stance may simply encourage the adversary to redouble his or her efforts to force them to yield. For instance, after surrounding Indian outposts in 1961, Chinese forces withdrew in an effort to signal a desire to be conciliatory. Unfortunately, Indian leaders "interpreted the Chinese withdrawal as a sign of timidity [and] became even bolder in their efforts to occupy as much of the disputed territory, east and west, as was possible" (Lebow, Jervis & Stein, 1984).

A structural change analysis of the conflict one is experiencing implies a number of possible tactics. Some of these are similar to the implications of conflict spiral analysis. For instance, people are likely to mitigate harsh words and heavy tactics when they believe such actions will encourage negative perceptions and the emergence of hawkish leaders on the other side. Other tactics are peculiar to structural change analysis. For example, one may try to avoid structural changes in one's own party that will contribute to further escalation of a controversy. Thus a leader who suspects that a permanent defense establishment will become a strong advocate for hawkish policies may insist that only temporary agencies be formed to meet a current threat.

In addition, structural change analysis implies the importance of *timing* in reversing any actions one has taken that are resented by the other party (Pruitt & Gahagan, 1974). For example, it seems reasonable to assume that the UB campus crisis would have dissipated quickly if the administration had publicly apologized for the initial violence by the campus police, made restitution to the students who were assaulted, and arranged to drop the charges against those initially arrested. Such actions would probably have prevented the formation of the Strike Committee. But once this committee had developed and numerous students had taken important positions in it, the campus was consigned to an extended period of heavy conflict.

The next chapter continues our discussion of escalation, focusing mainly on the question of how a conflict stays escalated once it has moved along this path.

CHAPTER 7

Persistence of Escalation

We saw in Chapter 4 that people in conflict sometimes resort to contentious tactics in an effort to prevail. The use of such tactics is both a cause and a symptom of conflict escalation. When conflict escalation does occur, it is accompanied by a series of incremental transformations; these transformations were discussed in Chapter 5, along with a set of conditions that prevent or retard escalation. In Chapter 6 we examined more closely the psychological and collective processes that produce escalation and its various transformations.

The present chapter closes the loop in our discussion of escalation by evaluating the reasons why conflicts continue to escalate and stay escalated once this process has begun.

THE TAIL OF CERBERUS: RESIDUES THAT CHANGE THINGS

According to Greek mythology, there stands near the entrance to Hades a three-headed dog named Cerberus. Cerberus has a scaly, spiked, powerful tail that allows the souls of the dead to pass into Hades with ease. Once a soul has passed the tail of Cerberus, however, the spines and scales of this tail make it impossible to return. Many animal traps have similar properties, allowing the quarry to pass unimpeded into the trap—perhaps in search of bait—only to find that it is not possible to get back out. The treadles in parking garages, which allow cars to pass smoothly in but damage the tires of any car that tries to drive out, operate on the same principle.

So it is with many escalating conflicts. In the process of waging a contentious struggle, relationships often change in ways that make it exceedingly difficult to reverse course. Up to a point, a rubber band may be stretched and, when released, still return to its original form and shape. Beyond that point, however, further stretching either breaks the rubber band or produces a change in the rubber band's elasticity that prevents it from resuming its original dimensions.

Another way of putting this is to say that many escalating conflicts are characterized by a series of semipermeable boundaries: thresholds that, once passed, do not readily permit retreat. Like a rubber band stretched beyond its normally tolerable limits, the relationship between individuals in an intensifying conflict may pass a psychological or collective threshold—a point of no return—that transforms the relationship into a new, more conflict-intensified state. Often several such thresholds are passed.

Consider this simple example. You and I are having an argument one day, and the exchange begins to heat up rather precipitously. You're assailing and yelling at me, and I'm doing the same to you. At some point during our angry exchange of words, I turn to you and say (with cool hostility) that I've never really respected or valued you. Eventually the argument subsides, as most arguments do, but our relationship is likely to have changed—and not for the better. The words I have uttered, perhaps primarily to goad and gall you and not out of deep-seated conviction, may well have changed things for you in ways that do not easily permit recovery. To be sure, we can continue the business of ordinary daily transaction with each other. But those words of disrespect have introduced a *residue that changes things*.

The identity of residues that change things was a major focus of our discussion in Chapter 6 of the structural change model of escalation. These residues include a desire to punish Other, negative attitudes and perceptions (such as distrust, zero-sum thinking, reduced empathy, and a tendency toward deindividuation), and the development of contentious group norms and goals.

Of course, not all conflicts escalate. Moreover, many that do escalate produce residues that are either negligible or more ephemeral than was implied by the spiked tail of Cerberus. We know this must be so because most conflicts do not continue escalating to the detriment of all concerned. The purpose of this chapter, however, is to examine that special and painfully costly set of escalating conflicts that do manage to produce residues that persist. The question is *why* they persist, and our threefold answer focuses on the persistence of attitudes and perceptions, the persistence of changes in group structure, and the process of overcommitment to an escalating course of action. We will consider each of these factors at some length.

THE PERSISTENCE OF NEGATIVE ATTITUDES AND PERCEPTIONS

Like all attitudes and perceptions, once established, negative attitudes and perceptions tend to endure. Part of the reason for this is that they support one another: Negative beliefs validate negative feelings, and negative feelings make negative beliefs seem right. Another part of the reason concerns the role of three important psychological mechanisms: selective perception, self-fulfilling prophecy, and autistic hostility. The way in which these three mechanisms operate is abstractly represented in Figure 7.1.

This figure is really little more than a combination of the two structural change models shown in Figure 6.2. Both selective perception and autistic hostility are best understood as self-reinforcing internal processes, whereas self-fulfilling prophecy is a kind of vicious circle.

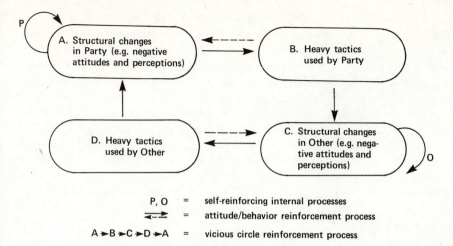

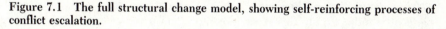

P, O	=	self-reinforcing internal processes
⇄	=	attitude/behavior reinforcement process
A ➤ B ➤ C ➤ D ➤ A	=	vicious circle reinforcement process

Figure 7.1   **The full structural change model, showing self-reinforcing processes of conflict escalation.**

Selective Perception

Once Party has formed a negative impression of Other—once the image of Other as an undesirable, unsavory, untrustworthy, unpleasant character has been shaped—the process of selective perception leads Party to search for and interpret information in ways that confirm the initial negative impression. In selective perception, we tend to see only those things that fit our needs or preconceptions. Once Party has articulated the hypothesis that Other is an undesirable, instead of gathering and evaluating data in scientific fashion in order to test this hypothesis, Party tends to locate *that* information that provides support for it. The net effect of such "hypothesis confirmation" is to support the original impression and sometimes to engender an even stronger, more negative hypothesis than before. An adversary who was first seen as a little rigid may now be regarded as stubborn, and eventually as hopelessly intransigent. Bad leads to worse, unattractive begets repulsive. Note that the structural changes created by selective perception are self-reinforcing and often quite independent of anything Other may say or do. Selective perception thus feeds on itself, as represented in Figure 7.1 by the two circular loops, P and O.

Although the terms "selective perception" and "biased perception" have a negative ring (implying, in effect, that Party deliberately or unconsciously distorts interpersonal information in ways that are undesirable), the process is actually a hallmark of effective social functioning. The world is an immensely complex place that floods each of us with far more social and nonsocial information than we can possibly hope to process. In response to this tendency toward information "overload," it is clearly necessary that each of us finds ways to process information selectively, thereby reducing this input to manageable proportions.

Offsetting this virtue is the obvious and important liability that stems from fitting one's impressions into a Procrustean bed—stripping away the rich individuality of other people in the service of developing a manageable impression. The pressures toward deindividuation (see page 104) are thus given a strong boost by the all-too-human tendency toward selective information processing. Moreover, in the midst of escalating conflict, selective perception is particularly dangerous. It can confirm negative views of the antagonist and hence maintain the existing level of escalation or even edge it upward.

The way in which selective perception operates in the service of escalating conflict has been addressed in a paper by Cooper and Fazio (1979). These authors discuss three interrelated forms that selective perception can take: distortion in the evaluation of behavior, the "discovery" of evidence that supports one's expectations, and the existence of attributional bias. Let us consider each in turn.

Selective Evaluation of Behavior. When feelings are strong, an identical item can be judged quite differently depending on whether the source of this behavior is seen as wearing a white hat or a black one (White, 1984). In an interesting study of student reactions to a Princeton–Dartmouth football game won by Princeton, Hastorf and Cantril (1954) found that the events of the game were judged very differently as a function of the viewer's allegiance. Hastorf and Cantril showed Princeton and Dartmouth students a film of the game and asked them to note all infractions. The Princeton students thought that the Dartmouth Indians had committed twice as many infractions as the Tigers, whereas the Dartmouth students saw no difference in the number of violations. In conflict, it appears, reality is all too often in the eye of the beholder.

Similarly powerful results have been obtained in other social psychology experiments, two of which are worthy of brief mention. Oskamp (1965) presented American college students with two parallel lists of conciliatory and belligerent acts that had been undertaken by both the United States and the Soviet Union. The same acts (for example, "The government has provided military training and assistance to smaller nations") that were rated favorable when performed by the United States (the white hats) were rated extremely unfavorably when attributed to the Soviet Union (black hats). Finally, the Sherifs (Sherif & Sherif, 1953, 1969; Sherif, et al., 1961), in a series of field experiments in boys' camps, examined judgmental distortion among rival groups as follows: A jelly bean hunt was sponsored by the researchers. At the conclusion of the contest, the boys were shown a standard slide photograph of a partially filled jelly bean jar and told that these beans had been collected either by one of their own group members or by one of the other group members. Then they were asked to judge the number of beans in the jar. Interestingly, the jar that was alleged to belong to their own group was seen to contain substantially more beans than the jar attributed to the enemy.

Supporting evidence is not confined to the experimental setting. In a Boston suburb recently, a neighborhood church proposed to establish a social service program for the less affluent, less fortunate members of society (in this case, a counseling program for the mentally retarded). This plan was seen by the church elders as an act of charity and love. But it looked quite different to a set of neighbors (community residents and tax payers who lived next to the church), who regarded the plan as a gross and inconsiderate violation of standards of neighborhood decency.

The "Discovery" of Confirming Evidence. It is one thing to attend selectively to those aspects of another's manner or behavior that conform to one's own preconceptions. It is quite another matter to "stack the deck" in such a way that, in Party's efforts to test hypotheses regarding Other, Party manages to ask those very questions that are most likely to skew the evidence in favor of Party's expectations. In the former case, Party is shown a glass of water and, depending on Party's slant or perspective, comes to view the glass as half full or half empty. In the latter situation, Party actually manages to arrange the process of information gathering in such a way that the glass that Party *expects* to be more empty than full miraculously turns out that way.

Case in point: The neighbors in the foregoing example proceeded from the assumption that the church consisted of a bunch of inconsiderate territorial imperialists. Given this assumption or hypothesis about the other side, if they had a chance to test this hypothesis by asking a few well-chosen questions, we might imagine the neighbors asking questions such as "Why exactly do you wish to ignore the views of the neighborhood in developing this plan?" or "How long have you been territorial imperialists?" The church, in turn, might ask such questions of the neighbors as "Why do you people always oppose efforts to take care of those who are in need of social assistance?" By thus skillfully framing questions in ways that can only confirm one's hypotheses—and by judiciously ignoring information that fails to confirm them—it is possible to "discover" only what one wants to find.

Mark Snyder and his colleagues have conducted several experiments that, although not directly related to the dynamics of conflict escalation, nevertheless shed light on the "discovery" of confirmatory evidence. In one of these studies, Snyder and Swann (1978) provided participants with hypotheses about other people and then allowed the participants to pick a set of questions to be asked of these people during subsequent interviews. In particular, some participants were initially given a description of what an extrovert is like, while others were given the personality profile of an introvert. Once these descriptions were provided, the participants were asked to match this general profile against the specific behavior of a target whom they would interview. To do so, they were to choose twelve questions to be posed to the target.

Snyder and Swann found that those people who were testing an "introvert" hypothesis (even though this hypothesis did not specifically apply to the target, about whom nothing yet was known), chose to pose interview questions that seemed to assume that the target was *already known* to be an introvert: "In what situations do you wish you could be more outgoing?" "What things do you dislike about loud parties?" Those in the so-called "extrovert" condition instead listed questions that presumed the target to be an extrovert: "What would you do if you wanted to liven up a party?" "In what situations are you most talkative?" When, in a subsequent study, the participants were actually permitted to pose the respective questions they had formulated, the response of their targets was such that the interviewers indeed concluded that the targets matched the profile they had been given at the outset.

It is clear, then, that people selectively locate evidence confirming their hypotheses about others. If this phenomenon is fairly powerful in the world of mundane, nonconflictual daily interaction, as Snyder and his colleagues have shown, we can reasonably expect it to be all the more powerful in an emotion-laden situation such as the conflict between the church and its neighbors. Party begins not with some vaguely articulated formulation of what Other may or may not be like, but with a sharply negative impression. This impression—be it the product of anger, fear, zero-sum thinking, wounded pride, or other states described in Chapter 6—is extremely likely to result in confirmatory evidence.

Attributional Distortion. Information about Other that supports Party's privately articulated hypotheses tends to be attributed to *dispositional* causes; behavior that is discrepant with Party's expectations is attributed to *situational* causes instead. That is, information in keeping with our expectations is seen as reflecting Other's enduring and stable characteristics, whereas information that violates our expectations is attributed to temporary environmental pressures on Other. In other words, data that confirm our views tend to be regarded as better data (more reliable, more consistent) than data that disconfirm them.

The net effect of this process in escalating conflict is that there is virtually nothing that Other can do to dispel Party's negative expectations. If Other behaves in a nasty way, this is taken as a true indicator of Other's nasty disposition. If Other turns the other cheek and displays friendly behavior, this is explained as a temporary fluke. Party's tendency to blame Other, to rarely give Other the benefit of the doubt, or to find it difficult to empathize with Other—all states that were discussed in detail in Chapter 6—are given a strong shot in the arm by this tendency to differentially explain the causes of Other's behavior. The phenomenon of attributional distortion has been demonstrated in a number of experimental studies (Regan, Straus & Fazio, 1974; Hayden & Mischel, 1976).

Again, consider the community conflict between the church and its neighbors as a case in point. Imagine that, in a meeting between representatives of the two sides, the neighbors offer to be a bit more flexible on an issue of importance to the church (say, parking privileges on the street adjacent to the church). In an escalating conflict, a concession on an issue such as this would probably be regarded as a Trojan Horse, a gift with strings attached. Or perhaps it would be seen as the result of the church's own hard bargaining. In any event, it would not be regarded as an indication that the neighbors are really a friendlier group than the church initially assumed. Similarly, tough bargaining, the use of threats, and name-calling by either side would probably be regarded by the other as confirming their worst fears and expectations.

Given these three forms of selective perception—selective evaluation of information, distorted hypothesis testing, and attributional bias—it is small wonder that conflicts can more easily escalate than move back down the ladder. Once that genie emerges from the bottle, these three processes combine to make it exceedingly difficult to lure it back in. As represented by the loops (P and O) of Figure 7.1, these are internal processes that are self-reinforcing. They feed on themselves in ways that lead conflict escalation to persist.

Before we leave the topic of selective perception, one additional comment is in order. Although we have here discussed the role of various cognitive processes that operate in the service of conflict escalation, it is important to bear in mind that these very processes may also serve more positive ends. Two people who are wildly and relentlessly in love, for example, may be expected to see one another "through rose-colored glasses"; to continually find support for the hypothesis that each is the most wonderful person in the world; to bias the explanations for their beloved's behavior in ways that discount negative information ("He was very grumpy this morning—must be the damp weather"); and to overstate the stability of positive information ("He just cracked another joke. What a wit he is!"). In other words, these processes are capable of reinforcing both positive and negative impressions.

The Self-Fulfilling Prophecy

Negative attitudes and perceptions sometimes reinforce themselves by having an impact on Other's behavior. The sequence of events by which this occurs is shown in Figure 7.1. First, Party's negative attitudes and perceptions (A), and particularly Party's expectation of negative behavior from Other, lead Party to take hostile actions toward Other (B). These actions produce negative attitudes and perceptions in Other (C), leading Other to respond in ways (D) that confirm and strengthen Party's negative attitudes and perceptions (A). This circular process is the *self-fulfilling prophecy*. This sequence (A → B → C → D → A . . .) constitutes a clear and powerful vicious-circle reinforcement process. Note that, if the circle were begun at point B in Figure 7.1, with Party's use of heavy contentious tactics, we would have the structural change model diagrammed in Figure 6.2.

The self-fulfilling prophecy is more than an hypothesis. It has been demonstrated experimentally, both in the psychologist's laboratory and in a variety of natural settings. Whether we cite the expectations of teachers about the performance of their pupils (Rosenthal & Jacobson, 1968), the prior expectations of students about the maze-learning abilities of their albino rats (Rosenthal & Fode, 1963), or the admitting diagnosis of a mental patient (Rosenhan, 1973), it is clear that Party's expectations generate behavior that in turn prods Other to behave in ways that reconfirm Party's initial expectations.

For example, the neighbors may believe that the church consists of a group of inconsiderate and nasty folks who are likely to do nasty things to the neighbors if given half a chance. These beliefs (A) may well lead the neighbors to preempt the church's presumed nastiness by doing unto them a few nasty things of their own first. For example, they may threaten to go to court to prevent the church from getting necessary permits. This hostile behavior (B), quite independent of the church's actual intentions, may anger and provoke members of the church (C) and lead them to respond with defensive behavior (D). For example, they may go ahead with plans for the Neighborhood Care program, completely ignoring the wishes of the neighbors. This behavior, in reality only a response to the neighbors' behavior, will serve to confirm what the neighbors believed all along (A). The net effect of such a self-fulfilling prophecy—in which Party's attitudes or expectations lead to behavior, which begets behavior by Other, which begets attitudinal confirmation—is to cause conflict escalation to persist. Not only have the neighbors' worst suspicions about the church been confirmed by the latter's behavior, but this behavior is also likely to drive the neighbors to intensify their dislike for the church, leading to new and more dire self-fulfilling prophecies.

An Aside on the "Tar Baby" Effect. It is often (perhaps typically) the case that self-fulfilling prophecies are driven along by the things that Other actually *does*, which confirm Party's own worst suspicions. Occasionally, however, the prophecy is fulfilled not because of things that Other does but because Other does nothing to disconfirm Party's expectations. In effect, this variant of the self-fulfilling prophecy is fueled by the *absence* of behavior by Other. For example, if I regard you as a cold and indifferent person and therefore avoid you at a social gathering, your very ignorance of my hypothesis may lead you to unwillingly behave in ways (such as paying no attention to me) that confirm my hypothesis and fulfill the prophecy.

In order to understand how this paradoxical form of self-fulfilling prophecy actually operates, recall the old tale of Brer Rabbit and the tar baby in one of Joel Chandler Harris's Uncle Remus stories (1955, first published in 1880). One day Brer Fox decided to trap his perennial adversary, Brer Rabbit, by fashioning a likeness of a baby out of tar. Brer Rabbit spotted this "tar baby" by the side of the road and tried to engage it in a bit of friendly conversation. The more Brer Rabbit talked to the tar baby, who of course had nothing to say in return, the angrier he got. "Mawnin! Nice wedder dis mawnin'," said old Brer Rabbit. No response. "Is you deaf? Kaze ef you is, I kin holler louder." No response. "Ef you don't take off dat hat and tell me howdy, I'm gwine ter bus' you wide open." No response. At last Brer Rabbit could stand it no longer. He punched the tar baby in the nose, only to get his fist stuck and find himself increasingly irate. So he hauled off and hit the tar baby with the other fist, and it too got stuck in the tar. Punch led to kick, and before long Brer Rabbit was completely entangled. Indeed, the harder he tried to extricate himself, the more enmeshed he became.

Just as the tar baby knew nothing of Brer Rabbit's feelings or intentions, so Other is often unaware of Party's intentions when Party makes many an influence attempt. The probable outcome of such a situation is that Party's worst expectations about Other are confirmed, even though Other is quite oblivious of this fact.

The pathos of the so-called "tar baby effect" stems from the fact that—were it not for misunderstanding, miscoordination. and miscommunication—the negative inferences might never be made. If Brer Rabbit had known that the tar baby could not react, or if the tar baby had not been so "dense," Brer Rabbit's attitudes and behavior would surely have been different. Too many strikes have persisted, to the detriment of all concerned, because each side held expectations of which the other was oblivious. Each side in the church–neighborhood conflict may have been willing to make concessions to end their conflict, but each may have taken the other's lack of initiative in this regard as confirmation of the other's intransigence. If ever there were a situation in which communication could not help but benefit the concerned parties, it is a situation such as this.

Autistic Hostility

As we mentioned in Chapter 6, there is a tendency to stop interacting and communicating with people we do not like or respect. An extreme example is the perhaps apocryphal case of two brothers who ran a store. One brother accused the other of stealing a dollar from his cash register; the other denied it, whereupon the first brother stopped talking to the other. Thirty silent years later a stranger walked in, confessed to the theft (which had been preying on his conscience), and made restitution. Communication between the brothers was restored.

The problem with an interruption of communication—between two brothers or between a church and its neighbors—is that it makes it impossible to resolve the issue that fostered the initial breach. The parties are consigned to maintain their prior views of each other, including the ones that brought communication to a screeching halt. In effect, these views have initiated a process by which they have perpetuated themselves. This is called the phenomenon of *autistic hostility* (Newcomb, 1947). It is a self-reinforcing internal process, again represented by the two circular loops, P and O, in Figure 7.1.

THE PERSISTENCE OF STRUCTURAL CHANGES IN COLLECTIVES

We have described a number of mechanisms by which the psychological residues of conflict tend to be self-perpetuating and even self-enhancing. There are other mechanisms that have the same effect for collective residues—for the structural changes in groups that are central to the escalation of many intergroup controversies. These are also modeled by loops P and O.

Norms of all types, including those that encourage aggressive behavior toward the outgroup, tend to be self-perpetuating and hence often outlive the reasonable purpose for which they were first developed. This occurs because people who challenge a norm tend to be punished by the group. It also occurs because others who doubt the validity of a norm tend to remain silent for fear of being labeled deviants or, in the case of intergroup conflict, traitors. Still other group members then continue to follow the norm without question, because they do not realize that it is a proper matter for controversy.

New struggle groups and new struggle programs within old groups also tend to become self-perpetuating because they foster vested interests. Group membership and participation in organized activities give some people status, others occupation and wealth, and still others a sense that life is meaningful. People do not easily surrender such benefits, and they often take action to ensure the survival of their group or program. If the raison d'être for that group or program is the conduct of contentious conflict, there are vested interests in the persistence of such conflict. This is another mechanism by which escalation tends to be self-perpetuating. An example is the Strike Committee that was organized during the student demonstrations described in Chapter 5. This committee gave status and meaning to the lives of hundreds of students who participated in it and who would otherwise have been consigned to the round of unromantic activities that are the usual lot of undergraduates. Once formed, the Strike Committee would not easily be disbanded, and its formation was clearly a point of no return in the controversy (Pruitt & Gahagan, 1974).

Similar events have occurred many times in history (Schumpeter, 1955, first published in 1919), and the danger is not necessarily far from home. In his farewell address to the nation, President Eisenhower warned about the development of a built-in lobby for international conflict centered in what he called the "military–industrial complex."

Vested interests extend as well to leaders, who are usually motivated to maintain their leadership positions. If they have gained these positions because of their militancy or skill at waging contentious conflict, they have a vested interest in the perpetuation of contentious conflict. Hence they have incentives for resisting conflict resolution and for starting new conflicts. Here, then, is another mechanism by which escalation tends to be self-perpetuating. This mechanism was probably at work in the Japanese attack on Pearl Harbor in 1941. According to Russett (1967), the Japanese leaders knew this attack was very risky. Indeed, in advocating the attack, one of them commented that "Sometimes it is necessary to close one's eyes and jump from the temple wall." But the alternative was apparently worse. These leaders were military men who had gained high government positions in the late 1930s as a result of the great importance to the Japanese of the war they were waging in China and Indochina. In 1941 the United States began to block the shipment of oil from what is now Indonesia, which made it difficult to continue the war effort. Had the war effort stopped, these generals and admirals would almost surely have been demoted. They were willing to take what would otherwise have been an unconscionable risk in order to perpetuate the war effort and hence maintain their positions.

OVERCOMMITMENT AND ENTRAPMENT

There is one other reason why the transformations that occur during escalation tend to persist. This is because commitments to contentious behavior tend to produce confirmatory changes in psychological and group processes that further strengthen these commitments. This process is represented in Figure 7.1 by the loop of arrows that starts at B, goes to A, and then returns to B (and by the comparable loop between D and C). It is due in part to the pervasive tendency to rationalize one's behavior (see Festinger, 1957) and in part to a process of "overcommitment" that has been extensively studied in research on entrapment, a dysfunctional but pervasive human phenomenon.

An Aside on the Dollar Auction Game. In order to understand better the dynamics of overcommitment to an escalating course of action, let us briefly consider a simple parlor game, first proposed by Shubik (1971) and extensively researched by Teger (1980). This game, known as the Dollar Auction, is played as follows: Several people are invited to participate in the auction of a dollar bill by calling out bids until a high bid has been reached. The high bidder is then awarded the dollar bill, in exchange for paying the amount that he or she bid. Thus, if the winning (high) bid were 15 cents, the winner would be awarded 85 cents (1 dollar minus 15 cents). The "catch" in this game is that the *second-highest* bidder is also required to pay the auctioneer the amount he or she bid but does not receive a dollar bill in return. So, if the bidding for the dollar stopped with a high bid of 35 cents and a next-highest bid of 25 cents, the winner would receive a total of 65 cents, and the next-highest bidder would have to pay the auctioneer 25 cents.

People typically start this game by calling out a small amount of money. And why not? If the dollar bill can be won with a bid of 10, 20, or 30 cents, why not give it a try? Perhaps no one else will elect to play the game. Unfortunately, other people typically reason in much the same way, and the result is that several people begin to bid. Eventually the bidding approaches 1 dollar (the objective value of the prize), and at this point two important things happen: The number of players typically decreases until only the two highest bidders remain in contention. And the attentional focus of the each remaining bidder shifts from the initial concern about maximizing gain (doing as well for oneself as possible) to a concern with minimizing losses instead. As the bidding passes 1 dollar, the issue is no longer how much one can win, but how much one can keep from losing.

Why do people not quit at this point? Largely, it appears, because they are all too well aware of how much time and money they have already spent and are reluctant to give up on this "investment." Moreover, each continues to hold out hope that the other will stop playing, take the loss graciously, lick his or her wounds, and depart the scene—leaving victory to the surviving player. How do I know, each reasons, that I can't still manage to snatch victory from the jaws of defeat by persisting just a bit longer? The problem is that, if each player reasons this way, neither is apt to quit, and conflict escalation is likely to continue.

As the conflict grows with each bidding increment, yet another transformation—one described in Chapter 5 on escalation—begins. The concern with maximizing winnings, which first gave way to a concern with minimizing losses, is now supplanted by the determination to make certain that, even though one is sure to lose oneself, the other player is going to lose at least as much. Each now knows for sure that he or she is certain to "go down in flames," and each is more determined than ever to pull the other player down at least as far, at least as fast. It is in this last stage of the Dollar Auction that concerns about looking foolish in the eyes of the adversary come to the fore, as the players become increasingly preoccupied with the issue of "image loss."

This illustration of Shubik's Dollar Auction game suggests that people in escalating conflicts may tend not merely to commit themselves to some goal (such as defeat of the other person) but also to *overcommit* themselves in ways that appear quite irrational to most external observers. Shubik has reported, for example, that a dollar bill is often auctioned off for as much as $5 or $6. Surely this is an illustration of commitment in the service of irrationality. But what is it that explains overcommitment? Why do people commit themselves and their resources above and beyond reason? To develop a partial answer to these queries, we must explore some of the underlying conceptual features of the process of "entrapment."

Defining Characteristics of Entrapment. Entrapment is simply a special form of escalation in which the parties expend more of their time, energy, money, or other resources in the conflict than seems appropriate or justifiable by external standards. According to Brockner and Rubin (1985), there are three major defining characteristics of situations that lead to entrapment.

First, it must be possible for Party to regard the same parameter (be it time, money, or human lives) as either an investment or an expense. In the Dollar Auction game, for example, the money spent on escalating one's bidding may be regarded simultaneously as an investment (moving one closer to one's goal of winning the auction) and as an expense (money spent that cannot be retrieved, at least if one is the second-highest bidder). Party is thus a Janus-faced creature, able to look forward toward an apparently accessible goal *and* forced to look backward at the costs that are accruing.

Second, as time passes or as additional resources are invested in entrapping situations, the cost associated with continuing increases, but so does the presumed proximity to the desired goal. As a result, the longer Party remains in an entrapping situation, the more Party is caught between two opposing forces.

Third, of the two possible extreme decisions that can be made—total commitment and total withdrawal—the former is favored by the circumstances. Thus the pressure restraining Party from continued involvement (represented by the total accumulated cost incurred) is *more* than offset by the pressures that drive Party to persist, such as the reward associated with obtaining the goal, the belief that the goal is just ahead, and the cost associated with giving up one's investment. Although a player in the Dollar Auction game is continually restrained from further participation because of the amount of money that he or she has already committed, this restraint is offset by the desire to win that rotten dollar bill, the hope or belief that such victory lies just a bid or two away, and the conviction that the money already spent needs to be justified by even more expenditure.

Some Examples of Entrapment. As it turns out, there are a great many situations that exhibit the characteristics of entrapment. Some of these situations (such as an individual trying to decide how much more money to sink into an old car, how much longer to wait for a bus or a friend, or how much longer to hold onto a failing stock investment) are essentially nonsocial in nature. They pit Party against himself, herself, or nature—not against another person. The situations of greatest interest in this book, however, are those that entail a competitive relationship between two or more individuals, groups, or nations. The Dollar Auction game is a quintessential illustration of an entrapping interpersonal conflict. At an intergroup level, consider the illustration of the SST negotiations of some years ago, in which the designers of, and investors in, supersonic transportation felt increasingly compelled to justify the many millions of dollars they had already spent by investing even more—despite growing worldwide opposition. Or consider the example of two sides persisting in a strike, partly because each has suffered so much already that to give up would be to have suffered in vain. Or, for that matter, recall our example of community conflict between the church and the neighborhood. The longer each side has clung to an intransigent position, the more compelled each may feel to justify this position through continued intransigence.

Finally, at the level of international decision making, one can analyze the role and extended involvement of the United States in Vietnam as an illustration of entrapment. Indeed Halberstam (1969), in his book *The Best and the Brightest,* analyzes U.S. involvement in very much these terms. The "doves" argued time and again that the United States had embarked on a fool's journey (let alone an unethical one) and that we should withdraw our forces from Southeast Asia immediately before another American (or Vietnamese) life was lost. But this is exactly why we should remain in Vietnam, retorted the "hawks," exactly why we *should* persist. To withdraw now, they argued, would be to have sacrificed countless lives in vain, for nothing, on an escapade that would be regarded as meaningless. And anyway, victory in Vietnam, and the security of an anti-communist regime in Southeast Asia, seemed just a battle or two away. A similar analysis is possible of the aftermath of Israel's 1982 invasion of Lebanon, the Argentine campaign in the Falkland Islands, Soviet intervention in Afghanistan, and United States involvement in Central America.

Some Factors Leading to Entrapment. In one form or another, both in the psychologist's laboratory and in the field, entrapment has been the object of investigation by a number of researchers over the last decade. The Dollar Auction game has been studied extensively by Teger (1980); Rubin, Brockner, and their associates have devised other laboratory paradigms in order to study very much the same phenomenon; and Staw (1981) and Lewicki (1980), among others, have studied entrapment in field settings. The results of these studies need not concern us here (see Brockner and Rubin, 1985, for a detailed review of this literature), but it may be useful to conclude our discussion by commenting on a few of the many factors that promote entrapment, thereby leading escalation to persist.

1. *Absence of limits.* Research by Brockner, et al. (1979) and by Teger (1980) indicates that people who are not asked to specify the limits of their involvement in a potentially entrapping task become more entrapped than those who set a limit beforehand. Moreover, when people make a show of public commitment to a limit, by announcing it for others to see and hear, they are least likely to become entrapped.
2. *Absence of chunking.* A particular problem arises when the resource expended in an entrapping situation is *time*—for example, when one is placed "on hold" by a telephone receptionist. The problem is that there are no natural points of decision about whether to continue that line of investment. One is passively involved in the expenditure and does not have to decide whether to commit further resources. People are particularly vulnerable to entrapment in such situations.

   There is research evidence to support the view that one way of avoiding entrapment in such situations is by introducing mechanisms that allow involvement to be "chunked" in ways that invite periodic appraisal of the process. As evidenced by the findings of a study by Rubin, et al. (1980), even the minimal provision of such opportunities for chunking can help. Participants in this entrapment task were stopped once every three minutes by the experimenter, who inquired whether they wished to continue or to quit. Merely posing this question had the effect of leading participants to quit the entrapment situation more than twice as soon as those who were allowed to participate without interruption.
3. *Nonsalience of costs incurred.* The stopping points introduced by Brockner, et al. (1980) not only allowed decision makers to chunk their involvement but also reminded them of the costs associated with continued participation. In the absence of such reminders, entrapment is likely to increase. This point was demonstrated in a study by Brockner, et al. (1981) in which participants were given a "payoff chart" that depicted their investment costs at each of a number of possible stopping points. Although people were informed of the chart's availability, they were not required to refer to or utilize it in any way. Those who did not have access to this chart—that is, those for whom costs were not made salient—became significantly more entrapped than their counterparts. Findings by Brockner, et al. (1982) indicate that this effect is particularly striking when cost-salience information is either introduced or kept unavailable *early* in an entrapping task, before the pressures toward overcommitment come into play.
4. *Excessive need to save face.* As we have already seen, in the last stages of the Dollar Auction, Party seems to persist largely in order to make sure that Other is forced to lose at least as much as Party itself. It is in this last phase that protagonists become excessively concerned with the image of toughness that they project to their

adversary and to any observing audience. Although we have used the Dollar Auction game to develop this point, it applies to virtually all forms of escalating conflict. As conflict continues to intensify between individuals, groups, or nations, the parties become extraordinarily concerned that any conciliatory or friendly gesture will be taken to imply weakness and invite future exploitation. In entrapment terms, we may say that to the list of forces pressuring Party to persist in an escalating conflict (nearness to goal, value of goal, cost of giving up on one's investment) may be added the concern that Party not be humiliated by Other. Experimental support for the observation that face-saving motivation leads to increased entrapment has been provided in studies by Brockner, et al. (1981, 1982).

In summary, then, quite apart from the selective perception, self-fulfilling prophecies, and structural changes that cause escalation to persist, there are important forces at work that urge people not to give up their tactical investments. A commitment that may initially have been made with some modicum of restraint is too often followed, in escalation, by the fancy cognitive footwork that leads Party to justify this commitment and the costs incurred by renewing the commitment in ways that are not sensible. And when two people play the game of competition in this way, the results can be incendiary.

CONCLUSIONS

In this chapter, we have described a number of mechanisms that maintain and sometimes augment the transformations that occur during conflict escalation. These mechanisms perpetuate the changes in individual psychology, group process, and community structure that are both antecedent and consequent to contentious interaction.

It should be noted that most of these mechanisms affect the *broad relationship* between the parties under consideration in addition to the way in which conflict over a particular issue is handled. They cause feelings, attitudes, perceptions, norms, and types of leadership to persist as residues beyond the end of a particular conflict incident. These residues then encourage the development of further conflict and the use of contentious tactics when further conflict arises. This point is well illustrated by the sequence of events producing the Cold War, as described in Chapter 6. The negative attitudes and suspicions engendered on both sides by earlier encounters encouraged actions that produced new issues and fostered the use of even heavier tactics to gain victory on these issues. In a sense, it may be more proper in such circumstances to speak of the *escalation of a conflictual relationship* than to speak of the escalation of conflict.

In escalating conflict, it is clearly easier to squeeze the toothpaste out of the tube than to put it back in. And yet we know that conflicts do not continue escalating forever. At some point the turmoil subsides, and conflict begins to abate. The next chapter examines the transitional circumstances that make it possible for escalation to stop and for settlement of the conflict to begin.

CHAPTER 8

Stalemate and De-escalation

For the last several chapters we have told the story of how and why conflicts escalate. Our tale has often been a gloomy one, tracing the nasty, seedy, and perverse aspects of human behavior. We have seen some of the many ingenious ways in which people manage to exploit others in the service of prevailing in a competitive struggle, and we have charted the processes that drive and perpetuate conflict escalation. It is at the point of stalemate, however (the focus of the present chapter), that things ever so grudgingly begin to take a turn for the better.

To be sure, *not all* conflicts are addressed through contentious strategy and tactics. Many, perhaps most, conflicts move to solution through problem solving, withdrawal, outright yielding, or inaction. Furthermore, *not all* conflicts in which contentious tactics are used lead to escalation. One side may give in, or both may realize that contentious tactics often spell destructive consequences. And *not all* escalating conflict persists. The many powerful and effective pressures toward stability may restrain antagonists from excessive head-bloodying, from widening the conflict, and from slipping into the transformations that accompany escalation. Finally, *not all* conflict escalation results in stalemate. Disputants are capable of pulling back from the brink either without trying to club each other into submission or at some point before they have battled to stalemate. In short, there are ample opportunities for conflict to be addressed productively, often to the mutual benefit and satisfaction of the parties, without conflict escalation. (This nonescalatory pathway is represented by curve B in Figure 5.1.)

Having said all this, we turn our attention to the *other* curve in Figure 5.1, curve A. Here conflict continues to escalate despite the availability of more productive strategic alternatives and despite powerful restraining forces toward stability. Yet even in this worst of all worlds, we will argue, there is room for hope. For if it is sadly the case that most good things eventually come to an end, it is happily true that bad things come to an end as well. People in an escalated conflict can do only so much damage to each other, and for only so long. Eventually, after each has heaped on the other's head all the nastiness, manipulativeness, and abuse that he or she can muster, there comes at last a time of *stalemate*.

At the point of stalemate, neither party can or will escalate the conflict further, though neither is yet able or willing to take the actions that will eventually generate an agreement. The point of maximum conflict intensity has at last been reached, the relationship has at last plummeted to its destructive nadir—and if things are to take a turn, it can only be for the better. Stalemate is a highwater mark for the conflictual ark. The waters will probably rise no more, nor have they yet begun to subside in de-escalation.

To be sure, even in stalement the parties may continue to employ contentious tactics in an effort to prevail. Their behavior, for a while at least, may appear unchanged. What begins to change, in stalemate, is the protagonists' outlook. As much as each might like to knock the other's block clean off, such an outcome is finally understood to be unattainable. Out of the grudging realization that Party can or will do no more damage to Other than has already occurred, and out of the realization that things can and must change, emerge the elements that eventually permit the conflict to be reduced or solved. In this chapter we will examine some of the whys and wherefores of stalement: why it occurs, what it encourages people to do, and how people in conflict can move toward de-escalation.

WHY DOES STALEMATE OCCUR?

There are four major reasons for the emergence of stalemate: failure of contentious tactics, exhaustion of necessary resources, loss of social support, and unacceptable costs. Contentious tactics that were used with some success in the past may begin to fail because they have lost their bite. Perhaps Party has tried once too often to feather-ruffle, threaten, or become committed to some irreversible position, and Other no longer finds such moves believable or worth heeding. Another possibility is that, like two people who have lived together for many years, the adversaries have come to know each other's moves and gestures so well that it is no longer possible to seize the advantage. Each move has its properly orchestrated, well-learned countermove; thrust and parry fit neatly together.

Exhaustion of the resources necessary to continue the struggle is also related to the failure of contentious tactics to work as intended. Like two boxers, bloodied and weakened after many rounds of pounding each other against the ropes, the disputants in an escalating conflict simply run out of steam. There is no lack of determination to defeat the adversary, nor is there lack of insight into the necessary moves. Each would still like nothing more than to knock the adversary out and snatch a last-minute victory from the jaws of impasse. But it just isn't possible. The verbal and tactical blows that once landed with such force and effect now have little impact on an adversary who is similarly weakened. Would that those arms could be raised once more to deliver a *coup de grâce*, but by now they are heavy with fatigue.

There are several sorts of resources that may be exhausted as the parties enter a stalemate. One, suggested by the prizefighter illustration, is *energy*—the physical and/or psychological stamina necessary to sustain continued struggle. Another important resource in many competitive struggles is *money*—the ability to sustain the continued financial costs incurred by investment in those tangibles used to wage competition. When the bidders have no more funds to continue their struggle, the auction is over. When both combatants supply lines are cut, the battle must come to an end. Finally, *time* in and of itself often comprises a limited resource which, once exhausted, forces the adversaries into stalemate. As the hands of the clock march toward midnight, the protagonists may feel uncomfortably close to a point of no return.

Related to the exhaustion of resources is the possibility that the parties are forced into stalemate because they are no longer able to obtain the social support necessary to continue. People in conflict often rely on the support of constituencies of "backers" in order to sustain a competitive struggle. Labor and management negotiators can bargain with each other only so long as each continues to have the endorsement—passive though it may be—of the parent organizations that they represent in the proceedings. International diplomats, as the news media continually remind us, are limited and occasionally hamstrung in their effectiveness by lack of support back home. Even prizefighters are best thought of not as individuals but as representatives of their respective financial and social interests; whether to continue fighting is typically not the fighter's decision alone. Thus escalating conflicts often end in stalemate because the protagonists are no longer able to secure the confidence and/or support of a necessary constituency.

Finally, there are important occasions in which stalemate occurs not because the parties are unable to continue their competitive struggle, but because they are no longer willing to do so. We are not speaking here of a change of heart leading each to regard the erstwhile adversary as a friend and colleague. Rather we are addressing those situations in which Party very much continues to wish for the defeat or destruction of Other but suspects that the costs likely to be incurred by continuing the struggle will be so great that further conflict escalation must be avoided. Perhaps the risks of continued competitive struggle are simply too large. Possibly there is fear that, unless escalation ends promptly, new issues and people will become involved, poisoning the broader relationship between the parties.

As an illustration of a stalemate engendered by such cost estimates, consider the Cuban missile crisis of 1962. Several months prior to the crisis proper, the Soviet Union had begun to send shipments of medium-range missiles and nuclear warheads to the island of Cuba, with the clear and unmistakable intention of targeting these weapons, once assembled, at the major urban centers of the eastern United States. The crisis itself began when incontrovertible photographic evidence of this activity was brought to the attention of President John F. Kennedy. The President responded by threatening to impose a naval blockade of all Soviet shipments to Cuba unless the Russians immediately stopped all further shipments and destroyed those weapons and sites already on the island. The response was Soviet silence. So the stage was set for one of the most dramatic superpower confrontations in the history of either nation.

President Kennedy announced that the naval blockade would be put into effect on Wednesday, October 24th. American cruisers and aircraft carriers were dispatched to the waters off Cuba. As the hour of 10:00 A.M. approached, two Russian ships were detected, proceeding toward the 500-mile quarantine barrier. As the two ships, the *Gagarin* and the *Komiles*, neared the barrier, it was learned that a Russian submarine had moved into position between them. The American carrier *Essex* was ordered to signal the submarine to surface and identify itself; if it refused, depth charges were to be used.

The President's brother Robert F. Kennedy was at his side during these events, and he described them in some detail in his moving history, *Thirteen Days* (1969):

> I think these few minutes were the time of gravest concern for the President. Was the world on the brink of holocaust? Was it our error? A mistake? Was there something further that should have been done? Or not done? His hand went up to his face and covered his mouth. He opened and closed his fist. His face seemed drawn, his eyes pained, almost gray. . . We had come to the time of final decision (pp. 69–70).

At 10:25 came the message that the Russian ships had stopped dead in the water. The President immediately issued an order that no Russian ships were to be stopped or intercepted, giving the ships ample opportunity to turn back. RFK concludes:

> Then we were back to the details. The meeting droned on. But everyone looked like a different person. For a moment the world had stood still, and now it was going around again (p. 72).

The United States and the Soviet Union had ample opportunity and ample resources to continue waging their contentious struggle off the shores of Cuba in October 1962. The probable costs of doing so, however, were perceived by each as so great that continued struggle was not possible. The result was a classic stalemate, in which each side had carried the escalation as far as it dared go. In the aftermath of this eyeball-to-eyeball confrontation, steps were set in motion that led to an agreement by which the United States promised not to invade Cuba in exchange for a Soviet commitment to withdraw and/or destroy its missiles in Cuba.

Stalemate and the Capacity to Push. It was Sir Isaac Newton who observed that for each action there is an equal and opposite reaction. In the language of an escalating conflict, what this means is that, as a stalemate is approached, Party's capacity to push the other any further is matched by a corresponding resistance to further yielding on the part of Other. Stalemate occurs because Party, as actor, can push Other no further and because Party, as target, can in turn be pushed no further. Stalemate is thus the stopping point in this process of push and counterpush.

Another way of describing such a situation is to say that the two parties are relatively equal in current power. Such may not always have been the case; one party may have been more powerful than the other at first. But if the originally less-powerful party has yielded further than the more powerful party, his or her resistance to further yielding is likely now to be sufficiently great to outweigh the other's initial advantage. The two parties are now equal in *effective* power.

WAYS OUT OF STALEMATE AND INTO DE-ESCALATION

Thus far we have described the reasons why people, in an escalating conflict, so often finally fall into a stalemate. But what happens next? What happens once stalemate is reached? To understand the various answers to this query, let us return to our earlier analysis of the possible approaches to conflict.

In the introductory chapter of this book, we suggested that there are five different strategies people can employ for coping with conflict: contending, inaction, yielding, withdrawing, and problem solving. Almost by definition, stalemate is characterized by the discrediting of the first of these alternatives: Neither party can prevail through the use of contentious tactics. What, then, of the other four possibilities?

Inaction

Consider an illustration from the fairy-tale world of Dr. Seuss. Two imaginary creatures, a North-Going Zax and a South-Going Zax, are making tracks one day in opposite directions, and they encounter each other along the way. The North-Going Zax complains that its counterpart is blocking the path and in the way: "I'm a North-Going Zax and I always go north. Get out of my way, now, and let me go forth." To which the South-Going Zax quickly retorts that it has business in a south-bound direction: "So you're in MY way! And I ask you to move. And let me go south in my south-going groove." But neither is willing to budge, creating an inevitable stalemate. All day they persist, stopped in their tracks—the North-Going Zax and the South-Going Zax. And as the years go by, the Zax continue to stand firm, until at last a highway comes through the area, and an overpass (the Zax bypass) is built around the two stubborn creatures.

Inaction, it appears, is a tolerable state of affairs for the two Zax. Neither pushes forward or backpedals by the smallest step, and the two continue forever to adhere to the positions that each held when they first met. Some labor–management controversies, as well as some marriages, exhibit this property: the parties adhere almost indefinitely to the positions that characterize their stalemate. However, inaction is usually not tolerable. Labor and management can suffer the costs of a protracted strike for only so long. Similarly, marital impasse tends eventually to become so painful or costly that inaction is seen as an intolerable option. Such a "hurting stalemate" (Touval & Zartman 1985) motivates the parties to some other kind of action.

Yielding

It is always possible for a stalemate to be settled through yielding. One side can simply capitulate, bringing a quick and timely end to what would otherwise be a protracted, costly impasse. It is also plausible to imagine both sides in an exchange of concessions, acknowledging the unacceptability of continued stalemate and mutually consenting to a compromise solution in which each yields. Witness the denouement of the Cuban missile crisis, in which the Soviets agreed to withdraw their nuclear missiles, while the Americans agreed not to invade Cuba and to remove NATO missiles from Turkey. Each side yielded, and the result was compromise.

Note, however, that yielding may sometimes be deemed an unacceptable way out of statement. The two sides may have poured so much energy and ego into their contentious struggle that they are entrapped by their commitment. They simply have too much invested in beating the other, and in preventing the other from emerging the victor, to quit now. To yield even a jot is to surrender one's pride and run the risk of profound humiliation. So, although yielding is often an acceptable solution to statement, it is no panacea.

Withdrawing

What, then, of withdrawing? Can one or both parties to a stalemate not respond through literal or psychological withdrawal? This is indeed a possibility in many situations, though by no means all. Consider international affairs, for example, where there is nowhere else to go!

The implications of withdrawing are varied because they depend on the value of the status quo to which one withdraws. Sometimes the status quo is favorable to one's interests and withdrawal has much the same impact as victory. Under these conditions withdrawal seems like an attractive way to end an impasse. At other times, the status quo favors one's adversary and withdrawal is tantamount to defeat, making it an unattractive solution. Most of the time, withdrawal is costly to both parties and hence not an attractive option for either of them unless all other approaches, including problem solving, fail.

Problem Solving

What remains, once the alternatives of inaction, yielding, and withdrawing have been dismissed as undesirable or unacceptable by the parties, is the possibility of problem solving. If we cannot push each other any harder than we already have, if we refuse to end the stalemate through yielding or withdrawing, and if doing nothing is simply too costly, then we must try to work together to find a mutually acceptable way out.

Perhaps the most important consequence of stalemate, then, is that the parties are often forced into a grudging acceptance of their adversary as an interdependent partner with whom some *quid pro quo* will have to be worked out. The adversary does not come to be seen as a beloved partner with whom collaboration is an exciting and welcome opportunity, but as an enemy whose cooperation is needed. It was Winston Churchill who, when asked about Great Britain's decision to form an alliance with the Soviet Union in an effort to defeat Nazi Germany, responded by saying, "To beat the Nazis I would form an alliance with the devil himself." As the parties take the first tentative steps out of stalemate toward problem solving, each regards the adversary as the devil that he or she needs, the enemy who must nevertheless be catered to and leaned on if the conflict is to be resolved. In the next chapter, we will discuss the nature of problem solving. Here we wish merely to emphasize the fact that the first steps taken in the direction of problem solving after escalation emerge not out of good feeling but out of perceived necessity.

Earlier in this chapter, we briefly considered the important role of power equality in creating stalemate. Such parity, we observed, signifies that, regardless of the history that led the parties to escalate their conflict to the point of stalemate, they have now arrived at the point where they cannot push each other around. We can carry this reasoning one step further on the basis of the conclusions reached just above. Because problem solving is often the most acceptable way out of deadlock, it follows that power equality commonly leads to problem solving.

The likelihood of adopting a problem-solving strategy also depends to some extent on the apparent chances of success with problem solving. To echo what was said in Chapter 2, problem solving seems more feasible to the extent that there is perceived common ground (PCG)—resulting from the belief that the aspirations on both sides are not too high or too rigid or that there is potential for the development of integrative alternatives. Without some assurance along these lines, one or both parties may prefer to withdraw rather than engage in a fruitless sequence of problem-solving activities. Third parties can sometimes enhance PCG by vigorously intruding themselves into the stalemate situation. Trust in the mediator can substitute for trust in the other party in the early stages of third-party intervention (Underhill, 1981).

Stalemate and Problem Solving in the Middle East.   The role of power equivalence and PCG in the creation of stalemate and subsequent problem solving are perhaps nowhere better demonstrated than in the October War in the Middle East of 1973. The war began with a stunningly effective surprise attack launched simultaneously by the Egyptians and the Syrians against Israel while most Israelis were religiously observing their holiest day, Yom Kippur. Both the Egyptians and the Syrians made striking advances through territory that had been in Israeli possession since the so-called "Six Day War" of 1967—a war in which Israel had seized control of the Sinai Peninsula, the West Bank of the Jordan River, and the strategically important Golan Heights.

American Secretary of State Henry Kissinger seems to have well under-stood the antecedents of problem solving, because he helped orchestrate an outcome to the October War that left Egypt and Israel in a position of relative power equality. Safran (1978), in his history of American relations with Israel, indicates that Kissinger systematically manipulated the flow of arms to Israel during the days of the October War, deliberately timed American pressure to declare a cease-fire, and timed the American declaration of a world-wide alert (in response to the Soviets' stating their intention to enter the war)—all in order to create a stalemate that was characterized by relative equality and interdependence.

It appears that Kissinger believed the Israelis were so powerful in the wake of the 1967 campaign that they were unlikely to come to the bargaining table. Why should they consider yielding when the other side(s) had so little to offer in return? Egypt and Syria, in turn, had been so badly defeated in 1967 that they could not possibly hope to negotiate successfully with Israel and so preferred to avoid such a process. The 1973 October War changed all this. Israel now discovered that it could be defeated (at least temporarily) by a worthy adversary, while Egypt and Syria discovered that they had a few more "teeth" than they realized. When a cease-fire was struck at the end of thirteen days of vicious fighting, a stalemate was created under conditions that were propitious for subsequent resolution through the intervention of a third party.

In his analysis of this period, Zartman (1981) points out that the Israelis, Egyptians, and Syrians were stalemated at the war's end in a number of differ-ent ways. For one thing, an Israeli counterattack had completely encircled the Egyptian Third Army, whereas the Israelis themselves were encircled by other Egyptians. At another level, the Israelis had territory (the Sinai) but not the recognition and legitimacy that they desired from their Arab neighbors. For their part, the Egyptians and the Syrians lacked the territory but had the advantage of growing numbers on their side, as well as the ability to withhold recognition of Israel as a legitimate sovereign state. As Zartman writes,

> The 1973 war showed that the Israelis did not always win, nor did the Egyptians always lose. It reversed the fickle play of images under which each side operated, so that even the resounding Israeli comeback and the short-lived quality of the Egyptian and Syrian advances could not destroy this new appreciation of capabili-ties and potentialities (p. 150).

Thus Kissinger helped to engineer a stalemate that set the stage for subse-quent problem solving.

As the hostilities ceased, Kissinger moved immediately into high gear, serving for a period of months as a mediator, shuttling back and forth between Israel and its adversaries. His constant argument was that neither side could hope to move further through force and that their relative equality of power made genuine trade-offs possible. He also chose easy issues to mediate first, thus fostering a sense of momentum in the negotiators. In these ways he kept alive the sense of stalemate and added to it an element of PCG—a belief on the part of the principals that a mutually acceptable agreement could be reached if they would only stay the course with Henry. Zartman (1981) writes of Kissinger's skill in this regard as follows:

> Even as Kissinger was fostering the perception of stalemate, his real tactical skill came from an ability simultaneously to convince the parties that compromise was theoretically possible and that, wherever it lay, such compromise was preferable to the dire alternatives of unilateral action and inaction (p. 152).

PROBLEMS WITH GETTING TO PROBLEM SOLVING

The best answer to the question of how people in an escalated conflict move from stalemate to problem solving is probably "very carefully." Showing too much interest in problem solving can affect Other's perceptions about the power relations and about Party's dependence on reaching agreement. Proposing meetings, suggesting a possible compromise—even proposing mediation—can subtly convey the impression that Party is overly eager for settlement and must be playing a losing hand (Pruitt, 1971). Let us consider an example from the world of championship chess.

It was early in the seventies that Bobby Fischer of the United States and Boris Spassky of the Soviet Union participated in a series of classic confrontations in Reykjavik, Iceland, to determine the world chess champion. As one of the early games in the match was drawing near a close, it became abundantly clear that neither Fischer nor Spassky had even the slightest chance of winning. Each had been reduced to a king and a pawn, and neither had the board position necessary to queen his pawn. Yet, despite the clear inevitability of a draw, neither player gave even the slightest sign of relenting. The two great chess experts stubbornly refused to show any awareness of the other's presence in the room, not to mention across the board. Instead, as chess commentator Shelby Lyman observed at the time, the two men continued to play "forehead to forehead."

The moves dragged on, the referee apparently becoming increasingly impatient about the behavior of the two players, whose game was so obviously headed for a draw. Why would neither propose the compromise solution under these circumstances? Apparently because to do so would have been to signal less self-assurance than was shown by one's adversary, thereby possibly weakening one's position in the games that were to come. How, then, was a draw eventually reached? As Lyman tells the story, Fischer and Spassky stopped playing forehead to forehead at precisely the same instant, looked up and into the other's eyes, smiled, simultaneously nodded their heads, and agreed to a draw without a word ever having been said!

The coordination process leading to calling this game a draw can be thought of as a very simple form of problem solving, resulting from the fact that neither party had the capacity to win and leading to a simple compromise agreement. The broader point is that, because power equality is often very delicate, the parties to this arrangement are likely to go out of their way to avoid the appearance of having a strong interest in problem solving or compromise. The trouble with showing such interest is that it may undermine the impression that Party is a tough and opportunistic opponent who cannot be forced into doing things against his or her will. Far better to wait a while in the hope that some way will emerge to escape from the stalemate than to suffer image loss in Other's eyes. Again, a third party can often be useful in coordinating a simultaneous entry into problem solving.

Given the massive concern with image loss that is characteristic of many parties in stalemate, it is obviously essential that an effective third party—or the disputants themselves, for that matter—find ways of addressing this concern. Although we will discuss a number of techniques in the book's remaining chapters, two ways of cutting through face-saving concerns are particularly appropriate for discussion at this point: the judicious use of contact and communication, and the introduction of superordinate goals.

Contact and Communication

Direct contact between antagonists and the communication that often goes with it can have a number of beneficial effects. First, contact and communication allow the parties to explain actions and proposals that might otherwise elicit defensive reactions or retaliation. Second, they contribute to understanding the other party's motives, sensitivities, and the like; this makes it easier to deflate concerns with image loss and to act in ways that will not upset the other. Third, contact and communication permit problem-solving discussions in which substantive and procedural issues can be resolved. Without such discussions, the search for a mutually acceptable formula must take the form of trial and error, which has many pitfalls. The surest way to achieve an integrative agreement is through discussion of needs and priorities. Finally, contact and communication usually contribute to interpersonal attraction and hence to the development of positive bonds. Research (Festinger, Schachter & Back, 1950; Zajonc, 1968) shows that contact encourages attraction more often than antagonism.

As we will see in the Chapter 10 discussion of third-party intervention, despite their potential advantages, contact and communication should not be regarded as panaceas. Under some circumstances, they tend to be useless or worse than useless (Rubin, 1980). In intense conflict, people often will not use available communication channels (Deutsch, 1973). They see no point in doing so when they cannot believe what the other party says and are too angry to consider any solution that is acceptable to the other. When they use communication channels, it is often to threaten or try to trick the adversary rather than to engage in problem solving (Worchel, 1979). Indeed, when people are severely at odds with each other, communication can be exceedingly explosive, allowing angry, insulting interchanges. This effect was observed in an experimental boys' camp run by the Sherifs (Sherif & Sherif, 1953, 1969; Sherif, et al., 1961). The boys were separated into cabins and encouraged to frustrate one another, producing considerable antagonism. Thereafter, contact between the cabins produced only arguments and name-calling, which served to exacerbate the controversy.

These points qualify the value of contact and communication but do not completely invalidate these processes. They suggest, for example, that if parties are very angry with each other, a cooling-off period may be needed before communication is productive. They also suggest that a third party may have to shuttle between the two parties for a period of time, improving mutual images and laying the groundwork for agreement, before direct contact is of value.

Cooperation on Other Issues: Superordinate Goals

After experimenting with a number of unsuccessful approaches to conflict resolution, including the provision of opportunities for communication, the Sherifs hit on a method that succeeded in breaking down the antagonism between the two cabins of boys in their camps. This was to have the boys cooperate on issues other than those involved in the controversy. For example, the counselors arranged for a breakdown in the water supply to the camp. To fix it, the boys had to work together to disassemble the water tower and carry it to a truck that would take it to town to be repaired. Performance of these tasks reversed the prior escalation, building bonds between the groups.

The Sherifs call this the method of *superordinate goals*, because it involves development of an objective that is common to both parties and beyond the capability of either party alone. Probably the most effective superordinate goals result from the emergence of a common enemy. Such a development was seen in the United States during the Second World War, when the negative sentiments toward the Soviet Union rapidly shifted to positive feelings in the face of the common enemy, Nazi Germany.

Some superordinate goals result from common opportunities for gain rather than common enemies. For example, young married couples who are quarreling sometimes decide to have a child so as to develop a common cause. This is seldom a good idea, because children can also put a strain on a relationship and can be the innocent losers if the tactic does not work. But it is, nevertheless, a commonly applied "remedy."

Having and working on superordinate goals enhances bonds with the other party in a number of ways. One is by the principle of psychological balance—my enemy's enemy is my friend (Aronson & Cope, 1968). Another is by reducing the salience of group boundaries; people who are working toward common goals are in some sense members of the same group and hence are not so likely to be antagonistic toward one another (Turner, 1981). A third is by a reinforcement mechanism; as we work together, each of us rewards the other and produces a sense of gratitude and warmth in the other. Pursuing superordinate goals also means that Party sees itself as working on behalf of Other, a view that is likely to foster positive attitudes toward Other and cut through the concerns with image loss that are often characteristic of stalemate.

The existence of superordinate goals is a powerful contributor to stability under most conditions—but not all. If cooperation toward these goals is unsuccessful (for example, if the common enemy wins), unity may disintegrate and an argument ensue about who is to blame for the loss. This is particularly likely to happen if there was prior tension in the relationship, because previously established images have a way of reintroducing themselves (Worchel, Andreoli & Folger, 1977).

How can superordinate goals be developed in conflict situations? Sometimes circumstances force them on the parties, as when two nations are attacked by a third. Even a military crisis between two nations can have such an effect if it is sufficiently frightening on both sides. It was shortly after the Cuban missile crisis that the United States and the Soviet Union began to negotiate in earnest the terms of the détente that developed between them. This crisis made nuclear war seem imminent in many people's thinking. Sometimes third parties arrange superordinate goals, as the counselors did in the Sherifs' camps. It is also possible for one or both principals to arrange for the development of such goals. A classic example is the government that starts a conflict with another country in order to quell internal challenges to its legitimacy. This occurred in 1982, when the government of Argentina took over the Falkland Islands during a period of severe internal controversy. Married couples who try to resolve a blowup by planning a vacation trip are another case in point.

It is often hard for the principals in a controversy to agree on common goals because they are so antagonistic toward one another. People who are engaged in a struggle may have difficulty cooperating on anything, even on the development of superordinate goals to curb the struggle. Thus superordinate goals, like contact and communication, cannot be viewed as a cure-all. They can help, however, in the often painful process of moving from stalemate through de-escalation and into problem solving.

CONCLUSIONS

A number of theorists (including Douglas, 1962; Gulliver, 1979; Kochan, 1980; Morley & Stephenson, 1977; and Stevens, 1963) have concluded that negotiation, a form of conflict, typically proceeds through several stages. Though there are differences in the number of stages that these theorists postulate, they agree in identifying two stages: an early contentious stage and a later problem-solving stage. Pruitt (1981) suggests further that lying between contention and problem solving is a middle stage, stalemate. These points can be extended to other forms of conflict in addition to negotiation.

The ideas presented in this and earlier chapters help us understand why conflict so often goes through these stages. Intent on fostering their own interests and with little or no concern about the other party's interests, the parties initially gravitate toward contentious tactics. The idea at this first stage is to see how many concessions can be wrested from the adversary. Some of these tactics prove effective, and both parties yield on certain issues. But there comes a time of diminishing returns at which "all of the threats, commitments and debating points that can be made have been made; and the opponent, while duly impressed, is unwilling to make further concessions" (Pruitt, 1971, p. 210). This is the point of stalemate. There is a temptation at this point to allow the stalemate to continue. But this is often infeasible or unacceptable. Costs are mounting—negotiators must be paid, customers are being lost, there is a danger of further alienating the opponent—and a deadline is sometimes approaching at which agreement must be reached or dire consequences (such as a strike) will result. Hence, assuming that neither party is ready to withdraw, they must turn to the only remaining strategy, problem solving. This is the focus of the next chapter.

CHAPTER 9

Problem Solving

The theme of Chapter 8 was that escalating conflict often reaches the point where both parties find the further use of contentious tactics either unworkable or unwise. If yielding, withdrawing, and inaction are also ruled out, as they frequently are, the solution to such a stalemate must eventually be found in problem solving, the only remaining one of the five strategies. Problem solving can be defined as any effort to locate a mutually acceptable solution to the controversy.

Problem solving is by no means always the last step in a controversy. Indeed, it is often the approach taken first, especially when relations with Other are valued and there is perceived common ground. (This is because it does not run the risk of antagonizing Other in the way that heavy pressure tactics do.) Many controversies are resolved through initial problem solving and never escalate. Still other controversies display a picture-frame progression of events: Problem solving is tried first but it fails. The parties then turn to contentious behavior, and the controversy escalates for a while, until a stalemate is reached and problem solving is reasserted.

At its best, problem solving involves a joint effort to find a mutually acceptable solution. The parties or their representatives talk freely to one another. They exchange information about their interests and priorities, work together to identify the true issues dividing them, brainstorm in search of alternatives that bridge their opposing interests, and collectively evaluate these alternatives from the viewpoint of their mutual welfare.

However, a full problem-solving discussion of this kind is not always practical because of the realities of divergent interests. One or both parties may fear that such openness will deny them an opportunity for competitive gain or give the other party such an opportunity. When these fears exist, individual problem solving is a practical alternative. A single person or small partisan group can perform all the functions just described: seeking insight into the other party's interests, identifying the true issues, devising mutually beneficial alternatives, and evaluating these alternatives from a joint perspective. Another approach is for a third party to do the problem solving.

There are many arguments for engaging in problem solving. One is that this strategy reduces the likelihood of runaway escalation. This is because it does not pose a threat to Other and is psychologically incompatible with the use of heavy contentious tactics. As the saying goes, "It is better to jaw-jaw than to war-war." Problem solving also encourages the discovery of compromises and integrative options that serve both parties' interests.

Problem solving is not without its risks, however. Individual efforts to find a mutually acceptable solution tend to weaken Party's own resolve and may also (if there is ambiguity about Party's strength) telegraph weakness to Other. Also, problem solving discussions can be more advantageous to one party than the other. For instance, they are likely to provide greater benefit to the more verbal of the two parties, who is often better armed with statistics and other persuasive devices (Pruitt & Syna, 1983). An example is a discussion between labor and management in which union leaders are poorly educated. If the less verbal party has greater threat capacity, as is sometimes true of the labor representative, that party may be able to achieve a larger outcome from contentious behavior than from problem solving.

These are real risks, but they are not insuperable. It is often possible to engage in problem solving and at the same time cope directly with these risks by means of such devices as communicating covertly with the other party, combining problem solving with contentious behavior, equalizing the parties in verbal ability, or paying greater attention to the needs of the party with greater threat capacity so as to discourage that party from resorting to a contentious approach. The first two of these devices will be discussed in greater detail later in this chapter.

The next section deals with the impact of problem solving on the outcome of conflict. One possible outcome, the development of an integrative solution, receives special emphasis. Following that, we examine the techniques people use to fashion integrative solutions. Five types of integrative solutions are described, along with the refocusing questions that make it possible to devise these solutions. Methods that can be used to analyze one's interests are also examined. Next, we offer some theoretically based advice about how to get the most out of problem solving. Four steps in formulating the problem are outlined, a firm but conciliatory strategy is advocated, and suggestions are made about how to structure the agenda, search for an overarching formula, and break "rigidifying linkages." Then we describe some methods of covert problem solving that are available when overt problem-solving approaches seem too risky. The chapter closes with a discussion of tactics that can be used to persuade the other party to join oneself in problem solving.

OUTCOMES OF PROBLEM SOLVING

Successful problem solving can lead to three broad classes of outcomes: compromise, agreement on a procedure for deciding who will win, or integrative solution.

Compromise

A *compromise* is an agreement reached when both parties concede to some middle ground along an obvious dimension. A good example is a decision to settle a wage dispute by splitting the difference between the two parties' proposals or to resolve a dispute about whether to vacation in Maine or Florida by going to a beach in North Carolina. The popular use of the term "compromise" is somewhat broader; it often means any agreement in which the parties abandon their initial demands. But, following the lead of Follett (1940), we have adopted a narrower definition in order to distinguish compromises from integrative solutions.

Compromises can sometimes be very good for both parties and sometimes very bad. But most commonly they provide both parties a middling outcome—by no means as good as what they had hoped for or as bad as what they might have got. Where it can be achieved, an integrative solution is usually much better for both parties than a compromise. Yet many controversies end in compromise. Among the reasons for this are aspirations that are not sufficiently high, time pressure that makes it hard to embark on a search for new options (Yukl, et al., 1976), fear of prolonged conflict, and a societally endorsed fetish for "fairness" that often attracts unwarranted attention to the 50–50 division. In addition, compromises sometimes grow out of an unduly escalated episode. So much energy has been devoted to trying to beat the other party, and so much attention is focused on partisan options, that the parties cannot engage in creative efforts to devise new alternatives. Hence, when they finally see that they are in a hurting stalemate, they reach out in desperation for an obvious compromise.

Agreement on a Procedure for Deciding Who Will Win

Compromise is not the only kind of solution that seems fair. Sometimes the outcome of problem solving is a procedure for deciding who will win—that is, a rule for awarding one party all it is asking while the other gets little or nothing. Examples of such a procedure include:

- Tossing a coin, with victory for the winner.
- Comparing needs, with victory for the party who feels most strongly about the issue under consideration.
- Submitting to a third-party decision, with victory for the disputant whose position seems most cogent to a judge or arbitrator.
- Voting, with victory to the party who can command a majority of some deliberative body.

It is sometimes essential to use one of these procedures—for example, when there are only two possible outcomes (such as I go first or you go first). But in most cases, more integrative solutions are available if the parties will only seek them out. This means that norms of fairness and legitimate procedures like voting can sometimes be snakes in the grass, undermining the parties' will to look for more integrative solutions and the benefits that come with such solutions.

Integrative Solutions

An integrative solution is one that reconciles (that is, integrates) the two parties' interests. Integrative solutions produce the highest joint outcomes of the three types of agreement. Consider, for example, the story of two sisters who are quarreling over an orange. A compromise agreement is reached to split the fruit in half—whereupon the first sister squeezes her half for juice while the other uses the peel from her half in a cake. Both would clearly have profited more from the integrative solution of giving the first sister all the juice and the second all the peel. But, intent on compromise, they never found it.

In this story, it is possible for a *fully* integrative solution to be reached, one that totally satisfies both parties' aspirations. However, most integrative solutions are not quite so successful. They *partially* reconcile the parties' interests, leaving them fairly content but not quite so happy as if they had achieved all they had hoped for.

Integrative solutions sometimes entail known alternatives, but more often they involve the development of novel alternatives and hence require some creativity and imagination. For this reason, it is proper to say that they usually emerge from a process of creative thinking. Integrative solutions can be devised by either of the parties acting separately, by the two of them in joint session, or by a third party such as a mediator.

Situations that allow for the development of integrative solutions are said to be high in "integrative potential" (Walton & McKersie, 1965).[1] Not all situations have such potential. For example, there is little integrative potential when a tourist dickers with a North African merchant about the price of a rug; one party's gain is almost surely the other's loss. But there is more integrative potential in most situations than is usually assumed. Hence a skilled and sustained problem-solving effort is often richly rewarded.

Although it is true that problem solving can lead to any of the three possible outcomes—compromise, agreement on a procedure for deciding who will win, or integrative solution—parties to conflict are strongly advised to pursue integrative solutions if at all possible. This advice is given for four main reasons.

1. If aspirations are high and there is resistance to yielding on both sides, it may be impossible to resolve the conflict unless a way can be found to join the two parties' interests.
2. Agreements involving higher joint benefit are likely to be more stable. Compromises, coin tosses, and other mechanical agreements are often unsatisfying to one or both parties, causing the issue to come up again at a later time (Thomas, 1976).
3. Because they are mutually rewarding, integrative solutions tend to strengthen the relationship between the parties. Strengthened relationships usually have inherent value and also facilitate the development of integrative solutions in subsequent situations.
4. Integrative solutions ordinarily contribute to the welfare of the broader community of which the two parties are members. For example, a firm usually benefits as a whole when its departments are able to reconcile their differences creatively.

---

[1] The reader will recall that the concept of perceived integrative potential (PIP) was introduced earlier to describe the likelihood of finding an integrative solution as this likelihood is perceived by the parties to a conflict. The term "integrative potential" used here refers to the *true* likelihood of finding such a solution.

The discovery of an integrative solution diminishes, and can even abolish, perceived conflict of interest. This point can be demonstrated with reference to the graphs in Figure 2.2 on p. 12. The graph in Figure 2.2(d) shows a fairly severe perceived divergence of interest. There is a possible compromise with the center alternative, but it comes nowhere near satisfying the two parties' aspirations (which are shown by the dashed lines). This divergence of interest disappears in Figure 2.2(a) as a result of developing an integrative solution. It follows that, if an integrative solution is known at the outset of concern about an issue, conflict can be avoided. Had the sisters in our example thought immediately about exchanging peel for pulp, there would have been no conflict.

In summary, of the three outcomes that can result from problem solving, integrative solutions are almost always the most desirable. They tend to last longer and to contribute more to the relationship between the parties and the welfare of the broader community than do compromises and agreements about how to choose the winner. In addition, they tend to diminish the sense of conflict. Integrative solutions are not always available, but there is more integrative potential in most situations than meets the eye. Problem solving is especially likely to lead to integrative solutions when aspirations are high, time pressure is low, fear of conflict is low, and the parties are not overly impressed by the importance of fairness.

TYPES OF INTEGRATIVE SOLUTIONS

If integrative solutions are so important to achieve, how do they emerge? What are the routes for moving from opposing demands to an alternative that reconciles the two parties' interests? We have identified five such routes, leading to five types of integrative solutions: expanding the pie, nonspecific compensation, logrolling, cost cutting, and bridging. In addition to its theoretical value, this typology should be useful as a check list for any bargainer or mediator seeking a way to settle a controversy.

In order to increase the theoretical and practical value of our presentation, we shall mention in connection with each type of solution the kind of information that is needed in order to formulate such a solution and several refocusing questions that can aid in the search for such a solution. The types of solutions will be listed in order of the difficulty of getting the necessary information—with the least difficult listed first.

Our typology of integrative solutions is illustrated by a running example concerning a husband and wife (or any two people) who are trying to decide where to go on a two-week vacation. The husband wants to go to the mountains, the wife to the seashore. They have considered the compromise of spending one week in each location but are hoping for something better. What approach should they take?

Expanding the Pie

Some conflicts hinge on a resource shortage. Time, money, space, automobiles, handsome men, or what have you—all are in long demand but short supply. In such circumstances, integrative solutions can be devised by expanding the pie, which means increasing the available resources. For example, our couple might solve the problem by persuading their employers to give them two additional weeks of vacation so that they can spend two weeks in the mountains *and* two weeks at the seashore. Another example (cited by Follett, 1940) is that of two milk companies who were vying to be first to unload cans on a platform. The controversy was resolved when somebody thought of widening the platform.

Expanding the pie is a useful formula when the parties find one another's proposals inherently acceptable but reject them because they pose opportunity costs. For example, the husband rejects the seashore because it keeps him away from the mountains, and the wife rejects the mountains because they deny her the pleasures of the seashore. However, expanding the pie is by no means a universal remedy. If there are inherent costs, as opposed to opportunity costs, in the other party's proposal (the husband cannot stand the seashore or the wife the mountains), broadening the pie may yield strikingly poor results. Other types of integrative solutions are better in such cases.

The information requirements for expanding the pie are very slim. All that is required is knowledge of the parties' demands. No analysis of the interests underlying these demands is needed. However, this does not mean that such a solution is always easy to find. There may be no resource shortage, or it may be expensive to enlarge the pool of resources. Furthermore, it may not be apparent that the problem hinges on a resource shortage. In an argument over who goes first on the loading platform, it may not be clear that the real issue is the size of the platform.

Several refocusing questions can be useful in seeking a solution by expanding the pie. How can both parties get what they want? Does the conflict hinge on a resource shortage? How can the critical resource be expanded?

Nonspecific Compensation

In nonspecific compensation, Party gets what he or she wants, and Other is repaid in some unrelated coin. Compensation is "nonspecific" when it does not deal with the precise costs incurred by the other party. For example, the wife in our example might agree to go to the mountains—even though she finds them boring—if her husband agrees that some of the family resources can be spent on buying her a new car. Another example is a supervisor giving an employee a bonus for going without dinner in order to meet a deadline.

Compensation usually comes from the party whose demands are granted, because that party is "buying" concessions from the other. But it can also originate with a third party or even with the party who is compensated. An example of the latter is an employee who pampers himself or herself by finding a nice office to work in while going without dinner.

Two kinds of information are useful for devising a solution via nonspecific compensation: (1) information about one or more realms of value to the other party, for example, knowledge that he or she values love or attention or is money-mad; (2) information about how badly that party is hurt by making the concessions; such information is useful for devising adequate compensation. If only one of these kinds of information (or neither) is available, it may be possible to conduct an "auction" for the other party's acquiescence, changing the sort of benefit offered or raising one's offer in trial-and-error fashion, until a formula is found to which he or she can agree.

Refocusing questions that can help locate a means of compensation include: What does the other party value that I can supply? How valuable is this to the other party? How much is the other party hurting in conceding to me?

Though it is often useful, nonspecific compensation has its limitations. These are mainly due to normative constraints. For example, it is not proper to pay a government employee for food stamps. Foa and Foa (1975) have developed a general theory about the kinds of compensation that are considered appropriate as repayment for certain kinds of concessions. They classify resources on two dimensions: concreteness (tangibility) and particularism (the extent to which the value of the resource depends on the identity of the person delivering it). Status and love are examples of abstract, particularistic resources; goods and money are concrete, nonparticularistic resources. These authors have shown, in a series of studies, that a form of compensation appears more appropriate the closer it is in this dimensional space to the resource received. Thus goods can properly be exchanged for money and status for love. But money cannot properly be exchanged for love.

When there are normative constraints against a compensatory scheme that is nevertheless desired by the parties, three strategies are available for avoiding community awareness of the transaction: making a secret agreement, secretly transferring one or both benefits, and delayed sequential enactment of the benefits (such that the two parties' actions are so separated in time that outsiders do not see the connection). A traveler who places a $20 bill in his or her passport at a foreign airport is making a secret transfer. An example of a secret agreement that was also sequentially enacted can be seen in the American pledge to withdraw missiles from Turkey during the Cuban missile crisis. This withdrawal was delayed for four months after the Russians took their missiles out of Cuba, presumably so that the connection would not be obvious. One can only assume that the American president feared that, if this agreement became known, he would be criticized by opposition politicians or nervous allies.

Compensatory schemes often take the form of promises—guarantees of later benefit in exchange for present compliance. Promises were earlier described as contentious tactics aimed at eliciting a concession from Other. Hence promises must be viewed as an unusual hybrid of contentious and problem-solving tactics.

Logrolling

In a solution by logrolling, each party concedes on issues that are of low priority to itself and high priority to the other party. In this way, each gets that part of its demands that it deems most important. Like the other types of solutions, logrolling is not a universal route to integrative solutions. It is possible only when several issues are under consideration and the parties have different priorities among these issues. Suppose that, in addition to their disagreement about where to go on vacation, the wife in our example prefers a first-class hotel and the husband wants to go to a tourist home. If accommodations are most important to the wife and location is most important to the husband, they can reach a fairly integrative solution by agreeing to go to a first-class hotel in the mountains.

Another example is a hypothetical case of bargaining between labor and management in which labor initially demands a 20 percent increase in overtime rate and 20 more minutes of rest breaks, and management indicates unwillingness to provide either concession. If the overtime rate is especially important for labor and if long rest breaks are particularly abhorrent to management, a reasonably integrative solution can be achieved by labor dropping its demands for more rest breaks in exchange for management giving in on the overtime rate. This sort of solution is typically better for both parties than a compromise on the two issues, such as a 10 percent increase in overtime rate and 10 more minutes of rest time.

Logrolling can be viewed as a variant of nonspecific compensation in which each party is compensated for making concessions desired by the other.

To develop solutions by logrolling, it is useful to have information about the two parties' priorities among the issues so that concessions can be matched up, but it is not necessary to have information about the nature of the interests (goals and values) underlying these priorities. Information about priorities is not always easy to get. One reason for this is that people often try to conceal their priorities for fear that they will be forced to concede on issues of lesser importance to themselves without receiving compensation. Another reason is that people often erroneously project their own priorities onto others, assuming that what they want is what the other wants also.

Solutions by logrolling can also be developed by a process of trial and error in which one systematically offers a series of possible packages, keeping one's own aspirations as high as possible, until an alternative is found that is acceptable to the other party (Kelley & Schenitzki, 1972; Pruitt & Carnevale, 1982).

Refocusing questions that can be useful for developing solutions by logrolling include: Which issues are of higher priority and which of lower priority to myself? Which issues are of higher priority and which of lower priority to the other party? Are some of my high-priority issues of lower priority to the other party and vice versa?

Cost Cutting

In solutions by cost cutting, Party gets what he or she wants, and Other's costs are reduced or eliminated. The result is high joint benefit, not because Party has changed his or her position but because Other suffers less. For instance, suppose that the husband in our example dislikes the beach because of the hustle and bustle. He may be quite willing to go there on vacation if his costs are cut by renting a house with a quiet inner courtyard where he can read while his wife goes out among the crowds.

Cost cutting often takes the form of specific compensation, in which the party who concedes receives something in return that satisfies the precise values frustrated. For example, if the wife's main objection to the mountains is the absence of seafood, it may be possible to reach agreement by locating a mountain hotel that serves seafood. Specific compensation differs from non-specific compensation in that it deals with the precise costs incurred rather than providing repayment in an unrelated coin. The costs are actually cancelled out rather than being overbalanced by benefits achieved in some other realm.

Information about the nature of the other party's costs is, of course, helpful for developing solutions by cost cutting. This is a deeper kind of information than knowledge of that party's priorities. It involves knowing something about the interests—the values and needs—underlying that party's overt position.

Refocusing questions for developing solutions by cost cutting include: What costs are posed for the other party by my proposal? How can these costs be mitigated or eliminated?

Bridging

In bridging, neither party achieves its initial demands, but a new option is devised that satisfies the most important interests underlying those demands. For example, suppose the husband in our vacation example is mainly interested in fishing, and the wife wants mainly to swim. These high-priority interests might be bridged by finding an inland resort with a lake that is close to woods and streams. Follett (1940) gives another example of two women reading in a library room. One wants to open the window for ventilation, the other to keep it closed in order not to catch cold. The ultimate solution involves opening a window in the next room, thereby letting in the fresh air while avoiding a draft.

Bridging typically stems from a reformulation of the issue(s) on the basis of an analysis of the underlying interests. For example, a critical turning point in our vacation example is likely to come when the initial formulation "Shall we go to the mountains or the seashore?" is replaced by "Where can we find opportunities for fishing and swimming?" This new formulation becomes the basis for a search model (Simon, 1957) that is employed in an effort to find a new alternative. The reformulation process can be carried out by either or both parties or by a third party who is trying to help.

It is rare that a solution can be found that bridges all of the two parties' interests, as the window in the next room of the library does. More often, higher-priority interests are served while lower-priority interests are discarded. For example, the wife who agrees to go to an inland lake may have foregone the lesser value of smelling the sea air, whereas the husband may have given up his predilection for spectacular mountain vistas.

It follows that people who seek to develop bridging solutions must usually have information about the nature of the two parties' interests and about their priorities among these interests. Information about priorities among interests is different from information about priorities among issues (which is useful for developing solutions by logrolling). Issues are the concrete matters under discussion now; interests are the hidden concerns that underlie preferences with respect to issues.

To achieve an optimal solution by bridging, the information just described should be used as follows: In an initial phase, one's search model should include all of the interests on both sides. But if this does not generate a mutually acceptable alternative, some of the lower-priority interests should be discarded from the model and the search begun anew. The result will not be an ideal solution, but it is likely to be one that is mutually acceptable. Dropping low-priority values in the development of bridging solutions is analogous to dropping low-priority demands in the search for a solution by logrolling. But the latter is in the realm of concrete proposals, while the former is in the realm of the interests underlying these proposals.

Refocusing questions that can be raised in seaching for a solution by bridging include: What are the two parties' basic interests? What are the priorities among these interests? How can both sets of high-priority interests be achieved?

THE ANALYSIS OF INTERESTS

To devise an integrative solution involving cost cutting or bridging, it is usually necessary to know something about the interests underlying one party's position (in the case of cost cutting) or both parties' positions (in the case of bridging). The most obvious way to get this information is to persuade the parties to talk about their interests. However, there are two problems with this method. One is that people do not always understand the precise nature of the interests underlying their own preferences. Their position in a controversy is often a matter of what feels best; they feel good about their own proposal or uneasy about the other party's proposal without knowing precisely why. For example, the wife may feel comfortable at the seashore and uncomfortable in the woods but not be sure why she feels this way. The other problem is that people are often unwilling to reveal their interests for fear that the other party will use this information to personal advantage—for example, for constructing threats. This problem arises when there is distrust between parties. An example is unwillingness to tell one's spouse that one is greatly in need of affection for fear that the spouse will later threaten to withdraw affection whenever he or she wants a concession.

Fortunately, there are other approaches to gathering information about people's interests besides getting them to talk directly about these interests. These include:

1. Listening "with the third ear"—that is, being attentive to the points they emphasize, the places where they become emotional, and the issues they neglect to mention (Fisher & Ury, 1981).

2. Employing stereotypes based on what is known about others similar to the people under study (Harsanyi, 1962). For example, if a small boy asks for money, one might guess—on the basis of stereotypes—that he wants to buy food or toys.

3. Drawing inferences from the people's behavior outside the conflict situation.

4. Asking third parties about the people's values and standards.

Interests Underlying Interests

Learning about the first-level interests that underlie a party's proposals is often not enough. One must seek the interests underlying these interests, or the interests underlying the interests underlying these interests, etc. The point is that interests are often organized into hierarchical trees, with more basic interests underpinning more superficial interests. If one goes down the tree far enough, one may locate an interest that can be easily bridged with an interest of the opposing party.

An example of an interest tree appears on the left of Figure 9.1. It belongs to a hypothetical boy who is trying to persuade his father to let him buy a motorcycle. At the right are listed those of the father's interests that conflict with the son's interests. At the top of the tree is the boy's initial position (buy a motorcycle), which is hopelessly opposed to his father's position (no motorcycle). Analysis of the boy's proposal yields a first-level underlying interest: to make noise in the neighborhood. But this is opposed to his dad's interest in maintaining peace and quiet. Further analysis of the boy's position reveals a second-level interest underlying the first level: to gain attention from the neighbors. But again this conflicts with one of his father's interests, to live unobtrusively. The controversy is resolved only when someone (the father, the boy, the boy's mother, or someone else) discovers an even more basic interest underlying the boy's desire for a motorcycle: the desire to impress important people. This discovery is significant because there are other ways of impressing important people that do not contradict the father's interests—for example, the bridging solution of going out for the high school soccer team.

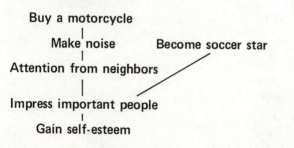

SON'S INTERESTS   FATHER'S INTERESTS

Buy a motorcycle   No motorcycle

Make noise   Become soccer star   Peace and quiet

Attention from neighbors   Live unobtrusively

Impress important people

Gain self-esteem

Figure 9.1   Son's interest tree in a controversy with his father.

At the bottom of the boy's preference tree is a fourth-level interest, self-esteem. But it is unnecessary to go down this far, because the controversy can be resolved at the third level.

Same Issue—Different Meaning

When one seeks the interests underlying divergent positions, one often finds that the issue under consideration has a different meaning to each of the two parties. Though there appears to be disagreement, there is no fundamental opposition in what they are really asking. Figure 9.2 shows some dimensions that leave room for bridging.

An example of a controversy that was resolved when a mediator discovered that one party was seeking substance while the other was seeking appearance is given by Golan (1976). A cease-fire in the Yom Kippur War found the Egyptian Third Army surrounded by Israeli forces. A dispute arose about the control of the only road available for bringing food and medicine to this army, and the two parties appeared to be at loggerheads. After careful analysis, the mediator (Henry Kissinger) concluded that Israel wanted actual control of the road, whereas Egypt wanted only the appearance that Israel did not control it to avoid embarrassment back home. A bridging solution was found that involved stationing Israeli soldiers unobtrusively on the sides of the road (so that they actually controlled it) and having United Nations checkpoints on the road itself (to give the impression of international control).

Another controversy was resolved when it was discovered that one party had immediate concerns whereas the other's concerns were more distant. This situation involved a strike by public transit workers in Buffalo. The mayor of the city, who was asked to mediate the dispute, found that the bus company's refusal to pay stemmed from insufficient funds, whereas the motormen's main

ONE PARTY CARES MORE ABOUT	THE OTHER PARTY CARES MORE ABOUT
substance	form, appearance
economic considerations	political considerations
internal considerations	external considerations
symbolic considerations	practical considerations
immediate future	more distant future
ad hoc results	the relationship
hardware	ideology
progress	respect for tradition
precedent	this case
prestige, reputation	results
political points	group welfare

Figure 9.2 Polar opposites that are not necessarily in conflict (from **Fisher & Ury, 1981, p. 77**).

concern was their salary in future years. Hence he recommended that the workers get half of what they were asking immediately and the other half a year later, after the company had had a chance to petition the city for an increase in the bus fare. This was another bridging solution.

To summarize the last two sections, we have described five types of integrative solutions: expanding the pie, nonspecific compensation, logrolling, cost cutting, and bridging. These, and the refocusing questions that make them possible, provide five routes along which the disputants or a third party can move from an apparent divergence of interest to an agreement that satisfies both parties' major interests. These solutions differ in the information required to attain them. Expanding the pie requires only knowledge of the parties' current demands. Nonspecific compensation requires information about a realm of value to the other party outside the current controversy. Logrolling requires knowledge of the parties' priorities among the issues under discussion. And cost cutting and bridging require information about the interests that are served by the parties' current demands. Interests are often organized hierarchically; hence it is frequently productive to seek the interests underlying the interests that are served by current demands and the interests further underlying those interests, etc. Quite often, when one digs down into underlying interests, it turns out that the issue in dispute has a different meaning to each of the two parties, which makes agreement easier to reach.

HOW TO GO ABOUT PROBLEM SOLVING

It clearly makes sense to search for integrative solutions in most conflicts. How should one go about this search—how should it be organized? This is the question of creative problem solving.

Steps in Creative Problem Solving

The following sequence of steps makes most sense in the search for creative solutions to apparent conflicts of interest.

STEP 1. Ask Whether There Really Is a Conflict of Interest. An apparent conflict of interest may be *illusory*. If there is a misunderstanding about the circumstances, or if one or both parties misconstrue the other party's proposals or interests. If the parties can grasp this point, the conflict will go away and problem solving will be unnecessary. Hence, asking whether there is a real conflict of interest is the logical first step.

Illusory conflict can arise in at least three ways. Party may have a false impression about Other's intentions or aspirations. For example, a carpenter who came to look at a job in the home of one of the authors said that the estimate would cost $50. When asked why he expected a fee, he indicated that he feared homeowners would file for an insurance payment on the basis of his estimate and then do the repairs themselves. When assured that this homeowner was all thumbs with tools, he withdrew the request for a fee. Second, Party may think Other's intended actions will create costs that they actually will not create. For example, parents may oppose a teenage party because of the anticipated noise until they learn that the proposed party will take place while they are away. Third, Party may view Other's intentions as arbitrary or illegitimate when they really are not. For example, a university department chair thought she was in conflict with the Dean of Continuing Education over the division of some student fees. At the "showdown" meeting between these two administrators, the dean argued that Continuing Education should get the larger share because more of its budget depended on "soft money." Once this argument had been presented, the dean's claims seemed nonarbitrary, and there no longer seemed to be a conflict in the eyes of the chair.

STEP 2. Analyze One's Own Interests, Set Reasonably High Aspirations, and Be Ready to Stick to Them.   If one concludes that a conflict really exists, the next step is to carefully examine one's own interests—one's basic goals and values. This avoids the danger of going off half-cocked and getting involved in controversy over inessential issues. The methods for analyzing interests described earlier can be useful in this enterprise. Having done so, one must set reasonably high aspirations with respect to these interests and be ready to stick to them. In short, one must be both ambitious and stubborn about one's basic interests.

We acknowledge that by endorsing ambition and stubbornness we are saying that protracted conflict is often necessary for the development of truly integrative solutions (Filley, 1975). Party must maintain high aspirations fully cognizant of the fact that, in the last analysis, they may not be compatible with Other's aspirations. This seems paradoxical, but we hasten to add that we are not talking about heavily competitive conflict. Creative conflicts are in the category of vigorous discussions or mild arguments, in which both parties state their preferences and stick to their goals while remaining flexible about their means of attaining them.

We are also not endorsing bull-headedness. Aspirations should start and stay high, but not so high as to outrun any reasonable integrative potential. If they remain too high, time will be lost and Other may withdraw because the conflict seems hopeless.

STEP 3. Seek a Way to Reconcile Both Parties' Aspirations.   Having set high aspirations, Party should seek a way to reconcile these aspirations with those held by Other. In other words, party should engage in problem solving—in a search for an integrative solution. The various refocusing questions discussed in the prior section should be posed, and one or more search models should be developed in an effort to achieve the goals that both parties find most important.

It is not clear that any one of the five kinds of integrative solutions is better or easier to achieve than the others. Hence we do not recommend starting the search with any particular type of solution in mind. The right type of solution depends in part on the kind of information available. If Party cannot fathom Other's reasons for making his or her demands, cost cutting and bridging are not possible and Party must be content with the other three approaches. On the other hand, if this information *is* available, it may make sense to pursue several kinds of solutions at once—for example, to seek a way to expand the pie at the same time that one seeks a bridging solution.

Sometimes there is too little information about Other's situation to permit a thoughtful approach to the development of integrative solutions. For example, Other may reject Party's proposals but refuse to give reasons or make a counterproposal. When this happens, a policy of trial and error must be adopted (Kelley & Schenitzki, 1972; Pruitt & Carnevale, 1982), in which Party proposes a sequence of alternatives that satisfy his or her own aspirations in the hope of finding one that appeals to Other as well.

STEP 4. Lower Aspirations and Search Some More. If agreement is not reached at step 3, a choice should be made between two further options. Party can reduce his or her own aspirations somewhat—that is, concede on low-priority issues or discard low-priority interests—and try again. Alternatively, if Party's search model includes Other's aspirations as well as his or her own, Party can lower these aspirations and then, if a solution is found, try to persuade Other that such a reduction is desirable.

Step 4 should be repeated over and over again until an agreement is reached or withdrawal becomes inevitable.

Being Firm but Conciliatory

The policy described in steps 2 and 3 of the sequence just given can be viewed as *firm but conciliatory*. Party is advised to be firm about his or her own basic interests—yielding only when it is clear that they cannot be attained—but conciliatory toward Other in the sense of being responsive to Other's basic interests also. An important aspect of being conciliatory is to be flexible about how one's own interests are achieved in order to be open to new ideas about how to reconcile them with Other's interests. Hence, this policy can also be described as involving *firm flexibility;* Party should be firm with regard to ends but flexible with regard to the means used to reach these ends. A quotation from Fisher and Ury (1981) captures the essence of firm flexibility: "It may not be wise to commit yourself to your position, but it is wise to commit yourself to your interests. This is the place . . . to spend your aggressive energies" (p. 55).

A firm but conciliatory strategy is often employed with success in child rearing. Wise parents are strict and even punitive about ethical standards and such minimal goals as cleanliness, safety, and parental peace of mind. Their children are urged to order their lives within the framework of these values and disciplined for moving outside of them. Yet the same parents are concerned about their children's welfare, so they are flexible about the means by which their values are achieved, allowing and even helping their children to accomplish the children's own goals within the framework of the parents' values. For example, a father may be strict with his son about straightening up his room yet lenient about when and how this work will be done. The result of such an approach is likely to be conformity to parental values, high joint benefit, and a good relationship between parent and child.

Structuring the Agenda

The firm but conciliatory approach and the step model to which it is related are useful for dealing with either a single issue or a small group of related issues. But when many issues are being discussed in a joint problem-solving session, an agenda must be developed specifying the order in which the issues are to be taken up. Three guidelines for constructing such an agenda can be stated.

The first is that it often makes sense to put easier issues earlier in an agenda. This is because the success of problem solving is to some extent cumulative, in the sense that earlier achievement establishes the impression that later achievement is possible—that there is integrative potential. (We spoke of this impression as "momentum" in Chapter 3.)

For solutions involving logrolling to emerge from a problem-solving discussion, it is necessary for several issues to be under consideration at the same time, so that concessions on one issue can be traded for concessions on another. This implies the second guideline, that it is often desirable to expand the agenda to include seemingly extraneous matters. In doing so, problem solvers must be careful not to slip into the error of insisting that all issues be resolved before agreement is reached on any one issue. We are advocating discussing a number of issues in the same session, not trying to resolve them all.

The third guideline is useful when the agenda contains such a large number of items that logrolling opportunities may be missed because the issues on which it is possible to trade concessions are considered at different times. To avoid settling for a less attractive solution in such a situation, it may be possible at the beginning of problem solving to adopt the ground rule that no element of the agreement is finally approved until all issues have been thoroughly discussed. This allows earlier issues to be reconsidered in the light of later issues.

Searching for a Formula

When complex issues are under consideration, a twofold approach is often essential. The early stages of problem solving must be devoted to devising an overarching formula—a brief statement of common objectives that can serve as a road map to the eventual agreement. Only then is it possible to devise an efficient agenda for working out the details of the agreement (Zartman, 1977). If a formula is not developed, the proceedings are likely to get so mired down in details that momentum is lost and the parties withdraw or resort to a contentious approach.

An example of such a formula is the basic agreement in the Camp David talks between Israel and Egypt. In essence, Israel agreed to withdraw from the Sinai and begin talks about Palestinian autonomy in exchange for a peace treaty with Egypt. This formula was somewhat expanded in the Camp David Accords and became the basis for many years of further negotiation.

Breaking Linkages

Totally integrative solutions, in which both parties get all they were seeking, occasionally occur; but such agreements are quite rare. It is usually necessary for one or both parties to make selective concessions in search of a partially integrative solution. They must give up certain demands, diminish certain aspirations, or compromise certain values, while firmly adhering to others.

Demands, goals, aspirations, and values often come in bundles in the sense of being psychologically linked to other demands, goals, aspirations, and values. Hence, in order to make a concession, a process of unlinking must often take place in which some items in a bundle are psychologically separated from others. For example, consider the conflict between the son who wants a motorcycle and the father who opposes this purchase. There may be a close link in the son's thinking between making noise and making an impression on other people. To resolve the controversy, someone (such as his mother) must tell him, "It's not necessary to make noise to get attention." Another example concerns the married couple who disagree about where to go on vacation. If they cannot find a solution like those discussed earlier, unlinking may be helpful. Most couples assume that they must take a vacation together; that is, they link the concept of vacation to that of togetherness. Separating these concepts may yield the most integrative solution possible for some couples. It is not always necessary to go on vacation together.

In summary, the following four-step sequence of moves is suggested for problem solvers who are seeking integrative agreements: (1) Examine the situation to be sure that there is a conflict of interest. (2) Set reasonably high aspirations and be ready to stick to them. (3) Search for alternatives that satisfy both parties' aspirations. (4) If the third step fails to achieve a settlement, lower your own aspirations or your conception of the other party's aspirations and search some more. These recommendations imply a firm but conciliatory policy, in which a problem solver works hard to satisfy both parties' aspirations. Other advice to problem solvers is that they should put easier issues earlier in the agenda and expand the agenda to include issues that permit the exchange of concessions. When many issues are under consideration, it is advisable to search first for an overarching formula and to adopt the ground rule of not reaching an agreement on any issue until all issues have been discussed. To reach an integrative agreement, it is often necessary to break psychological linkages that make things seem to go together naturally.

COVERT PROBLEM SOLVING

Problem-solving behavior obviously makes a lot of sense in many situations. But what if Other has adopted a contentious approach and is unwilling to engage in problem solving? Might Party's problem-solving efforts be misinterpreted or exploited?

The answer to this question is yes. There are three risks in problem solving. All problem-solving behavior poses the risk of *image loss*—that is, a perception that Party is weak and irresolute and hence willing to make extensive concessions. This perception can actually undermine problem solving by encouraging Other to adopt contentious behavior in an effort to persuade Party to make those concessions. There is also some risk of *position loss* if Party, in pursuing a solution to the problem, makes tentative suggestions of possible options. Position loss is a perception by Other that Party has conceded from a previous position. A third risk is *information loss,* which can occur if Party talks about his or her interests or reveals information about his or her lower limit. The danger of providing such information is that Other may be able to use it to fashion threats or noncontingent commitments.

One solution to the problem of image loss, position loss, and information loss is to employ covert forms of problem solving. It is possible to conceive of a continuum of problem-solving tactics, ranging from the highly overt to the highly covert. On the overt end are such moves as openly engaging in a discussion of possible alternatives, making a concession on one issue in the hope of receiving a reciprocal concession on another issue, and proposing a compromise or integrative solution. On the covert end, there are three basic kinds of tactics: back-channel contacts, the use of intermediaries, and efforts to send signals to Other. Such tactics allow Party to explore possible problem solutions or to move toward overt problem solving without prematurely tipping his or her hand. If Party discovers, through such explorations, that Other is ready to accept a solution that is also acceptable to Party or to join in a problem solving process, Party can then become more overt—confident that there is no need to worry about image loss, position loss, or information loss.

Another value of covert problem solving is its compatibility with contentious behavior. If Party wants to explore the feasibility of problem solving or of certain problem solutions while maintaining an overtly contentious stance, covert problem solving is the answer. The point is that there are psychological contradictions between overt problem solving and highly contentious behavior. The attitudes required for these two kinds of performance are different. Covert problem solving is easier to reconcile with contentious behavior because it involves less commitment to cooperation. It is also less jarring for constituents if they are dedicated to a belligerent campaign. It is hard to rally one's forces around the battle cry that the other side is partly right. Hence leaders are often overtly contentious while engaging in covert problem solving—out of sight of their constituents.

It follows that covert problem solving is commonly found after a period of escalation when the conflicting parties have moved into stalemate. Each separately is groping for a different approach, but neither is fully clear about the other's frame of mind. Is the adversary ready for problem solving? If I make conciliatory moves, will he or she reciprocate or simply exploit my initiatives and turn them to competitive advantage? By employing covert initiatives, the parties can test each other's interest in problem solving without taking undue risks. If the other party "passes the test," they can then turn with confidence to more overt forms of problem solving.

If covert approaches were not available, stalemates would often be insoluble despite both parties' desire for problem solving, because neither party would have a low-risk way of checking out the other's readiness to cooperate.

The three types of covert problem solving behavior will now be described in greater detail.

Back-Channel Contacts

Back-channel contacts consist of informal problem-solving discussions behind the scenes. Such discussions usually involve a small number of people and often take place in relaxed and neutral settings, such as bars. Back-channel contacts commonly occur during negotiation, while seemingly rigid, contentious posturing is taking place on the official level. Reports of such contacts are found in accounts of negotiation in the international (Alger, 1961), industrial (Douglas, 1962) and domestic commercial (Pruitt, 1971) arenas. They were especially important during the Iranian hostage negotiations. Such contacts provide a more flexible arena for the development of integrative solutions than is usually available at the negotiating table. Back-channel contacts are also found outside the context of formal negotiation. For example, secret meetings between Secretary of State Henry Kissinger and Premier Chou En-lai laid the groundwork for President Nixon's trip to China, which was the watershed for improved Sino-American relations in the 1970s.

Back-channel contacts reduce the three risks mentioned earlier. Position loss is seldom a problem, because both parties ordinarily understand that ideas mentioned in a private discussion are not official positions unless or until they are formally labeled as such. Image loss and information loss cannot be completely averted, but they can be minimized by arranging for the participants to speak for themselves as individuals rather than for their organizations. This reduces the likelihood that their problem-solving activities will be seen as a sign that their constituents are ready to capitulate, or that information about the needs and values of their constituents will be derived from what they say. Additional insurance against these latter losses can be achieved by assigning to back-channel meetings lower-status members of the organizations (such as technical experts) who are capable of problem solving but cannot be assumed to speak definitively for their superiors.

There are certain trade-offs in assigning low-level personnel to such meetings and allowing participants to speak for themselves. Image loss and information loss are indeed minimized, but there is also a danger that these people will be less capable of engaging in effective problem solving because they are not fully acquainted with their organization's perspective or are not fully be-lieved when they speak about this matter. This danger can be minimized by a two-step progression in which informal problem-solving discussions are fol-lowed by more formal meetings where actual commitments can be made. The informal discussions make their contribution by increasing both parties' assur-ance that the other party is genuinely interested in problem solving and by indentifying possible directions in which the final agreement can go. The for-mal discussions put the finishing touches, and the official stamp of approval, on the agreement.

Back-channel meetings also have the virtue of being out of the public eye. Hence the participants can reveal information and take positions without worrying about the reactions of allies, third parties, and (to some extent) con-stituents. This allows a degree of flexibility that may not be possible in more open contexts.

Use of Intermediaries

When the risks seem too great for back-channel meetings, or when it is impos-sible for the parties to make direct contact, intermediaries can sometimes be used for problem solving. For example, an American newsman, John Scali, carried messages back and forth between the governments of the United States and the Soviet Union during the Cuban missile crisis (Young, 1968). A similar function was served by Christian Bourguet and Hector Villalon, a French lawyer and an Argentine businessman, respectively, during the nego-tiations that freed the American hostages in Iran (ABC News, 1981). Extended chains of intermediaries are sometimes necessary when the parties have very poor relations with each other. Thus, during the Vietnam War, a chain went from the United States government through officials in Great Britain to offi-cials in eastern Europe and finally to the government of North Vietnam (Kras-low & Loory, 1968). The relations between the parties at each link of this chain were better than the relations between the United States and North Vietnam.

Intermediaries provide greater protection against image loss and informa-tion loss than is found in back-channel meetings, because it is even less clear whether they represent the thinking of the people who sent them. If they seem soft, one cannot be sure that the other party is ready to make deep con-cessions; if they reveal information about underlying interests, one cannot be sure that it is accurate and hence that one can use it for constructing threats. Yet intermediaries are often able to find enough common ground and provide enough assurance of the other side's commitment to problem solving to make it seem worthwhile to launch more direct contacts.

Sending Conciliatory Signals

Conciliatory signals (also called tacit communication or sign language) are hints of a willingness to make a particular concession or to take some other cooperative action. Recall our description in Chapter 6 of Fischer and Spassky negotiating a draw in their chess match. Or consider Peters' (1952) account of an exchange between negotiators for labor and management—after a mediator had just suggested a compromise raise of 9 cents per hour:

> Frazier and Turner looked each other in the eye. Somewhere a communication established itself without a word between them. The question in each other's eye was, "If I move to 9 cents will you move to 9 cents?" Frazier said, "Well we are willing to give it some consideration for the sake of averting a strike." Turner nodded his acquiescence. The tension was gone as he buzzed his secretary to come in and take down a memorandum of agreement (p. 18).

Both the glances and the tentative statement by Frazier can be regarded as signals. The latter signal was less ambiguous than the former, presumably because the glances convinced Frazier that the risks were small enough so that he could afford to gamble on a tentative endorsement of the mediator's suggestions. Ping-pong-like sequences such as this, advancing to greater and greater clarity, are very common in conversations by signaling.

An effective signal must be both noticeable and disavowable. The latter is necessary so that image loss and position loss are minimized in the event that the other party is not ready to accept the proposal implied by the signal. One must be ready and able to deny that one intended to send a signal if the other party turns out to be uninterested in exchanging concessions. Otherwise one's negotiation position may be weakened.

Conciliatory signals are useful for sending up trial balloons about proposed compromises or integrative solutions. They are also useful for proposing that joint problem solving begin while minimizing image loss if Other is not interested. However, unlike back-channel contacts and the activities of intermediaries, signals cannot contribute directly to the development of new ideas for integrative solutions.

In summary, covert problem solving is often employed where there is fear of image loss, position loss, or information loss. This kind of activity takes three forms: back-channel contacts, sending messages through intermediaries, and sending conciliatory signals.

STRATEGIES FOR PERSUADING OTHER TO ENGAGE IN PROBLEM SOLVING

When Party is ready for problem solving (whether because of being in a perceived stalemate or because of feeling a genuine interest in Other's welfare), it is helpful if Other is also ready for problem solving. This is so for two reasons. First, Party can now employ more overt forms of problem-solving tactics, confident that Other will not take advantage of them. Such tactics are usually more effective. Second, joint problem solving—wherein the two parties exchange information about their values and perceptions and work together in search of a jointly acceptable solution—is usually more efficient than individual problem solving. If the two parties can talk things over, they can develop a search model that will represent a true melding of their separate interests.

As mentioned earlier, if Party is uncertain about Other's readiness for problem solving, he or she often adopts covert moves to explore this readiness. However, this is not the only possible approach. Party can sometimes actually take the initiative and try to convert Other to problem solving.

A major key to success in the latter enterprise is for Party to adopt *overtly* a firm but conciliatory stance (Komorita & Esser, 1975; McGillicuddy, Pruitt, & Syna, 1984). Earlier we argued that a firm but conciliatory stance is efficient in generating creative solutions. What we are arguing now is that such a stance, *if clearly telegraphed to Other*, encourages Other to follow Party into problem solving.

Our reasoning is as follows: The firm part of this strategy is needed to persuade Other that contentious tactics are infeasible, because Party is unalterably committed to achieving his or her basic interests, and to prevent Other from misinterpreting the conciliatory parts of Party's message as signs of weakness. The conciliatory part of this strategy is needed to convince Other that there is integrative potential in the situation—that Party can be trusted to help find a reasonable solution to the problems at hand and not to revert to contentious behavior if Other decides to initiate problem solving (see the discussion of trust in Chapter 3). There is a bumper sticker that says "Courtesy is catching." We are arguing that good problem solving is catching too.

An example of a firm but conciliatory stance can be seen in the statements made and the actions taken by President John F. Kennedy in 1961 during the Second Berlin Crisis. The Russians, under Premier Nikita Khrushchev, had been trying to end American occupation of West Berlin—and hence to end the rapid flight of skilled personnel from East Germany—by threatening to sign a separate peace treaty with East Germany and buzzing planes in the Berlin Corridor. Recognizing that some concessions had to be made, Kennedy "decided to be firm on essentials but negotiate on non-essentials" (Snyder & Diesing, 1977, p. 566). In a speech delivered on July 25, he announced three fundamental principles that ensured the integrity and continued American occupation of West Berlin. The firmness of these principles was underscored by a pledge to defend them by force and a concomitant military buildup. Yet Kennedy also indicated flexibility and a concern about Russian sensitivities by calling for negotiations to remove "actual irritants" to the Soviet Union and its allies. Two results were achieved. One was the building of the Berlin Wall. At the time, this action was seen in the West as a contentious move by the Soviet Union. But in retrospect, it can be viewed as an outcome of problem solving, because it was the culmination of a sequence of public statements on both sides hinting at the desirability of building a wall (Pruitt & Holland, 1972). It solved both parties' problems, stopping the population loss from East Germany without disturbing American rights in West Berlin. The second result was eventual negotiations, which made these American rights explicit in writing.

Specific guidelines for demonstrating that one has adopted the two sides of the firm but conciliatory stance are explored in the next four subsections.

Signaling Firmness

Our analysis suggests a variety of ways in which Party can signal a firm commitment to his or her basic interests. One is to make a vigorous verbal defense of these interests. A second is to be unwilling to make unilateral concessions (Komorita & Esser, 1975). A third is to arrange for one's constituents to make tough statements and to make it clear that one is accountable to these constituents (Wall, 1977). A fourth is to develop a moderate amount of threat capacity (Lindskold & Bennett, 1973) sufficient to impress Other with Party's firmness but not so formidable as to provoke Other into adopting fear-based countermeasures.

It may sometimes also be necessary to employ contentious tactics in order to underscore firmness with respect to basic principles. This can be particularly important when Party has recently yielded ground. Otherwise, Other may interpret Party's flexibility as a sign of weakness, maintain or raise his or her aspirations, and redouble his or her dedication to a contentious approach. Kennedy's performance is again a good example. His pledge to use force if necessary to defend Western rights in Berlin and the concomitant American military buildup served this function. Contentious tactics are also sometimes needed in conjunction with problem-solving overtures to motivate Other to take enough of an interest in Party's welfare to engage in problem solving.

In recommending the use of contentious tactics, we are mindful of the many problems associated with these tactics. Using these tactics can undermine problem solving by encouraging both the user and the target to become more rigid in their positions. These tactics also tend to alienate the target and hence to encourage the development of conflict spirals. In short, contentious tactics have the capacity of both contributing to and detracting from the development of mutually acceptable solutions. How can one obtain the advantages of these tactics while avoiding the pitfalls? There are at least four answers to this question.

1. Use contentious tactics to defend basic interests rather than a particular solution to the controversy. Thus Kennedy defended the American presence in Berlin without prejudging particular arrangements.
2. Send signals of flexibility and of concern about Other's interests in conjunction with contentious displays. Kennedy did this by offering to negotiate about "actual irritants." Such maneuvers are designed to make the integrative potential appear great enough to Other so that problem solving seems warranted.
3. Insulate contentious behavior from conciliatory behavior so that neither part of the strategy undermines the other. The most common form of insulation is the "bad cop/good cop" routine,[2] in which contentious behavior is assigned to one team member (the "bad cop") and problem-solving behavior to another (the "good cop").

[2]Also called the "black hat/white hat" and the "bad guy/good guy" routine.

In the context of the bad cop's threats, the good cop's offer of cooperation is more likely to be reciprocated by the target. In the context of the good cop's blandishments, the bad cop's escalation is less likely to produce a reciprocal escalation by the target. An example is the collection agent who indicates to a laggard creditor that his or her principal will sue unless the two of them can reach a mutually acceptable agreement.

4. Employ deterrent rather than compellent threats. Compellent threats require that Other adopt a specific option. Deterrent threats rule out an action or solution favored by Other but do not comment on the adequacy of other options, allowing Other to choose among them. For example, a mother who is losing sleep because of her son's late hours would be better advised to threaten to punish him for making noise (a deterrent threat) than for failing to come home on time (a compellent threat). In short, deterrent threats involve saying "no" to the other party without demanding that the other say "yes."

Signaling Conciliatory Intentions

Flexibility about the shape of the final agreement and concern about Other's outcomes can be signaled in a number of ways:

- Openly express concern about Other's welfare; "acknowledge their interests as part of the problem" (Fisher & Ury, 1981, p. 55).
- Indicate a willingness to change one's proposals if a way can be found to bridge the two parties' interests.
- Demonstrate problem-solving capacity—for example, by assembling an expert negotiating team so that it is obvious to Other that one has the capacity to develop useful new ideas.
- Maintain open communication channels to show Other that one is ready for cooperation.
- Reward Other for taking any cooperative initiatives (Deutsch, 1973).
- Reexamine any elements of one's supposed interests that are clearly unacceptable to Other to be sure that they are essential to one's welfare. If they turn out to be low in priority to oneself, it may be possible to drop them. If they turn out to be high in priority, it may be possible to discover interests underlying these interests that are not incompatible with Other's stance.

Unilateral Initiatives

Conciliatory signals are not always successful (LeBow, Jervis & Stein, 1984). One major problem with them is that Other may be so deeply suspicious of Party's goodwill that a simple show of flexibility and concern is not sufficient to break through. Osgood (1962, 1966) has outlined a general strategy that can be used at such times to underline one's conciliatory intentions. This strategy, which is called "Graduated and Reciprocated Initiatives in Tension-reduction" or simply "GRIT," requires Party to take a unilateral series of trust-building initiatives within the framework of certain rules. As summarized by Lindskold (1978), these rules are as follows:

1. The series of initiatives should be announced ahead of time in an effort to reduce tension.

2. Each initiative should be labeled as part of this series.
3. The announced timetable should be observed.
4. The target should be invited to reciprocate each initiative.
5. The series of initiatives should be continued for a while even if there is no reciprocation.
6. The initiatives should be clear-cut and susceptible to verification.
7. The strategist should retain a capacity to retaliate should the target respond by becoming more contentious.
8. The strategist should retaliate if the target becomes contentious.
9. The initiatives should be of various kinds, so that all they have in common is their cooperative nature.
10. The target should be rewarded for cooperating, the level of reward being pegged to the target's level of cooperation.

An example of a unilateral initiative can be seen in Egyptian President Sadat's dramatic 1977 flight to Jerusalem. Sadat said that his trip was designed to reduce tensions (that is, to improve Israeli trust in Egypt) so as to pave the way for negotiations. He apparently viewed the prior escalation between the two countries as mainly due to a conflict spiral in which the countries were alternately antagonizing each other. Not all of the Osgood rules were followed, but Sadat did announce his peaceful intentions ahead of time (rule 1) and he called for reciprocity (rule 4). The success of his trip can probably also be explained as due to the operation of some of the principles of attribution theory (Kelley, 1971). By making his trip, Sadat clearly suffered severe costs in terms of alienation from the rest of the Arab world and from some of his own citizens. Hence, as predicated by the augmentation principle, it was hard to doubt the genuineness of his interest in peace. Furthermore, it must have been hard for the Israelis to develop a rationale for explaining his trip in any other way. For example, it could not be seen as an act of obeisance, because Egypt was not in a militarily weak position compared to Israel. Hence, as predicted by the discounting principle, his trip appears to have engendered considerable trust among Israelis (Kelman, 1984). The development of this trust did not guarantee solution to all problems, but it contributed to the initiation and success of the subsequent negotiation.

It is important to note that Sadat made his trip to Jerusalem after the 1973 war. If he had done so before that war, it is questionable whether Israel would have responded in a conciliatory way. Before the war Egypt seemed militarily weak, so it seems unlikely that Israel saw itself as deadlocked in a no-win struggle with Egypt. Israel was "top dog" in the Middle East and had little reason for wanting to find a jointly acceptable solution to the Egyptian problem. Furthermore, Sadat's initiatives might well have been interpreted in Israel as manifestations of weakness rather than as evidence of a change of heart. But after the war, Israel was ready for problem solving.

The point is that GRIT is more likely to work—to elicit problem-solving behavior from Other—when it is part of a firm but conciliatory package. In addition to demonstrating trustworthiness, Party should demonstrate strength and a dedication to his or her own basic interests. This enhances the likelihood that Other will be motivated to reciprocate Party's conciliatory initiatives.

To summarize, it seems reasonable in most circumstances for Party to try to convert Other to problem solving—to persuade Other to work on Party's needs as well as Other's. This can often be done by adopting a manifestly firm yet conciliatory stance. Party must demonstrate to Other that Party is firm about defending basic interests *yet* flexible about the means for their defense and concerned about Other's interests as well. To send a message of firmness, it is sometimes necessary to use contentious tactics, but this should be done in such a way as to avoid unduly antagonizing Other. Conciliatory messages are often hard to get across because of the suspicion inherent in escalated conflict. Hence it is sometimes necessary to employ a dramatic and concerted tension-reducing program that involves striking unilateral initiatives such as that taken by Sadat in his 1977 trip to Jerusalem.

CONCLUSIONS: THE DEBATE BETWEEN THE HAWKS AND THE DOVES

Most communities (small groups, organizations, and nations) contain subgroups of hawks and doves who take opposing positions with respect to external relations. The hawks favor a tough, contentious defense of collective interests; the doves favor negotiation and problem solving with the outgroup in question. Our analysis of the importance of being firm but conciliatory suggests that both factions are needed to conduct external relations sanely: doves to work out agreements and hawks to avoid giving away the store.

Groups in conflict usually try to conceal the hawk–dove debate in an effort to present a united front to the adversary. Yet research suggests that revealing such internal divisions is more likely to encourage the outgroup to make a cooperative response than concealing them is (Jacobson, 1981). The presence of hawks sends a message of firmness and determination, while the presence of doves sends a message of readiness for conciliation. The convergence of these two messages encourages the outgroup to cooperate, so it is wise to show that the ingroup consists of both kinds of birds. This effect should be even stronger if one can demonstrate that these two factions are about equal in political strength—and hence that contentious behavior from the outgroup will backfire by leading to the ascendancy of the hawks, whereas cooperative behavior will be rewarded by encouraging political triumph by the doves. This effect is closely related to that produced by the bad cop/good cop routine described earlier.

In this chapter we have demonstrated the importance of problem solving as a technique for settling conflict. However, it is not always possible for the parties to a conflict to take this approach. Escalation may have made them too rigid and suspicious of one another to embark on such a course, or they may have little faith in the integrative potential of their situation. In such circumstances, it is often necessary to involve third parties in the controversy, a topic to which we now turn.

CHAPTER 10

The Intervention of Third Parties

In the course of this book, we have seen that people in the throes of escalation become heavily invested in waging conflict. Positions tend toward rigidity because the protagonists are reluctant to budge lest any conciliatory gesture be misconstrued as a sign of weakness. Moreover, the parties may lack the imagination, creativity, and/or experience necessary to work their way out of the pit they have jointly engineered—not because they don't want to, but because they don't know how. Thus, for a variety of reasons, disputants are sometimes either unable or unwilling to move toward agreement of their own accord. Under these circumstances, third parties often become involved at the behest of one or more of the disputants, or on their own initiative.

In this chapter, we examine more closely the important role played by third parties, particularly mediators.[1] We begin by considering what is meant by a third party and what it is about their very existence and inclusion in a conflict that has transforming implications. Next we review the range and variety of third-party roles that exist in interpersonal, intergroup, and international settings. Then we take a closer look at the kinds of things that third parties can do to bring about more effective dispute settlement. In other words, we try to address the important question of exactly how third parties can help. We conclude by examining some of the limits of third-party intervention—the circumstances in which such outside intervention is likely to prove ineffectual or even destructive.

WHAT IS A THIRD PARTY?

Stated most simply, a *third party* is an individual or collective that is external to a dispute between two or more others and that tries to help the disputants reach agreement.

It should be noted that the mere presence of a third party is likely to profoundly change the relationship between the disputants. Under most circumstances, such change is likely to be beneficial. The destructive path of

---

[1]Reviews of the theoretical and research literature on third-party functions will be found in Bercovitch (1984), Fisher (1983), Pruitt (1981), Rubin (1980, 1981), and Wall (1981).

the principals' escalating conflict is diverted, at least momentarily, by the third party's inclusion. The bluffs, threats, lies, and promises that characterize each disputant's efforts to prevail in an escalating struggle are apt to be interrupted by the third party's presence. This can help to shift the disputants in the direction of settlement. However, there are times when inclusion of the third party may have detrimental effects, such as when it occurs in the midst of efforts by the disputants to work directly toward settlement. In other words, a third party's involvement in a conflictual relationship that is characterized by genuine and effective movement toward settlement of differences may have the costly effect of breaking a newly established—and possibly quite fragile—momentum toward agreement.

The more general point is that *third-party intervention is not a panacea in conflict resolution.* Throughout this chapter we shall continue to hammer away at this important point. Third-party intervention is probably best likened to a strong medicine that may have undesirable side effects and that should therefore be employed with caution and some reluctance. The best, most effective third party is the one who becomes involved only when needed and who is so successful at helping the principals find a settlement and develop a working relationship with each other that they no longer need or want his or her services.

THE RANGE AND VARIETY OF THIRD-PARTY ROLES

As long as people have existed on this planet, they have managed to find ways of waging conflict. On occasion, as we have already seen, these competitive struggles have been pursued to the point of deadlock, where neither party finds contentious behavior of any further use because neither is able or willing to yield. It is at this point that third parties often become involved, and their input constitutes an important form of problem-solving behavior.

Third parties have probably been in business since the dawn of humanity; their various roles are well documented in such sources as *The Bible, The Iliad,* and *The Odyssey.* In examining the range and variety of these third-party roles, it may be useful to distinguish among a set of dimensions. The seven cited below are but a few of the many possibilities.

Formal vs. Informal Roles. The roles of many (perhaps most) third parties are defined on the basis of some formal understanding among the disputants or on the basis of legal precedents or licensing/certification procedures. Examples of such third-party roles are those of *mediator* (a person who attempts to help the principals reach a voluntary agreement), *arbitrator* (a person empowered to make binding recommendations for the settlement of a dispute), and *ombudsperson* (an individual charged with the resolution of conflicts that arise between individuals and institutions). Such formal third-party roles are likely to prove effective to the extent that they are acknowledged by the disputants as implying a legitimate right to be in the business of resolving conflicts.

In contrast are those more informal third-party roles, such as *intermediary* (a person whose job it is to communicate messages back and forth between the principals) and *special envoy* (a person dispatched to convey a particular message on behalf of one of the parties). Unlike their more formal counterparts, informal third parties typically function behind the scenes, out of the glare of the spotlight. During the 1979–80 Iranian hostage crisis, an Argentine businessman (Hector Villalon) and a French lawyer (Christian Bourguet) played two of the most important informal third-party roles: They served as behind-the-scene conduits between Iran and the United States at a time when all formal communication between the two nations had officially ground to a halt. Informal third parties can thus be enormously helpful and important in the shaping of a settlement, especially when the more formal roles have been discounted because the conflict is so intense that direct, public communication is deemed unacceptable.

Individual vs. Representative Roles. Third parties most often act as individuals, reflecting their own idiosyncratic points of view and concerns. On occasion, particularly in complex disputes involving multiple parties, such as labor-management negotiations or international affairs, third parties occupy representative roles instead. As representatives, such third-party intervenors speak for the interests of a constituency and can convey all the clout and legitimacy attendant on being the spokesperson for a potentially vast organization. For example, the Secretary of State of the United States, attempting to intervene in an international dispute between two nations, can do so with the full power of the United States squarely behind him.

As this illustration makes clear, however, a representative third-party role is likely to prove effective—even more effective than an individual role—only so long as the constituency represented is seen by the principals as having legitimate rights and interests. To the extent that such perceived legitimacy is absent, the representative role may prove quite ineffective. During the Iranian hostage crisis, for example, the United Nations Secretary-General (Kurt Waldheim) was quite ineffective in his intervention attempts, precisely because he was regarded by the Iranians as a representative of an illegitimate organization. Bourguet and Villalon could succeed as private individuals where representative third parties such as Waldheim inevitably failed.

Invited vs. Noninvited Roles. It often happens that a third party intervenes at the request of one or both of the principals, such as when the members of a divorcing couple agree to seek out the services of a divorce mediator. When this happens, the third party's recommendations are likely to prove quite effective, other things being equal, for two reasons. First, the invitation to intervene suggests that at least one of the parties is motivated to address the dispute in question. Second, the invitation makes the third party appropriate, acceptable, or desirable, thereby increasing the intervenor's clout and legitimacy.

In contrast are those uninvited roles, in which a third party (such as a bystander witnessing a playground tussle between two children) spontaneously intervenes or does so by virtue of legal requirement. Such uninvited third parties have none of the automatic benefit accruing to their invited counterparts, but they may nevertheless prove effective. This is especially likely to be so when the disputants regard the uninvited third party as impartial and genuinely motivated to help. Many an urban struggle has been resolved through the uninvited intervention of a prominent citizen who has offered to help identify the issues and to propose alternative settlements.

Impartial vs. Partial Roles. All other things equal, a third party who is seen as impartial is more likely to be successful than one who is not. However, impartiality is by no means an absolute requirement for effectiveness—and fortunately so, because impartiality in a third party may prove impossible to obtain. As Fisher (1981) points out, people in conflict often expect a third party to be some sort of "eunuch from Mars," but such pure, dispassionate, and disinterested individuals rarely exist. Instead third parties tend to have interests and areas of partiality that need to be taken into account, and that may even prove to be of some benefit in the dispute settlement process.

In addition, because of the value of power equality for conflict resolution, it is not unusual for third parties to take sides in the controversies they are mediating. As we saw in our earlier discussion of stalemate (Chapter 8), before people in conflict are motivated to work toward settlement, they often need to feel that they and their adversary are relatively equal in power. One of the things that a third party can do in this regard is to offset what appears to be a situation of power disparity by siding with the less powerful disputant, at least temporarily. Disputants who see themselves as equal in power are more likely to view the situation as in stalemate, which encourages them to employ problem-solving tactics, including collaboration with the third party. For example, by suggesting that discussions take place on the home turf of the weaker party, or even by appearing to favor the interests and positions of this less powerful disputant, the third party may be able to create more nearly ideal conditions for joint problem solving.

Advisory vs. Directive Roles. Sometimes third parties are placed in the position of giving advice only (mediators); on other occasions they are allowed to be directive (arbitrators). Third-party directiveness is sometimes needed, as when the principals are so hostile or have such high limits that they are incapable of reaching agreement. But third-party directiveness also has its drawbacks. Solutions devised by arbitrators are less likely to be integrative, in the sense of synthesizing the two parties' interests, than are those devised by the principals with the aid of a mediator. This is because the principals usually know their own interests better than any third party can. Also, the principals are more likely to be identified with agreements of their own devising—they can see the solution as their own, not the third party's. Both because the solutions tend to be integrative and because the parties tend to feel ownership, agreements reached through mediation tend to last longer than those reached through arbitration.

In general, then, the most effective third party is the one who exercises as little power as necessary in order to move the disputants in the direction of settling their differences.

Interpersonal vs. Intergroup Roles. Third parties, such as couple therapists, divorce mediators, and judges, typically intervene in disputes between individuals. Just as important, and far more complex, are instances of third-party intervention in disputes between groups and between nations. Sometimes these are disguised as disputes between individuals, but the individuals must still get agreement from other people (called constituents) to whom they are beholden. Whether disguised or not, constituent preferences must be taken into account, as any labor mediator will surely attest. Only a foolish labor mediator would assume that a strike can be resolved simply by meeting with the representatives of each side without taking into account the constituency pressures to which each side is subject.

Content-oriented vs. Process-oriented Roles. Some third-party roles focus primarily on the content of a dispute: the issues or substance under consideration. Others focus more on the process of decision making—the way in which discussions are taking place—quite independent of the substance of any possible agreements. Arbitrators and (to a lesser extent) mediators typically assume a content orientation, whereas marriage counselors and couple therapists assume more of a process focus. Whereas a content-oriented third party is likely to take charge of a dispute and try to push it toward settlement, a more process-oriented third party is likely instead to do whatever is necessary to help the disputants take charge of their own conflict and take care of themselves.

There are parallels between the advisory-directive dimension and the content-process distinction. Just as a directive third party is likely to produce more immediate dispute-settlement results than a more advisory intervenor, so too is a content focus likely to engender a quicker settlement than a process focus. Similarly, the process oriented third party, like the third party with the advisory, light touch, may be able to facilitate the development of agreements that are longer lasting and more satisfying to the principals involved largely because it is the principals, themselves, who have engineered an agreement.

EFFECTIVE THIRD-PARTY INTERVENTION

In this section, we shall develop the position that there are three kinds of things that third parties can do to intervene effectively: modify the physical and social structure of the dispute, alter the issue structure of the dispute, and take action to increase the parties' motivation to take their dispute seriously.

Modification of Physical and Social Structure

Third parties who wish to move the disputants closer to settlement can modify the physical and/or social structure of the conflict in many ways. The possibilities for such modification include structuring communication between the principals, opening and neutralizing the site in which problem solving takes place, imposing time limits, and infusing additional resources. Let us now consider each of these forms of physical and social modification in turn.

Communication.   At first blush it appears that a third party would be well advised to encourage communication between the disputants under any and all circumstances. What better way for parties to work through a conflict than by openly airing their differences? Unfortunately, social psychological research does not bear this out. Experiments by Krauss and Deutsch (1966) and others indicate that communication between people in conflict *does* help, but only so long as the intensity of the conflict is relatively small—in other words, hostility is low and the perceived common ground is large. Under these circumstances, the principals are likely to use the opportunity or requirement of communication for joint problem solving in order to work through those few differences that separate them and forge agreement.

Under conditions of intense escalated conflict, however, quite the reverse occurs. When required or encouraged to communicate with each other, people in an intense conflict use this opportunity to heap abuse on each other, to insult their adversary and his or her kinfolk, and to make an already bad interpersonal situation even worse. Under such circumstances, a third party would be well advised to actively prevent direct communication between the principals until a point is reached where it appears that such communication will improve the situation rather than exacerbate it.

When direct communication is ill advised, there are things a third party can do, working separately with the two principals, that will allow them to make better use of later communication opportunities. One is to try to improve the two parties' images of each other. In addition, the third party can play an educational role. In their classic research on the effects of communication in conflict-intensified relationships, Krauss and Deutsch (1966) found that conflict abated only when a third party (the experimenter in this case) actively tutored the disputants in the effective use of communication. In particular, it was only when the experimenter taught the disputants how to take the role of the other, to place themselves in the other person's shoes, and to understand the issues as the other person might that their competitive struggle ended. The same sort of effect has been observed in the more recent, potentially very important research of Herbert C. Kelman and his colleagues (Cohen, et al., 1977; Kelman, 1972; Kelman & Cohen, 1976). In one recent study, for example, four Israeli, four Egyptian, and four Palestinian participants were brought together for a meeting to discuss the ongoing Middle East conflict. By providing the three groups of participants with separate prenegotiation training in communication skills and perspective taking, the participants were better able better able to engage in a constructive discussion of the many differences among them.

In general, then, there are circumstances in which it makes good sense for a third party to bring the disputants together so that direct communication can take place. But there are also important occasions in which the better part of third-party wisdom is to keep them separate and to act as an intermediary who conveys messages back and forth, improves the parties' images of each other, trains them in communication skills, and encourages work on the *way* in which communication is—and ought to be—taking place. The primary advantage of such an arrangement is that it allows the third party to remain firmly in control of the interaction between the disputants. If direct communication is likely to work, the third party should encourage it; but if direct contact is instead likely to worsen matters, it should be discouraged and avoided, at least for a while.

Site Openness. Quite apart from introducing or restricting communication possibilities, an effective third party may be able to generate movement toward agreement by systematically varying the openness and/or neutrality of the site in which discussions between the principals take place. An open site is one that can be readily observed and influenced by a variety of external constituencies, audiences, and other publics. A closed site is characterized by limited access on the part of external observers to the discussions that take place.

An effective third party would do well to advise or require that all early discussions between the disputants take place under closed-site conditions. Only when an agreement has been struck, or is virtually certain to be struck, should the doors to the site be thrown open to the external world. The line of reasoning behind this conclusion is that site openness has the effect of "setting in concrete" whatever moves, gestures, or offers have just occurred. In the presence of an observing audience, including the media, disputants are likely to take far more seriously the image of strength or weakness that they project. As a result, premature site openness is apt to encourage the adoption of tough and intransigent bargaining positions, which make it difficult to reach agreement.

Paradoxically, site openness makes sense at a later time, when settlement is about to be reached. This is because the presence of external observers is likely to commit the parties to their tentative agreement in a way that does not permit facile reversal or subsequent efforts to unravel the agreement.

During the 1978 Camp David negotiations between Israel and Egypt, U.S. President Carter appears to have incorporated into the discussions virtually all aspects of the preceding analysis—and without ever having read our book! Thus, at the outset, and indeed throughout the thirteen days of negotiations, Carter went out of his way to shield Prime Minister Begin of Israel and Egyptian President Sadat from public view. Virtually nothing was made known to the public other than the fact that Begin was watching particular television programs at night, while Sadat was enjoying his stay in a particular cabin in the woods! Only at the conclusion of the meetings, when an agreement had been reached in principle, did the parties surface. At the very end of the negotiation, they appeared on the lawn of the White House, where multiple documents were signed with multiple pens, in full view of a world of onlookers.

Site Neutrality.   Regarding the matter of site neutrality, it is often in the interests of the third party to recommend or impose a site that is not on the home turf of either disputant but on neutral territory. This helps the third party control the access of various observers and/or constituencies to the negotiation, and it also prevents either side from gaining a tactical advantage by virtue of site location. The only exception occurs when one party is much weaker than the other. In that case, the effective third party may do well to offset this power discrepancy by deliberately staging discussions on the home turf of the less powerful party.

Time Limits.   A third party can attempt to get the principals moving by unilaterally suggesting or imposing deadlines. In the face of such time pressure, the disputants are forced to come to grips with the costs that will result if agreement is not reached in time. This makes them more likely to move toward settlement. Moreover, if time is more costly to the more powerful disputant, the third party can further the cause of power equalization by imposing a deadline. As an example of the effectiveness of time limits, consider the deadline imposed by President Carter on Begin and Sadat toward the end of the Camp David talks. Carter indicated that he would have to abandon his mediation and turn to other pressing activities in Washington if they were unable to reach agreement by a certain date. Agreement was reached shortly thereafter.

When imposing a deadline, third parties must be careful not to move too soon. The danger is that they may not give the principals enough time to reduce their aspirations or to engage in the creative thinking necessary to develop an integrative solution. The best advice for third parties is to make such a move at a time when a solution is just around the corner. The effect of such a judicious deadline is to inspire the parties to finish the process rather than waiting endlessly for the other to make the next move. Carter adhered to this principle at Camp David; he announced a deadline only after the negotiators had made considerable progress toward agreement.

Additional Resources.   An effective third party can judiciously manipulate at least three kinds of resources in an effort to generate pressure toward agreement. The first is his or her own time. As we have mentioned, by setting a limit to his or her participation, the third party can sometimes encourage the principals to move off the dead center of stalemate.

A second resource available to the third party is related to our earlier discussion of site openness. The third party often has access to the domain of public sentiment and can unleash the "mad dogs of the media" in an effort to present information about the ongoing discussion in ways that apply pressure for settlement. Thus the third party can reward a disputant for conceding by lavishing public praise on him or her (Wall, 1979). Alternatively, the third party can punish intransigence by judicious public criticism. Mediators worth their salt know the power of a timely press release.

Finally, a third party may be able to engender movement toward settlement by compensating the principals for their concessions. A good example is the role the United States played as mediator between Egypt and Israel over the past 12 years. Again and again the United States has promised military and economic assistance in exchange for flexibility in the negotiations between these countries. Increasing the size of the pie in this way transforms a zero-sum game into a non-zero-sum game, in which both disputants can do well. Of course, only a wealthy third party with a large stake in solution of the controversy will be willing and able to play such a role. This kind of role brings the third party into active negotiation with the two principals in ways that sometimes make it seem like a "three-cornered" conflict (Touval, 1975) rather than a two-sided conflict with third-party assistance.

Successful third parties always run the risk of becoming too important to the principals. Their actions increase the movement toward settlement, of course, but they also create conditions that may invite the principals' continued dependence on the third party. If agreement this time was possible because of third-party assistance, then why not lean on the third party for similar help next time? Moveover, to the extent that the third party compensates the principals for reaching agreement, the infusion of third-party resources may actually encourage a sort of "blackmail." The third party comes to be seen as wanting agreement so badly that he or she can be bullied into providing more and more assistance.

The history of American mediation in the Middle East illustrates these points. Beginning with Kissinger's intervention between 1973 and 1975, and continuing through Carter's assistance at Camp David in 1978, the United States has made it abundantly clear that it would facilitate the settlement process by providing military and economic assistance as needed. Needs have a way of becoming demands, and the Israelis and Egyptians have both proved quite adept at conceding to each other in exchange for American aid. American interest in developing Middle East agreements, and our determination to prevent the Soviet Union from asserting itself in the region, have created a condition that can be viewed as excessive dependence on the third party.

Modification of Issue Structure

As we have seen throughout this book, people in the throes of escalating conflict often lose sight of the issues with which they began their struggle, and they experience a lack of creativity and imagination that deprives them of the opportunity to work their way out of the hole that they have dug for themselves. An effective third party can be most helpful in this regard, assisting the disputants in the identification of existing issues and alternatives, helping them to package and sequence issues in ways that lead toward agreement, and introducing new issues and alternatives that did not occur to the disputants themselves. Let us consider each of these three forms of intervention.

Issue Identification. One of the most useful things a third party can do is help the principals identify the several issues in dispute. Because escalating conflict is often characterized by distorted perceptions of the other party and the issues in question, accurate information about preferences, expectations, and intentions should move the disputants considerably closer to agreement. As a result of issue identification, the principals should be better able to understand which issues require further work and which are easier to address.

Unfortunately, there are also some dangers in issue identification, in that certain issues are best left alone. When the disputants differ substantially on basic values or hold decidedly uncomplimentary views of one another, the third party must be very careful *not* to allow certain issues to come to the fore—lest the result be a rather unproductive explosion.

Closely akin to the matter of issue identification, but less fraught with the danger of backfiring, is third-party education of the disputants about the dynamics of conflict. Kochan and Jick (1978) have observed that third parties can teach bargainers about the general nature of the process in which they are involved and thus help them move more readily toward a mutually acceptable agreement. Similarly, Burton (1969), who has developed a workshop method for studying and resolving international disputes, points to the importance of instruction regarding conflict dynamics. Finally, Fisher and Ury (1981) observe that one of the most useful things a third party can do is help the disputants understand certain key concepts—such as the difference between the positions one takes in public and the interests one holds in private—and the way in which these concepts may be applied to facilitate dispute settlement.

Issue Packaging and Sequencing. Although disputants are occasionally required to address a single, monolithic issue, multiple issues more often exist. Under these conditions the principals—often with the assistance of a skillful third party—must decide whether to address these multiple issues all at once or sequentially.

Social psychological research on the bargaining process (Froman & Cohen, 1970; Kelley, 1966) has consistently indicated that bargainers do better, in terms of the quality of the agreements reached, when they negotiate multiple issues as a package rather than sequentially. Such holistic negotiating allows the principals to explore all possible types of concession exchange and thus, by logrolling (see Chapter 9), come up with a solution that is as close to optimal as possible.

Unfortunately, as issues proliferate, it becomes more and more difficult to deal with them as a package. In such cases, one needs a sequential agenda to keep one's sanity. Two principles should govern the third party's efforts to structure such an agenda. One is that the sequence should run from more general to more specific issues if at all possible—or from formula to detail, in

Zartman's (1977) terminology. This allows the parties to develop a road map before setting out on the difficult trip through the welter of specific issues. The other is that, when there is a choice, easier issues should be tackled earlier in the agenda. Success on these issues generates a running start, a kind of momentum that should carry over to the more intractable later issues and make them seem more amenable to problem solving.

New Issues and Alternatives. Perhaps the most creative thing a third party can do is introduce new issues and alternatives, thereby broadening the disputants' horizons and providing them with ideas for achieving integrative agreements.

Although a third party can introduce new issues and alternatives in a great many ways, several of these methods are particularly important. First, Fisher (1964) has pointed out that a third party may attempt to break a conflictual stalemate by dividing large, all-encompassing issues into smaller, more manageable pieces; Fisher refers to this technique as "fractionation." The 1962 Cuban missile crisis appeared, at first glance, to be comprised of a single issue: the relative toughness or weakness of the United States and the Soviet Union. Over the course of the thirteen days of the conflict, however, this monolithic, zero-sum issue was fractionated by the disputants themselves into a number of sub-issues (timing of missile removal, American compensation for this removal, and so on) that could be negotiated and that led eventually to a peaceful conclusion to the crisis.

Second, a third party may be able to introduce superordinate goals that help the disputants transcend the existing conflict (Sherif and Sherif, 1969). The nations of the Middle East, for example, although they have been at one another's throats for years and are clearly in the throes of an intense competitive struggle, share several concerns that are potentially superordinate in nature. These include a harsh climate, drought, shared economic concerns, and a number of common enemies. At some point, a skillful third party may be able to help the principals in this region to bridge at least a portion of their chronic, ongoing conflict by getting them to work on common objectives that offer possibilities for mutual cooperation.

Third, as we have already seen in our Chapter 7 discussion of the entrapment process, people in conflict may find themselves overcommitted to a course of action that privately makes no sense but from which they feel unable to escape. A skillful third party may be able to help in such circumstances by introducing a formula that allows one or both disputants to circumvent the commitment.

There are three ways in which a commitment can be thus circumvented. One way is by dividing a concept into two or more subconcepts that can coexist. For example, when the state of Texas was ready to join the Union, it was committed to retaining a navy—a commitment that was incompatible with statehood. This was circumvented by dividing the concept of navy into two subconcepts, naval personnel and naval vessels. This allowed Texas to have all the naval personnel it wanted, but no ships! A second way of circumventing a commitment is by relabeling an object or event so that it no longer falls within the scope of the commitment. Instead of demanding that the Israelis meet with the PLO, for example, the United States might be well advised to encourage preliminary discussions by Israel with an entity identified simply as Palestinians, thereby allowing the Israelis a face-saving way to meet with spokespersons for a group that has not yet recognized the right of Israel to exist as a sovereign nation. Finally, a third party can help the disputants circumvent commitments through an "agreement to disagree." The United States and the People's Republic of China appear to have agreed to disagree about the status of Taiwan, thereby allowing the two nations to develop talks on a great number of other topics. Agreeing to disagree permits the disputants to circumvent prior commitments to a competitive struggle by compartmentalizing those areas of disagreement in such a way that the remaining areas are available for work and discourse.

Increasing the Disputants' Motivation to Reach Agreement

When all is said and done, a third party's effectiveness hinges on his or her ability to move the disputants out of stalemate, in the direction of concession making and problem solving. The third party can sometimes goad the disputants into such movement, but it is far better if the disputants themselves are motivated to take their conflict seriously. Only then will a solution be engineered that is apt to last. How, then, can a third party induce the disputants to work toward settlement? The answer to this query, we believe, entails third-party work on five fundamental motivational concerns: concession making without loss of face, trust, irrationality, momentum, and autonomy.

Loss of Face. As we have repeatedly observed throughout this book, people in the throes of escalating conflict tend to develop a distorted sense of the importance of looking tough and unyielding in the eyes of their adversaries and various constituencies, and they tend to go out of their way to avoid doing things that might be construed as signs of weakness or image loss. All too often, the making of concessions—no matter how trivial or superfluous these concessions may be—is construed by each side as just such a sign of weakness. An effective third party can be enormously helpful in this regard, by allowing concession making without loss of face. By implicitly or explicitly requesting concessions, the third party can deflect the responsibility for compromise from the shoulders of the disputants onto his or her own shoulders instead. A concession that each side was unwilling to grant before, lest it be seen as a chink in the armor that invites exploitation in the future, can now be made with the understanding that it has been done at the behest of the third party. In effect, the parties can now say to each other that they have given something up not because they had to (because the other side forced them to do so) but because they chose to. In the spirit of being an obliging, cooperative, fairminded individual, each has gone along with the third party's request for concessions and in so doing has moved the pair closer to agreement.

Trust. For the disputants to be motivated to engage in problem solving, they must have some modicum of trust in each other; otherwise they will be too fearful of image loss, position loss, and information loss to proceed. There are several things that a third party can do to engender trust. First, he or she can encourage each side to make an irrevocable concession, no matter how small, in an effort to create tangible evidence of a willingness to give something up. The important consideration here resides in the concession's irrevocability, not in its magnitude. This is a miniature form of Osgood's (1962, 1966) GRIT strategy, which was discussed in Chapter 9. At another level, a third party can help to engender trust by pointing out areas of overlapping interests, while downplaying areas of disagreement and conflict. By drawing the principals' attention to the interests they have in common, the third party may be able to focus attention more on the possibilities of mutual gain than on the potential each party has for exploiting the other.

Irrationality. People in escalating, competitive struggles typically experience a great many angry, irrational feelings. Although these feelings may sometimes reflect deep-seated concerns that are not easily brushed away, at least as often they constitute "hot steam," the venting of which permits the principals to work more effectively toward a settlement of their differences. Hence a third party can sometimes prove invaluable by encouraging the disputants to vent their feelings and thus increase their motivation to work on their conflict.

Heavy venting, involving heated accusations and insults, should ordinarily not be allowed in the presence of the adversary, because that might poison the relationship. The third party should allow such venting only in private "caucus" sessions. In such sessions, the third party serves as a substitute target for the principals' irrational displays, thereby deflecting anger away from the adversary. A third party taking such a role has a function that is analogous to that of a psychotherapist dealing with negative transference. Serving as a substitute target for the client's anger and emotion, the therapist allows the client to experience catharsis and to adopt a more realistic outlook. Henry Kissinger's intervention in the Middle East was repeatedly characterized by just such a willingness to absorb the angry sentiments that each side intended for the other but that were directed toward him instead.

A final, important way in which a third party can help the disputants come to grips with their irrational feelings is through the timely infusion of humor. Obviously, humor can help to create a good mood in the midst of angry displays, and, in so doing, it may place the disputants in a state of mind that makes them more amenable to the possibility of reaching agreement. Social psychological research has indicated, not surprisingly, that people in a good mood tend to be both more persuasible (Janis, Kaye & Kirschner, 1965) and more generous (Isen & Levin, 1972). Similarly, Kressel (1972) has reported that humor contributes to willingness to trust a third party, and Carnevale and Isen (1983) have found that good mood facilitates creative problem solving. In short, the judicious use of third-party humor may actually facilitate movement toward settlement.

Momentum. For the principals to be motivated to engage in problem solving, each must believe that there is common ground—that agreement is ultimately possible. There is nothing more desperate or hopeless than the sense that one is working to no avail and that one's best, most conciliatory efforts have little chance of bearing the fruit of agreement. To create the sense that agreement is possible, a third party must be able to initiate and sustain momentum in the negotiations.

As evidenced by Kissinger's form of "step-by-step" diplomacy in the Middle East, perhaps the clearest way of establishing momentum is by engineering a series of small agreements, each of which leads to another agreement in chain-like fashion. Fed on a "diet" of small agreements, the principals in the Middle East moved from one disengagement arrangement to another, thereby establishing and maintaining a sense of movement and keeping the lines of communication and negotiation open at all times.

Autonomy. Students of conflict, as well as third parties themselves, too often have assumed that people in conflict automatically welcome the assistance of outside intervenors. The model that has too often been applied in this regard likens the conflict scenario to an old-time Western town rank with discord and violence. Into this troubled picture rides the squeaky-clean third party, bringing peace and justice to the beleaguered citizens. At the scene's conclusion, the third party rides off into the sunset, basking in the gratitude of the humble townfolk, and on into the next troubled community. A comfortable Panglossian view of conflict, perhaps, but not a good picture of reality!

A more accurate view of life in conflict, we suspect, is of a situation in which people wish to manage their own affairs without the intrusion of an outsider. People in conflict, we believe, typically want to mend their own fences and restore order to their own affairs. Hence they are apt to turn to a third party only (or primarily) in desperation. People do not like to ask for help if they don't need it. To do so involves putting their fate in somebody else's hands and running the risk of being seen as needy, helpless, or unduly dependent on others. People in conflict, like people in general, are guided by an intense need for autonomy. Third parties who wish to be effective would do well to keep this in mind.

Recent social psychological research on the effects of anticipated third-party intervention has generally supported the preceding analysis of autonomy, particularly when the intensity of conflict is moderate or low. As research by various scholars (Hiltrop & Rubin, 1982; Johnson & Tullar, 1972; Bigoness, 1976; LaTour, et al., 1976; Johnson & Pruitt, 1972; and Bartunek, et al., 1975) has indicated, when people are in the midst of a conflict of relatively low intensity, and are confronted with the possible intervention of a highly directive third party, they are more likely to come to agreement than they are when they anticipate less directive intervention. These results suggest that, when disputants anticipate the intervention of a third party who will take over (like the old-time Western hero), they move to avert such intervention by reaching agreement themselves—sooner and more readily the bossier the third party seems likely to be.

This is the situation that seems to prevail under conditions of small conflict. When conflict intensity is large, however—when people see little common ground and/or are hostile toward each other—the effects of anticipated third-party intervention look rather different. As we have already observed, people in intense conflict have face-saving concerns that make them reluctant to make concessions, lest these be construed by the adversary as a sign of weakness. Under conditions of intense conflict, the intervention of a third party (particularly a directive third party) is thus a welcome occasion. If the third party takes over and imposes a settlement, neither side will have been made to look foolish by giving in.

In summary, autonomy needs are characteristic of people in conflict and are particularly likely to surface under conditions of relatively small conflict. When conflict intensity is large, however, these autonomy needs may well be swamped by an even greater concern with face-saving, which in turn produces openness to third-party intervention.

As we have seen at several points in this chapter, the effectiveness of intervention techniques is powerfully influenced by the degree of conflict intensity. Another interesting and paradoxical point is that, under conditions of intense conflict, the anticipated involvement of a third party leads the disputants to freeze their bargaining positions, showing greater intransigence than they would otherwise exhibit.

CONCLUSIONS: THE LIMITS AND EVOLUTION OF THIRD-PARTY INTERVENTION

We began this chapter by observing that third-party intervention is no panacea. Third parties help enormously, but they can also hamper efforts by the principals to develop an agreement that makes sense for them. The most effective third party is the one who intervenes in conflict in such a way that the disputants do not become dependent on the third party for help in the future. Like the dodo, the roc, and the auk, an effective third party should be able to render himself or herself obsolete and extinct. The effective third party helps instill in the disputants a sense of autonomy and self-sufficiency. Beware the third party who lingers and loiters about the scene of conflict indefinitely; such a person is either intervening ineffectively or has a vested interest in keeping the third-party role alive.

Third parties may even get in the way. If the principals are moving toward agreement, third-party intervention may block this progress by forcing interaction with the mediator. In addition, because of their relative ignorance, third parties sometimes suggest inadequate, nonintegrative solutions. Finally, when the intensity of conflict is high, the anticipation of third-party intervention may make a bad situation worse by discouraging concession making.

In the last analysis, however, it is our view that third parties are enormously helpful and important in the reduction and resolution of differences. At a time when so very many conflicts—between individuals and among and between groups and nations—continue to plague all of us, at a time when our technological skills have dramatically outstripped our collective social skills, it is all the more important that alternatives to competitive, destructive conflict escalation be found. Third-party intervention is a crucial example of such an alternative.

We do not regard third-party intervention as a fixed, stable set of nostrums, tools, and techniques. Rather, we believe that methods of third-party intervention must change and grow in relation to the needs and adaptations of the disputants. A particular drug may be a powerful remedy at first and then become less effective as the organism against which the drug is directed begins to adapt to it. Similarly, a third-party tool or technique that proves effective at first may well lead disputants to accommodate and adjust in ways that weaken its effectiveness. Just as new drugs must be introduced when the old ones become ineffective, new methods of third-party intervention must sometimes be invented in response to the disputants' accommodations. Third-party intervention is thus probably best thought of as an evolving process. It is not merely the case that third parties do things to and with the objects of their intervention; those objects—the principals—do things in return, things that necessitate new third-party ideas and innovations.

Our assumption that third-party intervention is an evolutionary process can be illustrated most clearly in some of the transformations that have taken place in third-party methods of dealing with public-employment disputes. Starting with mediation, third parties have increasingly turned to conventional arbitration and then to final-offer arbitration. To be sure, mediation has been, and continues to be, an extremely influential and important intervention device. When used effectively, mediation can lead the disputants to evolve an agreement that makes good sense to them—and that is therefore likely to endure. The major problem with mediation, especially in public-employee disputes in which it is essential that agreement be reached (for instance, with policemen and firemen, without whose services the lives or well-being of thousands of citizens might be threatened), is that mediation lacks the teeth of third-party enforcement. There are times when mediation may simply fail to work and the disputants simply choose to ignore the advice of the mediator—to the detriment of the disputants and the public.

It is for this reason that, over the years, third parties in public-employee disputes have increasingly resorted to the use of conventional arbitration when possible. Under the rules of this form of intervention, the third party is empowered to impose any agreement that he or she sees as proper to resolve the issues under consideration. Such action in itself provides a settlement to the controversy. Furthermore, the anticipation of such action—with its implication that control will be wrested from the hands of the disputants—is capable of goading the disputants into working out their own agreements.

Unfortunately, conventional arbitration has several weaknesses. Many arbitrators, when confronted with the last demands of each side, tend to split the difference between these demands, thereby creating an apparently fair and equitable agreement. As disputants have come increasingly to expect an arbitrator to split the difference, the anticipation of conventional arbitration, instead of facilitating agreement, has often led each side to adopt a tough and extreme position (Magenau, 1983; Feuille, 1977; Stern, et al., 1975). By refusing to budge beyond a set of intransigent demands, the disputants incline the half-way point between the two positions in their own direction. Hence, if the arbitrator splits the difference, it will favor their welfare. This mechanism has been called the "chilling effect."

The problem of the chilling effect has led, in recent years, to yet another third-party innovation: a technique known as final-offer arbitration, which was first proposed by Stevens (1966). According to this technique, if disputants are unable to come to an agreement, they are required to submit to the arbitrator their best, most conciliatory offer. Unlike conventional arbitration—wherein the third party can decide on any final, binding settlement that he or she chooses—final-offer arbitration makes the third party choose one of the two final offers that have been submitted. He or she cannot improvise in any way.

Final-offer arbitration places the principals in the following bind: Each wants his or her own final offer to be the one selected by the third party. The only way to guarantee that this will happen is to figure out what the other person is likely to offer and then submit a proposal that seems slightly more reasonable. This is a tricky business. It is hard to guess what the other will offer, and one may lose one's shirt if the other's offer is chosen. Hence disputants often prefer to reach agreement on their own rather than take their chances on the third party's judgment. Final-offer arbitration, then, is a procedure designed to create so aversive a situation that disputants will reach agreement of their own accord rather than expose themselves to the vagaries of the final-offer procedure.

Most experimental evidence has lent support to the foregoing reasoning and to the generally greater effectiveness of final-offer arbitration than its conventional counterpart (Bazerman & Farber, in press; Bazerman & Neale, 1982; DeNisi & Dworkin, 1979; Magenau, 1983; Neale & Bazerman, 1983; Notz & Starke, 1978; Subbarao, 1978). Final-offer arbitration is now required by law in public-sector disputes in a number of states.

In the spirit of regarding third-party intervention as an evolving process, consider the following possible problem with final-offer arbitration that might arise in the long run and necessitate still a further change in third-party strategy: It is in the interest of each disputant to mislead the adversary into thinking that he or she is totally nonconciliatory, so that the adversary does not feel that it is necessary to make a truly reasonable final offer. Hence, there is some temptation for both disputants faced with final-offer arbitration to maintain extremely rigid offers during the negotiation and become reasonable only in the final offer that is privately submitted to the arbitrator. The problem with this strategy, if it is practiced on both sides, is that it creates more conflictual impasses than might have been necessary had the final-offer procedure not been in effect.

In short, there is no such thing as a perfect or ideal intervention procedure. Each procedure has its virtues and its liabilities. Moreover, each procedure is likely to give rise to clever adjustments and modifications on the part of resourceful disputants, necessitating the development of new and still more ingenious intervention techniques. This should prove to be no problem, in the ultimate analysis. Just as people in conflict are infinitely resourceful at finding ways to beat their adversary and/or the system rather than give up more than they have to, the people who are in the business of bringing about mutually acceptable agreements are infinitely resourceful too. Conflict may be a growth industry, but so too is the business of dispute settlement.

CHAPTER 11

Conclusions

Our aim in this, our last chapter, is not to summarize our book but to look back selectively in order to gain perspective and point the way to future theory and research. In approaching this task, we are mindful of a general characteristic of all theoretical ideas: *As they open some doors, they tend to close others*. To put this another way, there is a danger of unintended negative consequences in all concepts, models, and metaphors that are used in science. While illuminating some phenomena, they inevitably draw attention away from, and even at times confuse the analysis of, others.

The Three-Stage Sequence

As the title of our book reflects, we have told a story of conflict that resembles a play in three acts. In Act I, the central characters were introduced and the plot thickened. Here we defined conflict, indicated its sources, and told the story of *escalation*. Act II, a brief one-chapter flurry of enthusiasm, was the story of *stalemate*. In stalemate, the conflict gets to the point where it seems unwise to escalate further, and a stage of transition is reached. Act III was the denouement, the story of *settlement*. Here we described the ways in which conflict, once escalated and then stalemated, can be creatively moved back down the escalation ladder.

The dramaturgical metaphor, a play in three acts, has the virtue of simplicity, perhaps a touch of elegance, and more than a little symmetry. Although we have not said much about this metaphor per se, the truth is that it has helped guide our analysis at many points along the way. This metaphor fits many of the most important conflicts, yet we must acknowledge that it involves some oversimplification and hence runs the risk of limiting thought as well as illuminating it.

For one thing, a *symmetry* is suggested that is more illusory than real. In reality, it is a lot easier to move up the escalation ladder than to move back down. This is because (1) people are usually more frustrated by being deprived than they benefit from being rewarded, (2) experiencing inequity against us is more disturbing than experiencing inequity in our favor and, (3) fear is a more powerful motivator than is a sense of safety. As a result, people are more prone to retaliate and engage in defensive actions when challenged than to reciprocate when they are treated well. This means that vicious circles (conflict spirals) that deepen escalation are more readily achieved than benevolent circles that relieve escalation.

In retrospect, a valley or canyon metaphor might have been more appropriate than a play in three acts. This metaphor would involve the stages of descent (analogous to escalation), crossing to the other side (analogous to stalemate), and ascent (analogous to de-escalation). The pull of gravity makes it relatively easy to go down the side of a valley or canyon (one may not make it in one piece, of course, but that is another matter). But climbing up the other side can require real determination and effort—and, sometimes, considerable presence of mind.

Another problem with our three-stage model is that it implies an orderly, almost inexorable procession of phases that seems as lock-step as a Greek tragedy. Many conflicts do show this three-part sequence, including some of the most important and troublesome (such as the Vietnam War). But there are others that teeter on the brink of the escalative precipice, but never go over, and still others that are resolved so readily that they never get near the brink.

Perhaps a better metaphor than a play *or* a canyon is that of a tree with many branches. Here the changes that occur in conflict would be regarded not as progression along the tree's trunk but as movement from trunk to branch to sprig to leaf, along a variety of possible routes. We made a beginning at such a branching analysis in Chapter 5, suggesting that conflict in stable relationships differs from that in unstable relationships in that the intensity of conflict follows more of a sine-wave function than an escalative progression over time. But it was only a beginning.

The Lack of Attention to De-escalation

A second and related limitation of our analysis might be described as excessive negativity. We have paid a good deal more attention to escalation than to de-escalation, devoting twice as many chapters to the former topic. We had two basic reasons for taking this route: One was that escalation is the most dramatic and troublesome event that occurs in conflict. Escalation is what makes conflict a social problem. The other, perhaps more important, reason was that *there is so little theory about de-escalation*. Much more is known about how conflicts escalate than about how they de-escalate. For example, we can describe with some precision the processes by which an "enemy" image is established and empathy toward that "enemy" is destroyed, but we know little about the steps by which such an image is dissipated and empathy is reestablished. Indeed the literature on de-escalation is almost nonexistent, and our last two chapters are a good deal more tangential to this topic than we would have liked.

The abbreviated nature of the literature on de-escalation may partly reflect the unintended consequences of two very successful metaphors of the escalative process. These are the conflict spiral model and the structural change model, which are close cousins in that they both view escalation as largely a matter of vicious circles. The problem with these models is that they make no provision for the termination or reversal of a vicious circle and hence imply ever-lasting escalation. These models not only fail to address the phenomenon of de-escalation; they actually imply that it does not exist. (It is interesting to note that the third escalation metaphor, the aggressor–defender model, does allow for de-escalation, predicting that this process will occur when the aggressor has been effectively deterred. The problem with this model is it that illuminates only certain aspects of selected cases of escalation.)

We began to sketch a possible theory of de-escalation in Chapter 8 on stalemate. There we postulated that escalating conflict frequently reaches a point where both parties find further use of contentious tactics either unworkable or unwise. If yielding, withdrawing and inaction are also ruled out, as they often are, the solution to the controversy must eventually be found in the only remaining strategy, problem solving, and hence in de-escalation. But where do we go from this beginning? We still need theory about the processes that occur in the course of de-escalation and the circumstances that govern the likelihood and timing of this phenomenon.

One possible approach to constructing such a theory involves flipping around some of our observations about the processes underlying escalation. For example, the vicious circles that produce escalation may have their counterpart in benevolent circles leading to tension reduction (see Osgood, 1962, 1966). Similarly, one can sometimes point to structural changes that bring people together,[1] such as the development of admiration between former adversaries, the opening of peace talks, the swearing of blood brotherhood, and the establishment of a Peace Academy.

The Theory of Strategic Choice

Another major theme of our book concerns the choices people make among conflict strategies. We described five basic strategies (contending, yielding, problem solving, withdrawing and inaction) and developed, in Chapter 3, a theory about the forces that govern decisions among them.

Though we call the latter a theory of "strategic choice," we do not postulate a strictly rational process of decision making among the strategies. In our view, strategic choice is influenced by both rational considerations (such as perceived feasibility) and nonrational considerations (such as genuine concern about Other's outcomes).

Our strategic choice theory has been useful as an analytical tool at a number of points in the book—most notably in Chapter 8, where we argued that the decision to de-escalate is often a function of conditions that make strategies other than problem solving seem infeasible. Nevertheless, this perspective also has its limitations. The most obvious of these is its failure to shed light on the *combinations of strategies* that are sometimes encountered in conflict. For example, we indicated in Chapter 9 that the most effective approach to dealing with an adversary is often to combine problem solving with conten-

[1]This idea was suggested by Herbert C. Kelman in a private communication.

tious behavior that underscores an unwillingness to forsake one's basic interests. Strategic choice theory makes no provision for such a complex strategy, despite the fact that people sometimes act this way.

The Descriptive Character of Our Analysis

Yet another issue, in retrospect, concerns our heavy emphasis on *descriptive* theory as opposed to *prescriptive* theory. We have chosen, in most parts of the book, to indicate and explain how people *do* behave in conflict rather than how they *should* behave. Some prescriptive theory *is* presented in Chapters 9 and 10 on problem solving and third-party functions, but we could have done a lot more in this vein.

Our main reason for taking a descriptive approach is our conviction that good advice must be based on good cause-and-effect analysis. Without such analysis, recommendations for behavior may well be only nostrums. However, we also believe that the purveyor of descriptive theory should, where possible, indicate how his or her theory can be applied, and we admit to being somewhat remiss in this regard. Indeed, it is quite possible that our theoretical analyses would have been deepened had we more often taken the intellectually challenging route of asking questions about the practical applications of our analysis.

A good place to begin building more prescriptive theory might be found in our strategic choice theory. Unlike most prescriptive literature on conflict (such as Blake & Mouton, 1979; Fisher & Ury, 1981; and to some extent our Chapter 9), which emphasizes the value of problem solving above the other strategies, this theory treats all of the strategies equally. Accordingly, it might be used as a basis for developing a *contingency model* that specifies what strategy should be chosen in various circumstances. For example, one might argue that it is rational for Party to use contentious tactics rather than problem solving if he or she is not dependent on Other and has ample threat capacity. Even withdrawing and inaction can be defended under some conditions. For instance, Bettelheim (1960) indicates that he survived his harrowing experience in the German concentration camps by employing these strategies (and thus putting his affect on ice for a few years) rather than contending or problem solving with his captors.

The Emphasis on Individual Behavior

Our analysis has also placed heavy emphasis on the behavior of individual disputants rather than on the interaction between pairs of disputants viewed as a unit. This individual perspective has the virtue of encouraging us to reason precisely and permitting us to borrow many theoretical treasures from the rich storehouse of ideas that have been accumulated as a result of psychological research. But it also has its limitations, as all perspectives do. One limitation is that analyses of individual behavior have a way of ignoring action–reaction sequences, in which each party's behavior is responsive to the other party's.

We have partly compensated for this limitation by postulating three models of escalation (the aggressor–defender, conflict spiral, and structural change models) that emphasize action–reaction sequences. Another limitation is that the individual perspective generally fails to examine the effect on outcomes when two parties adopt different strategies. For example, when Party adopts a contentious approach and Other a problem-solving approach, does Other always convert to contending? Are there circumstances under which Party rather than Other is converted? We have not given such issues the attention they deserve.

The Effort to Produce a General Theory of Conflict

Perhaps the most pervasive assumption we have made in developing this book is that it is possible to develop a general theory of conflict that transcends the various levels and arenas of society. With the exception of a few mechanisms (such as the formation of struggle groups) that do not apply to the interpersonal level, we have assumed that most significant conflict processes are found equally in interpersonal, intergroup, interorganizational, and international relations. We have also been unwilling to distinguish in our theorizing between such distinct arenas as labor vs. management, Army vs. Air Force, and Shell vs. Texaco. We are comfortable with this broad perspective, because we feel that it maps well onto reality and because it encourages extrapolation of findings from one conflict arena to another, thus speeding the acquisition of knowledge. However, we are also aware of two possible dangers in pushing this perspective too far. One is that it may lead us to ignore real differences between conflict arenas. The other is that it may discourage empirical research. Most research on conflict must take place in a single arena (such as mediation sessions run by a community service), and the results may seem at first to be limited to that arena. Scholars who are striving too hard for general theory may find such results of little interest and hence be unwilling to embark on any research—to the severe detriment of the field.

In closing, we would like to believe that, in writing this book, we have opened more doors than we have closed—allowing fresh air and sunlight to find its way into a sometimes murky realm of theory. In doing so, we have inevitably chosen certain concepts and modes of analysis over others. These choices have had consequences that we have just explored with the hindsight that completion of our project allows and invites.

References

ABC News. 1981. America held hostage: The secret negotiations. New York, January 22, 1981.

Adams, J. S. 1965. Inequity in social exchange. In L. Berkowitz, ed. *Advances in experimental social psychology,* vol. 2. New York: Academic Press, pp. 267–99.

Alger, C. F. 1961. Non-resolution consequences of the United Nations and their effect on international conflict. *J. Conflict Resolution* 5: 128–45.

Allen, V. L., and Wilder, D. A. 1975. Categorization, belief similarity and intergroup discrimination. *J. Personality and Social Psychol.* 32: 971–77.

Apfelbaum, E. 1979. Relations of domination and movements for liberation: An analysis of power between groups. In W. G. Austin and S. Worchel, eds. *The social psychology of intergroup relations,* pp. 188–204. Monterey, Calif.: Brooks/Cole.

Aronson, E., and Cope, V. 1968. My enemy's enemy is my friend. *J. Personality and Social Psychol.* 8: 8–12.

Back, K. W. 1951. Influence through social communication. *J. Abnormal and Social Psychol.* 46: 9–23.

Baron, R. A. 1977. *Human aggression.* New York: Plenum.

Bartunek, J. M., Benton, A. A., and Keys, C. B. 1975. Third-party intervention and the bargaining of group representatives. *J. Conflict Resolution* 19: 532–57.

Bazerman, M. H., and Farber, H. A. In press. Arbitrator decision making: When are final offers important. *Industrial and Labor Relations Rev.*

Bazerman, M. H., and Neale, M. A. 1982. Improving negotiator effectiveness under final-offer arbitration: The role of selection and training. *J. Applied Psychol.* 67: 543–48.

Bem, D. J. 1972. Self-perception theory. In L. Berkowitz (ed.), *Advances in experimental social psychology,* vol. 6, pp. 1–62. New York: Academic Press.

Benton, A. A., and Druckman, D. 1973. Salient solutions and the bargaining behavior of representatives and nonrepresentatives. *International J. Group Tensions* 3: 28–39.

——————. 1974. Constituent's bargaining orientation and intergroup negotiations. *J. Applied Social Psychol.* 4: 141–50.

Ben-Yoav, O., and Pruitt, D. G. 1984a. Resistance to yielding and the expectation of cooperative future interaction in negotiation. *J. Experimental Social Psychol.* 20: 323–53.

——————. 1984b. Accountability to constituents: A two-edged sword. *Organizational Behavior and Human Performance* 34: 282–95.

Bercovitch, J. 1984. *Social conflicts and third parties: Strategies of conflict resolution.* Boulder, Col.: Westview.

Berkowitz, L. 1962. *Aggression: A social psychological analysis.* New York: McGraw-Hill.

Berkowitz, L., Cochran, S. T., and Embree, M. C. 1981. Physical pain and the goal of aversively stimulated aggression. *J. Personality and Social Psychol.* 40: 687–700.

Berkowitz, L., and Geen, R. G. 1966. Film violence and the cue properties of available targets. *J. Personality and Social Psychol.* 3: 525–30.

Berscheid, E., and Walster, E. 1978. *Interpersonal attraction.* 2d ed. Reading, Mass.: Addison-Wesley.

Bettelheim, B. 1960. *The informed heart: Autonomy in a mass age*. Glencoe, Ill.: Free Press.

Bigoness, W. J. 1976. The impact of initial bargaining position and alternative modes of third-party intervention in resolving bargaining impasses. *Organizational Behavior and Human Performance* 17: 185–98.

Black, T. E., and Higbee, K. L. 1973. Effects of power, threat, and sex on exploitation. *J. Personality and Social Psychol.* 27: 382–88.

Blake, R. R., and Mouton, J. S. 1962. Overevaluation of own group's product in intergroup competition. *J. Abnormal and Social Psychol.* 64: 237–38.

——————. 1964. *The managerial grid*. Houston, Texas: Gulf.

——————. 1979. Intergroup problem solving in organizations: From theory to practice. In W. G. Austin and S. Worchel, eds. *The social psychology of intergroup relations*, pp. 19–23. Monterey, Calif.: Brooks/Cole.

Blumenthal, M. D., Kahn, R. L., Andrews, F. M., and Head, K. B. 1972. *Justifying violence: Attitudes of American men*. Ann Arbor, Mich.: Institute for Social Research.

Bonoma, T. V., Schlenker, B. R., Smith, R., and Tedeschi, J. 1970. Source prestige and target reactions to threats. *Psychonomic Science* 19: 111–13.

Bonoma, T. V., and Tedeschi, J. T. 1973. Some effects of source behavior on target's compliance to threats. *Behavioral Science* 18: 34–41.

Bowers, J. W., and Ochs, D. J. 1971. *The rhetoric of agitation and control*. Reading, Mass.: Addison-Wesley.

Brehm, J. W., and Cole, A. H. 1966. Effect of a favor which reduces freedom. *J. Personality and Social Psychol.* 3: 420–26.

Brewer, M. B. 1979. Ingroup bias in the minimal intergroup situation: A cognitive motivational analysis. *Psychological Bulletin* 86: 307–24.

Brockner, J., and Rubin, J. Z. 1985. *The social psychology of conflict escalation and entrapment*. New York: Springer-Verlag.

Brockner, J., Rubin, J. Z., Fine, J., Hamilton, T. P., Thomas, B., and Turetsky, B. 1982. Factors affecting entrapment in escalating conflicts: The importance of timing. *J. Research in Personality* 16: 247–66.

Brockner, J., Rubin, J. Z., and Lang, E. 1981. Face-saving and entrapment. *J. Experimental Social Psychol.* 17: 68–79.

Brockner, J., Shaw, M. C., and Rubin, J. Z. 1979. Factors affecting withdrawal from an escalating conflict: Quitting before it's too late. *J. Experimental Social Psychol.* 15: 492–503.

Bronfenbrenner, U. 1961. The mirror-image in Soviet–American relations. *J. Social Issues* 17: 45–56.

Burton, J. W. 1962. *Peace theory*. New York: Knopf.

——————. 1969. *Conflict and communication*. New York: Macmillan.

Carnevale, P. J. D., and Isen, A. M. 1985. The influence of positive affect and visual access on the discovery of integrative solutions in bilateral negotiation. *Organizational Behavior and Human Decision Processes*, in press.

Cialdini, R. B., and Richardson, K. D. 1980. Two indirect tactics of image management: Basking and blasting. *J. Personality and Social Psychol.* 39: 406–15.

Clark, M. S., and Mills, J. 1979. Interpersonal attraction in exchange and communal relationships. *J. Personality and Social Psychol.* 37: 12–24.

Claude, I. L. 1962. *Power and international relations*. New York: Random House.

Cohen, S. P., Kelman, H. C., Miller, F. D., and Smith, B. L. 1977. Evolving intergroup techniques for conflict resolution: An Israeli–Palestinian pilot workshop. *J. Social Issues* 33: 165–89.

Coleman, J. S. 1957. *Community conflict*. New York: Free Press.

Cooper, J., and Fazio, R. H. 1979. The formation and persistence of attitudes that support intergroup conflict. In W. G. Austin and S. Worchel, eds. *The Social Psychology of Intergroup Relations*, pp. 149–59. Monterey, Calif.: Brooks/Cole.

Coser, L. A. 1956. *The functions of social conflict*. New York: Free Press.

Dahrendorf, R. 1959. *Class and class conflict in industrial society*. Stanford, Calif.: Stanford University Press.

Davies, J. C. 1962. Toward a theory of revolution. *Sociological Rev.* 27: 5–19.

DeNisi, A. A., and Dworkin, J. B. 1979. Final-offer arbitration. Unpublished manuscript.

Deutsch, K. W., and Singer, J. D. 1964. Multipolar power systems and international stability. *World Politics* 16: 390–406.

Deutsch, M. 1958. Trust and suspicion. *J. Conflict Resolution* 2: 265–79.

––––––––––. 1973. *The resolution of conflict: Constructive and destructive processes*. New Haven, Conn.: Yale University Press.

Deutsch, M., and Collins, M. 1951. *Interracial housing: A psychological evaluation of a social experiment*. Minneapolis, Minn.: University of Minnesota Press.

Deutsch, M., and Krauss, R. M. 1960. The effect of threat upon interpersonal bargaining. *J. Abnormal and Social Psychol.* 61: 181–89.

Deutsch, M., and Lewicki, R. J. 1970. "Locking in" effects during a game of chicken. *J. Conflict Resolution* 14: 367–78.

Dickoff, H. 1961. Reactions to evaluations by another person as a function of self-evaluations and the interaction context. Unpublished manuscript, Duke University.

Dion, K. L. 1973. Cohesiveness as a determinant of ingroup–outgroup bias. *J. Personality and Social Psychology* 28: 163–71.

––––––––––. 1979. Intergroup conflict and intragroup cohesiveness. In W. G. Austin and S. Worchel, eds. *The social psychology of intergroup relations*, pp. 211–224. Belmont, Calif.: Wadsworth.

Douglas, A. 1962. *Industrial peacemaking*. New York: Columbia University Press.

Dugan, M. A., ed. 1982. Special issue on conflict resolution. *Peace and Change* 8: 149 pp.

Feuille, P. 1977. Final-offer arbitration and negotiating incentives. *Arbitration Journal* 32: 203–20.

Festinger, L. 1950. Informal social communication. *Psychol. Rev.* 57: 271–92.

––––––––––. 1957. *A theory of cognitive dissonance*. Stanford, Calif.: Stanford University Press.

Festinger, L., Schachter, S., and Back, K. 1950. *Social pressures in informal groups: A study of human factors in housing*. New York: Harper & Row.

Filley, A. C. 1975. *Interpersonal conflict resolution*. Glenview, Ill.: Scott Foresman.

Fisher, R. 1964. Fractionating conflict. In R. Fisher, ed. *International conflict and behavorial science: The Craigville papers*. New York: Basic Books.

––––––––––. 1981. Playing the wrong game. In J. Z. Rubin, ed. *Dynamics of third-party intervention: Kissinger in the Middle East*, pp. 95–121. New York: Praeger.

Fisher R., and Ury, W. 1981. *Getting to YES: Negotiating agreement without giving in*. Boston: Houghton-Mifflin.

Fisher, R. J. 1983. Third-party consultation as a method of intergroup conflict resolution. *J. Conflict Resolution* 27: 301–34.

Foa, U. G., and Foa, E. B. 1975. *Resource theory of social exchange*. Morristown, N. J.: General Learning Press.

Follett, M. P. 1940. Constructive conflict. In H. C. Metcalf and L. Urwick, eds. *Dynamic administration: The collected papers of Mary Parker Follett*, pp. 30–49. New York: Harper.

Forcey, B., Van Slyck, M. R., Carnevale, P. J. D., and Pruitt, D. G. 1983. Looking strong: Gender differences in negotiation behavior under constituent surveillance. Poster presented at the American Psychological Association Convention.

Frank, J. 1982. *Sanity and survival*, rev. ed. New York: Vintage Books.

Freedman, J. L., and Fraser, S. C. 1966. Compliance without pressure: The foot-in-the-door technique. *J. Personality and Social Psychol.* 4: 195–202.

French, J. R. P., and Raven, B. H. 1959. The bases of social power. In D. Cartwright, ed. *Studies in Social Power,* pp. 150–67. Ann Arbor, Mich.: Institute for Social Research.

Froman, L. A., Jr., and Cohen, M. D. 1970. Compromise and logroll: Comparing the efficiency of two bargaining processes. *Behavorial Science* 15: 180–83.

Fry, W. R., Firestone, I. J., and Williams, D. L. 1983. Negotiation process and outcome of stranger dyads and dating couples: Do lovers lose? *Basic and Applied Psychol.* 4: 1–16.

Gahagan, J. P., and Tedeschi, J. T. 1968. Strategy and the credibility of promises in the prisoner's dilemma game. *J. Conflict Resolution* 12: 224–34.

Gahagan, J. P., Tedeschi, J. T., Faley, T., and Lindskold, S. 1970. Patterns of punishment and reactions to threats. *J. Social Psychol.* 80: 115–16.

Gandhi, M. K. *For pacifists*. 1949. Ahmedabad, India: Navajivan Publishing House.

Gerard, H. B., and Greenbaum, C. W. 1962. Attitudes toward an agent of uncertainty reduction. *J. Personality* 30: 485-95.

Gladwin, T. N., and Walter, I. 1980. *Multinationals under fire: Lessons in the management of conflict*. New York: Wiley.

Gluckman, M. 1955. *Custom and conflict in Africa*. Glencoe, Ill.: Free Press.

Golan, M. 1976. *The secret conversations of Henry Kissinger*. New York: Quadrangle.

Goldstein, J. H., and Arms, R. L. 1971. Effects of observing athletic contests on hostility. *Sociometry* 34: 93–100.

Gottman, J. M. 1979. *Marital interaction: Experimental investigations*. New York: Academic Press.

Greenberg, M. S., and Frisch, D. M. 1972. Effect of intentionality on willingness to reciprocate a favor. *J. Experimental Social Psychol.* 8: 302–11.

Gruder, C. L. 1971. Relationship with opponent and partner in mixed-motive bargaining. *J. Conflict Resolution* 15: 403–16.

Gulick, E. V. 1955. *Europe's classical balance of power*. Ithaca, N. Y.: Cornell University Press.

Gulliver, P. H. 1979. *Disputes and negotiations: A cross-cultural perspective*. New York: Academic Press.

Gurr, T. R. 1970. *Why men rebel*. Princeton, N. J.: Princeton University Press.

Halberstam, D. 1969. *The best and the brightest*. New York: Random House.

Hamilton, D. L., and Bishop, G. D. 1976. Attitudinal and behavorial effects of initial integration of white suburban neighborhoods. *J. Social Issues* 32: 47–67.

Hancock, R. D., and Sorrentino, R. N. 1980. The effects of expected future interaction and prior group support on the conformity process. *J. Experimental Social Psychol.* 16: 261–69.

Harford, T., and Solomon, L. 1967. "Reformed sinner" and "lapsed saint" strategies in the prisoner's dilemma game. *J. Conflict Resolution* 11: 104–9.

Harris, J. C. 1955. *The complete tales of Uncle Remus*. Boston: Houghton Mifflin.

Harsanyi, J. C. 1962. Bargaining in ignorance of the opponent's utility function. *J. Conflict Resolution* 6: 29–38.

Harvey, O. J. 1956. An experimental investigation of negative and positive relations between small groups through judgmental indices. *Sociometry* 14: 201–9.

Hastorf, A. H., and Cantril, C. 1954. They saw a game: A case study. *J. Abnormal and Social Psychol.* 49: 129–34.

Hatton, J. M. 1967. Reactions of negroes in a biracial bargaining situation. *J. Personality and Social Psychol.* 7: 301–6.

Haydon, T., and Mischel, W. 1976. Maintaining trait consistency in the resolution of behavorial inconsistency: The wolf in sheep's clothing? *J. Personality* 44: 109–32.

Heider, F. 1958. *The psychology of interpersonal relations*. New York: Wiley.

Hiltrop, J. M., and Rubin, J. Z. 1982. Effects of intervention mode and conflict of interest on dispute resolution. *J. Personality and Social Psychol.* 42: 665–72.

Hollander, E. P. 1978. *Leadership dynamics: A practical guide to effective relationships*. New York: Free Press.

Horai, J., Lindskold, S., Gahagan, J., and Tedeschi, J. 1969. The effects of conflict intensity and promisor credibility on a target's behavior. *Psychonomic Science* 14: 73–74.

Hornstein, H. A. 1976. *Cruelty and kindness: A new look at aggression and altruism.* Englewood Cliffs, N. J.: Prentice-Hall.

Hovland, C. I., and Sears, R. R. 1940. Minor studies of aggression. VI: Correlation of lynchings with economic indices. *J. Psychol.* 9: 301–10.

Isen, A. M., and Levin, P. F. 1972. Effect of feeling good on helping: Cookies and kindness. *J. Personality and Social Psychol.* 21: 384–88.

Jacobson, D. 1981. Intraparty dissensus and interparty conflict resolution. *J. Conflict Resolution* 25: 471–494.

Janis, I. L. 1972. *Victims of groupthink: A psychological study of foreign-policy decisions and fiascos.* Boston: Houghton Mifflin.

Janis, I. L., Kaye, D., and Kirschner, P. 1965. Facilitating effects of "eating-while-reading" on responsiveness to persuasive communications. *J. Personality and Social Psychol.* 1: 181–86.

Jervis, R. 1976. *Perception and misperception in international politics.* Princeton, N. J.: Princeton University Press.

Johnson, D. F., and Pruitt, D. G. 1972. Preintervention effects of mediation versus arbitration. *J. Applied Psychol.* 56: 1–10.

Johnson, D. F., and Tullar, W. L. 1972. Style of third-party intervention, face-saving and bargaining behavior. *J. Experimental Social Psychol.* 8: 319–30.

Jones, E. E., and Davis, K. E. 1965. From acts to dispositions: The attribution process in person perception. In L. Berkowitz, ed. *Advances in Experimental Social Psychology,* vol. 2, pp. 219–66. New York: Academic Press.

Jones, E. E., and Gordon, E. M. 1972. Timing of self-disclosure and its effects on personal attraction. *J. Personality and Social Psychol.* 24: 358–65.

Jones, E. E., Jones, R. G., and Gergen, K. J. 1963. Some conditions affecting the evaluation of a conformist. *J. Personality* 31: 270–88.

Jones, E. E., and Wein, G. 1972. Attitude similarity, expectancy violation, and attraction. *J. Experimental Social Psychol.* 8: 222–235.

Jones, E. E., and Wortman, C. 1973. *Ingratiation: An attributional approach.* Morristown, N. J.: General Learning Press.

Kahn, H. 1960. *On thermonuclear war.* Princeton, N. J.: Princeton University Press.

Kaplan, M. 1957. *System and process in international politics.* New York: Wiley.

Kelley, H. H. 1966. A classroom study of the dilemmas in interpersonal negotiations. In K. Archibald, ed. *Strategic interaction and conflict: Original papers and discussion.* Berkeley, Calif.: Institute of International Studies.

_____. 1973. The process of causal attribution. *Amer. Psychologist* 28: 107–28.

Kelley, H. H., Beckman, L. L., and Fischer, C. S. 1967. Negotiating the division of reward under incomplete information. *J. Experimental Social Psychol.* 3: 361–98.

Kelley, H. H., and Schenitzki, D. P. 1972. Bargaining. In C. G. McClintock, ed. *Experimental social psychology.* New York: Holt.

Kelley, H. H., and Stahelski, A. J. 1970. Social interaction basis of cooperators' and competitors' beliefs about others. *J. Personality and Social Psychol.* 16: 66–91.

Kelman, H. C. 1972. The problem-solving workshop in conflict resolution. In R. L. Merritt, ed. *Communication in international politics.* Urbana, Ill.: University of Illinois Press.

_____. 1984. Overcoming the psychological barrier: An analysis of the Egyptian–Israeli peace process. Unpublished manuscript.

Kelman, H. C., and Cohen, S. P. 1976. The problem-solving workshop: A social psychological contribution to the resolution of international conflicts. *J. Peace Research* 13: 79–90.

Kennedy, R. F. 1969. *Thirteen days: A memoir of the Cuban missile crisis.* New York: Norton.

Kimmel, M. J., Pruitt, D. G., Magenau, J. M., Konar-Goldband, E., and Carnevale, P. J. D. 1980. Effects of trust, aspiration and gender on negotiation tactics. *J. Personality and Social Psychol.* 38: 9–23.

Kleinke, C. L., Staneski, R. A., and Weaver, P. 1972. Evaluation of a person who uses another's name in ingratiating and noningratiating situations. *J. Experimental Social Psychol*. 8: 457–66.

Klimoski, R. J. 1972. The effects of intragroup forces on intergroup conflict resolution. *Organizational Behavior and Human Performance* 8: 363–83.

Kochan, T. A. 1980. *Collective bargaining and industrial relations*. Homewood, Ill.:Irwin.

Kochan, T. A., and Jick, T. 1978. The public sector mediation process: A theory and empirical examination. *J. Conflict Resolution* 22: 209–40.

Kogan, N., Lamm, H., and Trommsdorff, G. 1972. Negotiation constraints in the risk-taking domain: Effects of being observed by partners of higher or lower status. *J. Personality and Social Psychol*. 23: 143–56.

Komorita, S. S. 1973. Concession making and conflict resolution. *J. Conflict Resolution* 17: 745–62.

Komorita, S. S., and Esser, J. K. 1975. Frequency of reciprocated concessions in bargaining. *J. Personality and Social Psychol*. 32: 699–705.

Komorita, S. S., and Lapworth, C. W. 1982. Cooperative choice among individuals vs. groups in an *n*-person dilemma situation. *J. Personality and Social Psychol*. 42: 487–96.

Konečni, V. J. 1975. The mediation of aggressive behavior: Arousal level vs. anger and cognitive labeling. *J. Personality and Social Psychol*. 32: 706–12.

Kraslow, D., and Loory, S. H. 1968. *The secret search for peace in Vietnam*. New York: Vintage Books.

Krauss, R. M., and Deutsch, M. 1966. Communication in interpersonal bargaining. *J. Personality and Social Psychol*. 4: 572–77.

Kressel, K. 1972. *Labor mediation: An exploratory survey*. Albany, N. Y.: Association of Labor Mediation Agencies, 1972.

Kriesberg, L. 1982. *Social conflicts*. 2d ed. Englewood Cliffs, N. J.: Prentice-Hall.

Lamm, H., and Myers, D. G. 1978. Group-induced polarization of attitudes and behavior. In L. Berkowitz, ed. *Advances in experimental social psychology*, vol. 11, pp. 145–95. New York: Academic Press.

Lasswell, H. D. 1950. *A study of power*. New York: Free Press.

LaTour, S., Houlden, P., Walker, L., and Thibaut, J. 1976. Some determinants of preference for modes of conflict resolution. *J. Conflict Resolution* 20: 319–56.

Lebow, R. N., Jervis, R., and Stein, J. G. 1984. *Psychology and deterrence*. Baltimore: Johns Hopkins University Press, 1984.

Lewicki, R. J. 1980. *Bad loan psychology: Entrapment and commitment in financial lending* (Working paper 80–25). Durham, N. C.: Duke University Graduate School of Business Administration.

Lewicki, R. J., and Rubin, J. Z. 1973. Effects of variations in the informational clarity of promises and threats upon interpersonal bargaining. *Proceedings of the 81st Annual Convention of the American Psychological Association*, 8: 137–38.

Likert, R. 1961. *New patterns of management*. New York: McGraw-Hill.

Lindskold, S. 1978. Trust development, the GRIT proposal, and the effects of conciliatory acts on conflict and cooperation. *Psychol. Bull*. 85: 772–93.

Lindskold, S., and Bennett, R. 1973. Attributing trust and conciliatory intent from coercive power capability. *J. Personality and Social Psychol*. 28: 180–86.

Lindskold, S., Bonoma, T. V., Schlenker, B. R., and Tedeschi, J. T. 1972. Some factors affecting the effectiveness of reward power. *Psychonomic Science* 26: 68–70.

Lindskold, S., Bonoma, T., and Tedeschi, J. T. 1969. Relative costs and reactions to threats. *Psychonomic Science* 15: 303–4.

Lindskold, S., and Tedeschi, J. T. 1971. Reward power and attraction in interpersonal conflict. *Psychonomic Science* 22: 211–13.

Loftis, J. E. 1974. *Anger, aggression and attribution of arousal*. Ph.D. dissertation, Stanford University.

Longley, J., and Pruitt, D. G. 1980. A critique of Janis's theory of groupthink. In L. Wheeler, ed. *Review of personality and social psychology*, vol. 1, pp. 74–93. Beverly Hills, Calif.: Sage.

Loomis, J. L. 1959. Communication, the development of trust, and cooperative behavior. *Human Relations* 12: 305–15.

Lowe, C. A., and Goldstein, J. W. 1970. Reciprocal liking and attributions of ability: Mediating effects of perceived intent and personal involvement. *J. Personality and Social Psychol.* 16: 291–98.

Magenau, J. M. 1983. The impact of alternative impasse procedures on bargaining: A laboratory experiment. *Industrial and Labor Relations Rev.* 36: 361–77.

Major, B., and Forcey, B. 1985. Social comparisons and pay evaluations: Preferences for same-sex and same-job wage comparisons. *J. Experimental Social Psychol.* 21:393–405.

Mallick, S. K., and McCandless, B. R. 1966. A study of catharsis of aggression. *J. Personality and Social Psychol.* 4: 591–96.

Marshall, G. D., and Zimbardo, P. G. 1979. Affective consequences of inadequately explained physiological arousal. *J. Personality and Social Psychol.* 37: 970–88.

Maslach, C. 1979. Negative emotional biasing of unexplained arousal. *J. Personality and Social Psychol.* 37: 970–88.

McCallum, D. M., Harring, K., Gilmore, R., Drenan, S., Chase, J. P., Insko, C. A., and Thibaut, J. 1984. Competition and cooperation between groups and between individuals. Unpublished manuscript.

McGillicuddy, N. B., Pruitt, D. G., and Syna, H. 1984. Perceptions of firmness and strength in negotiation. *Personality and Social Psychol. Bull.* 10: 402–9.

Michener, H. A., Vaske, J. J., Schleifer, S. L., Plazewski, J. G., and Chapman, L. J. 1975. Factors affecting concession rate and threat usage in bilateral conflict. *Sociometry* 38: 62–80.

Milgram, S. 1974. *Obedience to authority: An experimental view*. New York: Harper & Row.

Mogy, R. B., and Pruitt, D. G. 1974. Effects of a threatener's enforcement costs on threat credibility and compliance. *J. Personality and Social Psychol.* 29: 173–80.

Morgenthau, H. J. 1967. *Politics among nations*. New York: Knopf.

Morley, I. E., and Stephenson, G. M. 1977. *The social psychology of bargaining*. London: Allen and Unwin.

Moscovici, S., and Zavalloni, M. 1969. The group as a polarizer of attitudes. *J. Personality and Social Psychol.* 12: 125–35.

Mulvihill, D. J., and Tumin, M. M. 1969. *Crimes of violence: Staff report to the National Commission on the Causes and Prevention of Violence* (vol. 11). Washington: U. S. Government Printing Office.

Neale, M. A., and Bazerman, M. H. 1983. The role of perspective-taking ability in negotiating under different forms of arbitration. *Industrial and Labor Relations Rev.* 36: 378–88.

Nemeth, C. 1970. Effects of free versus constrained behavior on attraction between people. *J. Personality and Social Psychol.* 15: 302–11.

Newcomb, T. M. 1947. Autistic hostility and social reality. *Human Relations* 1: 69–86.

North, R. C., Brody, R. A., and Holsti, O. R. 1964. Some empirical data on the conflict spiral. *Peace Research Society (International) Papers* 1: 1–14.

Notz, W. W., and Starke, F. A. 1978. Final-offer vs. conventional arbitration as modes of conflict management. *Administrative Science Quarterly* 23: 189–203.

Osgood, C. E. 1962. *An alternative to war or surrender*. Urbana, Ill.: University of Illinois Press.

——————. 1966. *Perspective in foreign policy*. 2d ed. Palo Alto, Calif.: Pacific Books.

Oskamp, S. 1965. Attitudes toward U. S. and Russian actions—a double standard. *Psychological Reports* 16: 43–46.

Peters, E. 1952. *Conciliation in action*. New London, Conn.: National Foremen's Institute.

Pilisuk, M., Kiritz, S., and Clampitt, S. 1971. Undoing deadlocks of distrust: Hip

Berkeley students and the ROTC. *J. Conflict Resolution* 10: 221–26.

Potter, S. 1948. *The theory and practice of gamesmanship: The art of winning games without actually cheating.* New York: Holt.

Pruitt, D. G. 1965. Definition of the situation as a determinant of international action. In H. C. Kelman, ed. *International behavior: A social-psychological analysis,* pp. 391–432. New York: Holt, Rinehart and Winston.

——————. 1971. Indirect communication and the search for agreement in negotiation. *J. Applied Social Psychol.* 1: 205–39.

——————. 1981. *Negotiation behavior.* New York: Academic Press.

Pruitt, D. G., and Carnevale, P. J. D. 1982. The development of integrative agreements in social conflict. In V. J. Derlega and J. Grzelak, eds. *Living with other people.* New York: Academic Press.

Pruitt, D. G., Carnevale, P. J. D., Ben-Yoav, O., Nochajski, T. H., and Van Slyck, M. R. 1983. Incentives for cooperation in integrative bargaining. In R. Tietz, ed. *Aspiration levels in bargaining and economic decision making,* pp. 22–34. Berlin: Springer-Verlag.

Pruitt, D. G., and Drews, J. L. 1969. The effect of time pressure, time elapsed, and the opponent's concession rate on behavior in negotiation. *J. Experimental Social Psychol.* 5: 43–60.

Pruitt, D. G., and Gahagan, J. P. 1974. Campus crisis: The search for power. In J. T. Tedeschi, ed. *Perspectives on social power,* pp. 349–92. Chicago: Aldine.

Pruitt, D. G., and Holland, J. 1972. *Settlement in the Berlin Crisis, 1958–62.* Buffalo, N. Y.: Council on International Studies, State University of New York at Buffalo.

Pruitt, D. G., and Snyder, R. C., eds. 1969. *Theory and research on the causes of war.* Englewood Cliffs, N. J.: Prentice-Hall.

Pruitt, D. G., and Syna, H. 1983. Successful problem solving. In D. Tjosvold and D. W. Johnson, eds. *Conflicts in Organization,* pp. 62–81. New York: Irvington.

Rabbie, J. M., and Wilkens, C. 1971. Intergroup competition and its effect on intra- and intergroup relations. *European J. Social Psychol.* 1: 215–34.

Rahim, M. A. 1983. A measure of styles of handling interpersonal conflict. *Academy of Management J.* 26: 368–76.

Ransford, H. E. 1968. Isolation, powerlessness and violence: A study of attitudes and participation in the Watts riot. *American J. Sociol.* 73: 581–91.

Raven, B. H., and Rubin, J. Z. 1983. *Social psychology.* 2d ed. New York: Wiley.

Regan, D. T., Straus, E., and Fazio, R. 1974. Liking and the attribution process. *J. Experimental Social Psychol.* 10: 385–97.

Richardson, L. F. 1967. *Arms and insecurity.* Chicago: Quadrangle Books.

Ring, K., and Kelley, H. H. 1963. A comparison of augmentation and reduction as modes of influence. *J. Abnormal and Social Psychol.* 66: 95–102.

Rogers, R. W., and Prentice-Dunn, S. 1981. Deindividuation and anger-mediated aggression: Unmasking regressive racism. *J. Personality and Social Psychol.* 41: 63–73.

Rosenhan, D. L. 1973. On being sane in insane places. *Science* 179: 250–58.

Rosenthal, R., and Fode, K. 1963. The effect of experimental bias on the performance of the albino rat. *Behavioral Science* 8: 183–89.

Rosenthal, R., and Jacobson, L. F. 1968. *Pygmalion in the classroom.* New York: Holt, Rinehart and Winston.

Rubin, J. Z., 1971. The nature and success of influence attempts in a four-party bargaining relationship. *J. Experimental Social Psychol.* 7: 17–35.

——————. 1980. Experimental research on third-party intervention in conflict: Toward some generalizations. *Psychol. Bull.* 87: 379–91.

——————. 1981. *Dynamics of third-party intervention: Kissinger in the Middle East.* New York: Praeger.

Rubin, J. Z., Brockner, J., Small-Weil, S., and Nathanson, S. 1980. Factors affecting entry into psychological traps. *J. Conflict Resolution* 24: 405–26.

Rubin, J. Z., and Brown B. R. 1975. *The social psychology of bargaining and negotiation*. New York: Academic Press.

Rubin, J. Z., and Lewicki, R. J. 1973. A three-factor experimental analysis of promises and threats. *J. Applied Social Psychol.* 3: 240–57.

Rubin, J. Z., Lewicki, R. J., and Dunn, L. 1973. Perception of promisors and threateners. *Proceedings, 81st Annual Convention of the American Psychological Association*, pp. 141–42.

Rubin, J. Z., Steinberg, B. D., and Gerrein, J. R. 1974. How to obtain the right of way: An experimental analysis of behavior at intersections. *Perceptual and Motor Skills* 39: 1263–74.

Ruble, T. L., and Thomas, K. W. 1976. Support for a two-dimensional model of conflict behavior. *Organizational Behavior and Human Performance* 16: 143–55.

Russett, B. M. 1967. Pearl Harbor: Deterrence theory and decision theory. *J. Peace Research* 2: 89–106.

Ryen, A. H., and Kahn, A. 1975. The effects of intergroup orientation on group attitudes and proxemic behavior: A test of two models. *J. Personality and Social Psychol.* 31: 302–10.

Safran, N. 1978. *Israel: The embattled ally*. Cambridge, Mass.: Harvard University Press.

Schachter, S. 1951. Deviation, rejection, and communication. *J. Abnormal and Social Psychol.* 46: 190–207.

_____. 1964. The interaction of cognitive and physiological determinants of emotional state. In L. Berkowitz, ed. *Advances in experimental social psychology*, vol. 1. New York: Academic Press.

Schelling, T. C. 1960. *The strategy of conflict*. Cambridge, Mass.: Harvard University Press.

_____. 1966. *Arms and influence*. New Haven, Conn.: Yale University Press.

_____. 1978. *Micromotives and macrobehavior*. New York: Norton.

Schlenker, B. R., Helm, B., and Tedeschi, J. T. 1973. The effects of personality and situational variables on behavioral trust. *J. Personality and Social Psychol.* 25: 419–27.

Schneider, D. J., Hastorf, A. H., and Ellsworth, P. C. 1979. *Person perception*. 2nd ed. Reading, Mass.: Addison-Wesley.

Schoorman, F. D., Bazerman, M. H., and Atkin, R. S. 1981. Interlocking directorates: A strategy for reducing environmental uncertainty. *Academy of Management Rev.* 6: 243–51.

Schumpeter, J. 1955. *The sociology of imperialism*. New York: Meridian Books.

Sharp, G. 1971. The technique of nonviolent action. In J. V. Bondurant, ed. *Conflict: Violence and nonviolence*, pp. 151–171. Chicago: Aldine.

Shaw, M. E., and Sulzer, J. L. 1964. An empirical test of Heider's levels in attribution of responsibility. *J. Abnormal and Social Psychol.* 69: 39–46.

Sherif, M., Harvey, O. J., White, B. J., Hood, W. R., and Sherif, C. W. 1961. *Intergroup cooperation and competition: The Robbers Cave experiment*. Norman, Okla.: University Book Exchange.

Sherif, M., and Sherif, C. W. 1953. *Groups in harmony and tension*. New York: Harper & Row.

_____. 1969. *Social psychology*. New York: Harper & Row.

Shubik, M. 1971. The dollar auction game: A paradox in noncooperative behavior and escalation. *J. Conflict Resolution* 15: 109–11.

Sillars, A. L. 1981. Attributions and interpersonal conflict resolution. In J. H. Harvey, W. J. Ickes, and R. F. Kidd, eds. *New directions in attribution research*, vol. 3, pp. 279–305. Hillsdale, N. J.: Erlbaum.

Simon, H. A. 1957. *Models of man: Social and rational*. New York: Wiley.

Snyder, G. H., and Diesing, P. 1977. *Conflict among nations*. Princeton, N. J.: Princeton University Press.

Snyder, M., and Swann, W. B., Jr. 1978. Behavorial confirmation in social interaction: From social perception to social reality. *J. Experimental Social Psychol.* 14: 148–62.

Solomon, L. 1960. The influence of some types of power relationships and game strategies upon the development of interpersonal trust. *J. Abnormal and Social Psychol.* 61: 223–30.

Staw, B. M. 1981. The escalation of commitment to a course of action. *Academy of Management Rev.* 6: 577–87.

Stern, J. L., Rehmus, C. M., Lowenberg, J. J., Kasper, H., and Dennis, B. D. 1975. *Final-offer arbitration.* Lexington, Mass.: Heath.

Stevens, C. M. 1963. *Strategy and collective bargaining negotiation.* New York: McGraw-Hill.

——————. 1966. Is compulsory arbitration compatible with bargaining? *Industrial Relations* 65: 38–52.

Subbarao, A. V. 1978. The impact of binding arbitration. *J. Conflict Resolution* 22: 70–104.

Sumner, W. G. 1906. *Folkways.* Boston: Ginn.

Syna, H. 1984. Couples in conflict: Conflict resolution strategies, perceptions about sources of conflict and relationship adjustment. Doctoral dissertation, State University of New York at Buffalo.

Tajfel, H. 1970. Experiments in intergroup discrimination. *Scientific American* 223: 96–102.

Teger, A. I. 1980. *Too much invested to quit.* New York: Pergamon.

Tetlock, P. E. 1983. Policymakers' images of international conflict. *J. Social Issues* 39: 67–86.

Thibaut, J. W., and Kelley, H. H. 1959. *The social psychology of groups.* New York: Wiley.

Thibaut, J. W., and Walker, L. 1975. *Procedural justice: A psychological analysis.* Hillsdale, N. J.: Erlbaum.

Thomas, K. 1976. Conflict and conflict management. In M. D. Dunnette, ed. *Handbook of industrial and organizational psychology*, pp. 889–935. Chicago: Rand McNally.

Touval, S. 1975. Biased intermediaries: Theoretical and historical considerations. *Jerusalem J. International Relations* 1: 51–69.

Touval, S., and Zartman, I. W., eds. 1985. *The man in the middle: International mediation in theory and practice.* Boulder, Col.: Westview Press.

Turner, J. C. 1981. The experimental social psychology of intergroup behavior. In J. C. Turner and H. Giles, eds. *Intergroup behaviour.* Oxford: Blackwell.

Underhill, C. I. 1981. *A manual for community dispute settlement.* Buffalo, N. Y.: Better Business Bureau of Western New York.

Uranowitz, S. W. 1975. Helping and self-attributions: A field experiment. *J. Personality and Social Psychol.* 31: 852–54.

Wall, J. A., Jr. 1975. Effects of constituent trust and representative bargaining orientation on intergroup bargaining. *J. Personality and Social Psychol.* 31: 1004–12.

——————. 1977. Intergroup bargaining: Effects of opposing constituent's stance, opposing representative's bargaining, and representative's locus of control. *J. Conflict Resolution* 21: 459–74.

——————. 1979. The effects of mediator rewards and suggestions upon negotiations. *J. Personality and Social Psychol.* 37: 1554–60.

——————. 1981. Mediation: An analysis, review and proposed research. *J. Conflict Resolution* 25: 157–80.

Walster, E. H., Walster, G. W., and Berscheid, E. 1978. *Equity: theory and research.* Boston: Allyn and Bacon.

Walton, R. E. 1969. *Interpersonal peacemaking: Confrontations and third-party consultation.* Reading, Mass.: Addison-Wesley.

Walton, R. E., and McKersie, R. B. 1965. *A behavioral theory of labor negotiations: An analysis of a social interaction system*. New York: McGraw-Hill.

Webster, N. 1966. *New Twentieth Century Dictionary*. 2d ed.

Wheeler, L., and Caggiula, A. R. 1966. The contagion of aggression. *J. Experimental Social Psychol*. 2: 1–10.

White, R. K. 1970. *Nobody wanted war: Misperception in Vietnam and other wars*. New York: Doubleday/Anchor.

——————. 1984. *Fearful warriors: A psychological profile of U. S.–Soviet relations*. New York: Free Press.

Worchel, S. 1979. Cooperation and the reduction of intergroup conflict: Some determining factors. In W. G. Austin and S. Worchel, eds. *The social psychology of intergroup relations*, pp. 262–273. Monterey, Calif.: Brooks/Cole.

Worchel, S., and Andreoli, V. A. 1978. Facilitation of social interaction through deindividuation of the target. *J. Personality and Social Psychol*. 36: 549–56.

Worchel, S., Andreoli, V. A., and Folger, R. 1977. Intergroup cooperation and intergroup attraction: The effect of previous interaction and outcome on combined effort. *J. Experimental Social Psychol*. 13: 131–40.

Worchel, S. and Norvell, N. 1980. Effect of perceived environmental conditions during cooperation on intergroup attraction. *J. Personality and Social Psychol*. 38: 764–72.

Young, O. R. 1968. *The politics of force*. Princeton, N. J.: Princeton University Press.

Yukl, G. A., Malone, M. P., Hayslip, B., and Pamin, T. A. 1976. The effects of time pressure and issue settlement order on integrative bargaining. *Sociometry* 39: 277–81.

Zajonc, R. B. 1968. Attitudinal effects of mere exposure. *J. Personality and Social Psychol. Monograph Supplement* 9 (2, Part 2): 2–27.

Zartman, I. W., ed. 1977. *The negotiation process: Theories and applications*. Beverly Hills, Calif.: Sage.

——————. 1981. Explaining disengagement. In J. Z. Rubin, ed. *Dynamics of third-party intervention*, pp. 148–67. New York: Praeger.

Zillmann, D. 1979. *Hostility and aggression*. Hillsdale, N.J.: Erlbaum.

Zillmann, D., Bryant, J., Cantor, J. R., and Day, K. D. 1975. Irrelevance of mitigating circumstances in retaliatory behavior at high levels of excitation. *J. Research in Personality* 9: 282–93.

Zimbardo, P. G. 1970. The human choice: Individuation, reason, and order versus deindividuation, impulse, and chaos. In W. J. Arnold and D. Levine, eds. *Nebraska Symposium on Motivation, 1969*. Lincoln, Neb.: University of Nebraska Press.

Zimbardo, P. G., Ebbeson, E. B., and Maslach, C. 1977. *Influencing attitudes and changing behavior*. 2d ed. Reading, Mass.: Addison-Wesley.

Zimbardo, P. G., Haney, C., Banks, W. C., and Jaffe, D. A. 1973. Pirandellian prison: The mind is a formidable jailer. *New York Times Magazine*, April 8.

Glossary

accountability. A representative's responsibility to report the outcome of his or her negotiations to powerful constituents.

aggression. Intentionally hurting another person.

aggressor–defender model. Explanation of escalation as due to one party's efforts to exploit another and the other's resistance to these efforts.

arbitrator. A third party who is empowered to make a binding decision in order to settle a dispute.

arousal. Activation of the autonomic nervous system.

aspirations. Goals and standards—what people are trying to achieve or avoid.

attitude. Positive or negative feeling toward a person or object.

attribution. Interpretation of the cause or motivation for another party's actions.

attribution theory. A body of psychological theory that explains how people interpret another party's actions.

augmentation principle. In attribution theory, the hypothesis that another party's actions will be viewed as expressing an underlying disposition to the extent that he or she incurs risks or costs in enacting them.

autistic hostility. Antagonism that perpetuates itself by blocking further communication with the other party.

back-channel contacts. Off-the-record meetings between disputing parties.

bad cop/good cop routine. A two-stage, two-person contentious tactic. In the first stage, person A punishes the target. In the second stage, person B rewards the target making it clear that person A will resume the punishment if the target fails to comply with a request.

balance of power. Distribution of resources such that all members of a community are deterred from attacking one another.

bond. Felt or perceived link between self and other. May be due to attraction, kinship, common group identity, perceived similarity, or the expectation of future dependence.

bridging. A type of integrative solution in which a new alternative is devised that satisfies the most important interests underlying the two parties' initial demands.

cohesiveness. Group solidarity; overall attractiveness of a group to its members.

collective. A set of people who are capable of coordinated action—a group, organization, community, or nation.

community polarization. Disappearance of neutral third parties from the community surrounding a controversy as a result of recruitment to one side or the other.

compellent threat. A threat that requests the target to adopt a particular action or solution.

compromise. An obvious alternative that stands part way between the parties' preferred positions.

concern about Other's outcomes. Importance placed on another party's interests.

concern about own outcomes. Importance placed on one's own interests.

conflict. Perceived divergence (conflict) of interest; a belief that the parties' current aspirations cannot be achieved simultaneously.

conflict spiral model. Explanation of escalation as due to a vicious circle of contentious action and reaction.

constituent. A party who is being represented.

contending. A strategy that involves an effort to impose one's will on another party.

coping strategies. Contending, yielding, and problem solving.

cost cutting. A type of integrative solution in which one party gets what it wants and the other's costs are reduced or eliminated.

covert problem solving. Problem solving that takes place behind the scenes or in the form of signals.

credibility. Believability of a threat, promise, or irrevocable commitment.

crosscutting group memberships. Configuration of bonds in which the major groups in a society have overlapping membership.

de-escalation. Reduction in the intensity of conflict.

deindividuation. Perception of a person as a member of a category rather than as an individual.

dependence. Reliance on another party for one's outcomes.

descriptive theory. Theory about how people behave.

deterrent threat. A threat that requests the target to avoid a particular action.

discounting principle. In attribution theory, the hypothesis that another party's actions are more likely to be attributed to cause X when alternative causes Y and Z can be confidently ruled out.

displacement. Diversion of aggression from the party who is blamed for an aversive experience to a convenient target.

disposition. A personality trait, attitude, or other characteristic of a party.

dissonance theory. A psychological theory explaining why attitudes and beliefs are consistent with prior actions.

distrust. Perception of another party as not caring about, or antagonistic toward, one's interests.

divergence of interest. A situation in which the parties cannot simultaneously achieve their aspirations.

dual concern model. A theory of strategic choice postulating that the strategy chosen is a function of the strength of one's concern about one's own outcomes and the strength of one's concern about the other party's outcomes.

entrapment. Persistence of unrewarding behavior.

escalation. An increase in the intensity of conflict.

ethnocentrism. Tendency to favor one's own group over other groups.

evil-ruler enemy image. Perception that the adversary consists of reasonable people who are dominated and misled by a small cotery of wicked leaders.

expanding the pie. A type of integrative solution in which a way is found to augment a scarce resource.

final-offer arbitration. Arbitration in which the third party must choose one party's position and reject the other party's position.

firm but conciliatory stance. Strategy of standing firm on one's basic interests while trying to be responsive to the other's basic interests.

firm flexibility. Firmness with respect to ends in conjunction with flexibility with respect to the means for achieving those ends.

formula. A brief statement of the essential features of an agreement, which serves as a guide for later work on the fine details.

gamesmanship. Contentious tactics that seek to win by throwing the target off guard.

geography of social bonds. Overall pattern of bonding and antagonism among the members of a community.

graduated and reciprocated initiatives in tension reduction (GRIT). Unilateral conciliatory actions designed to de-escalate a controversy with another party.

group changes. Changes in collectives that result from escalation and produce more escalation.

group polarization. Strengthening of the dominant attitude or belief in a group as a result of group discussion.

heavy tactics. Contentious tactics that impose great costs on the target.

illusory conflict. False perception of a divergence of interest.

image loss. Loss of status or credibility in the eyes of either an antagonist or an observer of the conflict.

inaction. A strategy that involves doing nothing.

information loss. Discovery by an adversary of the nature of one's interests or the location of one's lower limit.

ingratiation. Making oneself attractive to another party in order to be able to influence that party at a later date.

integrative potential. Availability of a mutually beneficial solution to a controversy.

integrative solution. An alternative that reconciles the parties' basic interests; a mutually beneficial solution.

interests. People's feelings about what is basically desirable—their values and needs.

interest tree. Hierarchical diagram showing more basic interests at lower levels and more superficial interests at higher levels.

intermediaries. People who carry messages between disputing parties.

invidious comparison. A perception that somebody else receives more reward in comparison to his or her worth than the perceiver does.

irrevocable commitment. Communication indicating that one will under no circumstances deviate from one's present position.

joint outcome space. Geometric representation of the perceived value to two parties of the available alternatives.

lightness of tactics. Lighter contentious tactics impose lower costs on the party at whom they are aimed.

linkage. Association of demands, goals, aspirations, and values in a package that seems inviolable. Unbundling such a package is often necessary for the development of an integrative solution.

logrolling. A type of integrative solution in which each party concedes on issues that are of low priority to itself and of high priority to the other party.

mediator. A third party who attempts to help conflicting parties reach a voluntary agreement.

mirror image. Similarity of attitudes and perceptions on both sides of a controversy.

momentum. A sense of forward motion in a controversy, resulting from prior success at achieving agreement.

nonspecific compensation. A type of integrative solution in which one party gets what it wants and the other is repaid in an unrelated coin.

norms. Rules of behavior that a group imposes on its members.

party. A participant in conflict. Parties can be individuals, groups, organizations, communities, or nations.

perceived common ground (PCG). The perceived likelihood of finding an alternative that satisfies both parties' aspirations.

perceived divergence of interest. A belief that the parties cannot simultaneously achieve their aspirations.

perceived feasibility. The extent to which a strategy seems capable of achieving one's aspirations at a reasonable cost.

perceived integrative potential (PIP). Belief about the availability of a mutually beneficial solution. PIP is higher the more likely it seems that such a solution is available and the more beneficial this solution seems to be.

perception. Belief about a person or object.

persuasive argumentation. A communication designed to change another person's attitudes or beliefs.

position loss. An adversary's perception that one has conceded from an earlier demand.

power. The capacity to persuade another party to yield.

prescriptive theory. Theory about how people should behave.

priorities. Preferences among interests, such as a preference for wealth over social approval.

problem solving. A strategy that involves seeking a mutually satisfactory alternative.

promise. Commitment to reward another party if that party complies with one's wishes.

psychological changes. Changes in individuals that result from escalation and produce more escalation.

selective perception. Seeing only things that fit one's needs or preconceptions.

self-fulfilling prophecy. An attitude or belief that reinforces itself by the impact it has on the other party's behavior.

social categorization effect. The finding that minimal differences between groups are usually sufficient to produce ethnocentrism.

social comparison. Assessment of another party's characteristics or situation in comparison with one's own.

stability. Used in two different senses: (1) a low likelihood that conflict will develop, and (2) a low likelihood that conflict will escalate.

stalemate. Condition in which both parties are no longer able or willing to expend the effort needed to sustain an escalated conflict.

strategic choice. Choice among the five basic strategies for dealing with conflict.

strategy. A broad type of conflict behavior; a class of tactics. Five strategies are distinguished: contending, yielding, problem solving, withdrawing, and inaction.

structural change model. Explanation of escalation as due to the residues of past conflict.

struggle group. A group that forms with the goal of achieving concessions from another party.

stubbornness. Reluctance to yield.

superordinate goal. An objective that is shared by the parties to a conflict and requires them to work together.

tactic. A narrow type of conflict behavior. Various possible tactics are implied by a single strategy.

tar baby effect. Reinforcement of an attitude or belief by the absence of behavior by the other party.

threat. Commitment to hurt another party if that party fails to comply to one's wishes.

trust. The perception that another party is concerned about one's interests.

vested interests. The motive to retain one's group membership or leadership position because of the benefits that accrue from it.

vigor. Amount of energy or effort put into strategy enactment.

withdrawing. A strategy that involves leaving the conflict, either physically or psychologically.

yielding. A strategy that involves lowering one's aspirations.

zero-sum thinking. The belief that my gain is your loss and your gain is my loss.

Author Index

Subject Index

About the Authors

DEAN G. PRUITT is Professor of Psychology at the State University of New York at Buffalo. He has published two books, *Theory and Research on the Causes of War* (with Richard C. Snyder) and *Negotiation Behavior*, and numerous articles on conflict and bargaining. He is currently engaged in research on third-party intervention in conflict.

Dr. Pruitt received his Ph.D. from Yale University in 1957 and went on to postdoctoral fellowships at the University of Michigan and Northwestern University. At the latter school, he was affiliated with the International Relations Program. He taught at the University of Delaware for five years before going to his present position in 1966. He is a Fellow of the American Psychological Association, a Vice President of the International Society of Political Psychology, and has held a Guggenheim Fellowship.

JEFFREY Z. RUBIN is Professor of Psychology at Tufts University and Associate Director of the Program on Negotiation at the Harvard Law School. A Columbia University Ph.D., he has been at Tufts since 1969, where he has held a number of positions including that of Director of the Center for the Study of Decision Making. He is editor of *Negotiation Journal: On the Process of Dispute Settlement*. A recipient of Guggenheim and Fulbright fellowships, he has authored books on negotiation, third-party intervention, and decision making, and is co-author of a textbook on social psychology.